Political Determinants of Corporate Governance

Political Determinants of Corporate Governance

Political Context, Corporate Impact

MARK J. ROE

OXFORD

UNIVERSITY PRESS

Great Clarendon Street, Oxford OX2 6DP

Oxford University Press is a department of the University of Oxford.
It furthers the University's objective of excellence in research, scholarship,
and education by publishing worldwide in

Oxford New York

Auckland Cape Town Dar es Salaam Hong Kong Karachi
Kuala Lumpur Madrid Melbourne Mexico City Nairobi
New Delhi Shanghai Taipei Toronto

With offices in

Argentina Austria Brazil Chile Czech Republic France Greece
Guatemala Hungary Italy Japan Poland Portugal Singapore
South Korea Switzerland Thailand Turkey Ukraine Vietnam

Oxford is a registered trade mark of Oxford University Press
in the UK and in certain other countries

Published in the United States
by Oxford University Press Inc., New York

British Library Cataloguing in Publication Data

Data available

Library of Congress Cataloging in Publication Data

Data available

Typeset by Newgen Imaging Systems (P) Ltd., Chennai, India
Printed in Great Britain
on acid-free paper by
Biddles Ltd., King's Lynn

ISBN 0–19–924074–4   978–0–19–924074–6
ISBN 0–19–920530–2 (pbk.)   978–0–19–920530–1 (pbk.)

10 9 8 7 6 5 4 3 2 1

PREFACE

The large business firm and its ownership structure is this book's general subject; the political impact on structure its specific focus. Too often the large firm's ownership structure is analyzed as a purely business institution, as one arising solely from organizational imperatives, technical foundations, and financial needs. The political and social predicates that make the large firm possible and that shape its form are not scrutinized as carefully, or at all, despite that variation in political and social conditions can deeply affect which firms, which ownership structures, and which corporate governance arrangements survive and prosper.

Yet if our goal is to *explain* why this or that business structure prevails, we would be wrong to ignore the national political and social environment surrounding the firm. Pierre Trudeau was once asked at the White House what it was like to lead Canada, a nation whose population is about one-tenth that of its big neighbor to the south. He replied, to paraphrase, that it was like sleeping next to an elephant. Even if the elephant is benevolent, and even if it is unaware of your existence, nevertheless small movements by the elephant at night deeply affect the quality of your sleep.

So it is with corporate ownership and governance. Two of the 'elephants' are the product and capital markets, and these two have long been properly seen as affecting firms' ownership and governance. But a big neighboring 'elephant' is also the firm's political environment, the degree to which the average voter wants government to affect the firm, how governments in fact affect firms, and the ways in which firms react to those political impulses. This 'elephant' is less often seen, and its effect hardly ever analyzed, but it can deeply affect the shape, structure, and governance institutions of the large business firm.

Figure P.1 shows an abstracted firm in its environment, with capital and labor markets affecting shareholder structure and managerial institutions, and with political institutions and product markets affecting the firm as well. Perhaps the picture shows the firm more beleaguered and confined than would be real: the firm shapes its environment too, and the way it reacts to pressures—defensively choosing this or that structure to ward off external threats or offensively seeking to mold a nation's politics—can affect corporate governance in important ways.

Among the rich democratic nations—the nations that can support large, public firms—some polities have encouraged the institutions that stabilize the large public firm with diffuse ownership. Some have not. These differences, arising

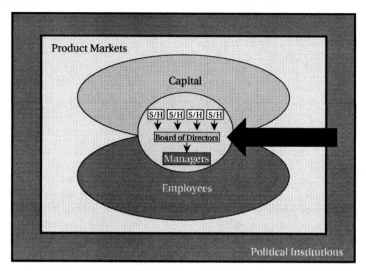

Fig. P.1. The corporate governance environment

from labor politics, orientation to shareholder value, and market conditions, can largely determine the ownership structure of large firms.

Consider nation-by-nation differences in how strongly governments support employee pressures on the firm. When employee pressures are weak—or when the government pays little attention to them—the firm has more options than when they are strong. Those kinds of employee pressures inside the American firm have been weak. Not so historically in most other Western nations, where employees have at times seized factories, where governments have sought to stabilize employment inside the firm by confining owners' discretion, and where national politics has at times vividly focused on the division of the economic spoils in ways that are pallid in American politics.

Before a nation can produce, it must have sufficient economic peace that the factory can function. The ways in which nations achieved—and maintained—that peace were not all identical; and these differences shaped corporate governance, ownership, and power inside the firm.

This political determinant, under-examined but tugging on the firm as strongly as the moon determines the tides, is the one that I focus on in this book. I do not offer a theory of *all* political determinants, but a theory and data on this one powerful political determinant. Our examining it should, I believe, greatly advance our understanding of the large firm. This political determinant—strong stakeholder pressure, whose political manifestation I call here, for lack of a better term, social democracy—affects the firm directly and also induces a counter-pressure inside the firm, usually for more focused, concentrated ownership. Perhaps a better title for this book, were it not for euphony, would have been 'A Political Determinant of Corporate Governance'.

* * *

One can look at this political dimension from differing angles. Each angle has the firm at its vertex, collecting capital-contributors, managers, and employees. One angle is of coalition-building: strong social democracies strengthen a managerial-employee coalition and weaken a capital-managerial coalition. Owners there would have even more reason than elsewhere to seek to weaken the first and strengthen the second. Another angle views the firm through the lens of basic agency cost literature, a literature that focuses on the flaws in managers' loyalty to shareholders' interests. The political focus here is that politics affects the size of the managerial agency costs that shareholders bear. When politics raises these costs, shareholders would demand more in the way of compensating firm structures that would make managers less likely to stray from shareholder loyalty. This agency cost perspective is the one we shall use for the most part, not because it's the only one but because it allows us to paint the issues quickly with a few brush-strokes. The agency cost style of analysis is common, and the vocabulary is regularly used in many academic disciplines.

Another angle is the perspective of micro-economic competition. Fiercely competitive markets support (or are supported by) one package of ownership structures and political orientation (namely, diffuse ownership and relatively con-servative economic politics). Or the angle of view might be that of labor: if a nation's labor markets are not fluid and employees 'own' their positions, that kind of a labor market calls forth countervailing ownership and governance structures of a kind differing from those prevailing in nations where labor markets are fluid and employees less protected by political institutions from the markets' ravages. Or, to take a last possible perspective, mechanically smooth corporate law is important for a nation in facilitating diffuse ownership and investor protection. But if the political environment is unfriendly to diffuse ownership, then even if the mechanical prerequisites, like a supportive corporate law, are in place, they will not be used if the political 'elephants' are restless and likely anyway to trample the small, diffuse shareholders.

CONTENTS

....

LIST OF GRAPHS AND FIGURES

Graphs

Figures

LIST OF TABLES

Introduction

Before a nation can produce, it must achieve social peace. Factories that fail to produce because of internal turmoil or external upheaval are less valuable than those that produce smoothly. If conflict is expected, investors invest reluctantly, or not at all, and the factory is not built. Or investors search for the organizational form that minimizes the chances and costs of conflict. Dampening turmoil, or insulating the firm from it, can be a strong force in shaping firms' ownership and governance. Perhaps secondary in the United States, these considerations have historically often been primary in other nations.

Social peace has been reached in different nations by differing means, some of which have then been embedded in business firms, in corporate ownership patterns, and in corporate governance structures. The ways to achieve and maintain social peace vary, and that variety explains quite a bit of why corporate governance structures vary around the world.

Politics can affect a firm in many ways: it can determine who owns it, how big it can grow, what it can produce profitably, how it raises capital, who has the capital to invest, how managers or employees see themselves and one another, and how authority is distributed inside the firm. For concreteness I focus on one key variable: the degree to which ownership separates from control. This is in itself a key aspect of the modern corporation, and emphasizing it gives us the discipline of dealing with a single variable, one for which finance theory is well developed and about which data can be had to test, probe, and better understand how the firm's political environment affects it. Ownership will be our primary focus, but it reflects the bigger claim, that much of the firm's structure is affected, sometimes determined, by its political environment, and if we fail to scrutinize the political impact on a firm, we are unlikely to get the full story.

The large publicly held, diffusely owned firm dominates business in the United States despite its infirmities, namely the frequently fragile relations between stockholders and managers. Managers' agendas can differ from shareholders'; and tying managers' actions tightly to shareholders' goals has been central to American corporate governance. But in other economically advanced nations ownership is not diffuse but concentrated. The problem to explain is why ownership of large

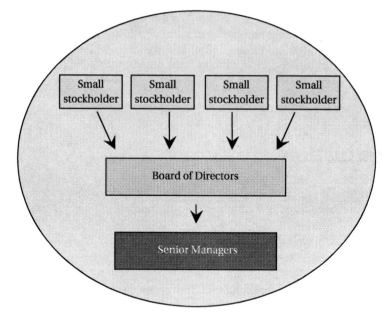

Fig. 1. Diffuse ownership

firms in the United States is diffuse, as depicted in Figure 1, while in so much of the rest of the wealthy West fewer firms go public at all, and of those that do, the firm's ownership is typically concentrated not diffuse, with a dominant stockholder as depicted in Figure 2. Although the American institutional investor has in recent years made the American stockholder less remote than it once was, even today ownership is much less concentrated in the United States than it is in the other nations in the wealthy West. It has been concentrated elsewhere in the wealthy West in no small measure because the delicate threads that tie managers to distant shareholders in the public firm fray easily in common political environments, such as those in the continental European social democracies.

Social democracies press managers to stabilize employment, to forgo some profit-maximizing but risky opportunities for the firm, and to use up capital in place rather than to downsize when markets no longer are aligned with the firm's production capabilities. Managers must have discretion in the diffusely-owned public firm, and how they use that discretion is crucial to stockholders, in that managers' actions produce the firm's profits. Social democratic pressures induce managers to stray further than otherwise from their shareholders' profit-maximizing goals: managers with discretion there are pushed away from being aligned with shareholders' typical profit-oriented goals. Moreover, the modern means that align managers with diffuse stockholders in the United States—incentive compensation, transparent accounting (whose recent failures highlight both its importance and its fragility), hostile takeovers, and strong shareholder-wealth maximization norms—have been weaker and sometimes denigrated by continental social democracies.

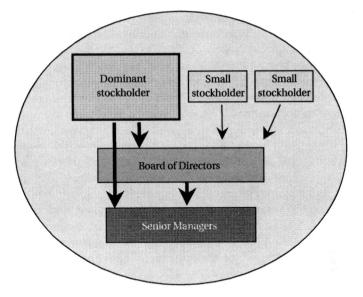

Fig. 2. Dominant stockholder in public firm

Hence, public firms there, all else equal, have had higher managerial agency costs, and large-block shareholding has persisted as shareholders' best remaining way to control those costs. Indeed, when we line up the world's richest nations on a left-right political continuum and then line them up on a close-to-diffuse ownership continuum, the two correlate powerfully.

True, the effects on total social welfare are ambiguous; social democracies may enhance total social welfare, but if they do, they do so with fewer public firms than less socially responsive nations. We thus uncover not only a political explanation for ownership concentration in Europe, but also a crucial political prerequisite to the rise of the public firm in the United States, namely the weakness of social democratic pressures on the American business firm.

* * *

That corporate governance structures around the world have differed is hardly contested. The very fact that many people talk today, at the beginning of the twenty-first century, about corporate convergence due to globalization tells us that people believe that corporate structures have sharply varied. The task here is to better explain why they varied. The thesis is straightforward: prevailing explanations—based on the level of economic and technological development, on differing economic tasks, on random variation, and on the quality of technical corporate law—while important and not to be discarded, are incomplete. One big explanation is absent from the literature, namely that how social conflict has been settled powerfully affects how firms are owned and how authority is divided.

Politics at times directly requires boardrooms and ownership structures to be a certain way. At other times it induces reactions, as, say, owners seek to mitigate political effects or employees react negatively to a political or economic result. At other times politics simply raises the costs of a particular structure, making that more costly structure less likely to arise and prosper.

No single explanation is going to dominate the others at all times: the level of economic wealth, the technological demands for large size, the institutions of capital-gathering, the prevailing tax rules, the legal institutions of the large firm are all important. My task here is hardly to refute the importance of these explanations for the rise of the large firm and the separation of ownership from control, but to focus on a deep, important, and missing political explanation.

I focus on two major corporate differences: the degree of separation of ownership from control, primarily and, secondarily, the degree of labor influence. The two are connected. In the United States ownership of the largest firms has been diffuse for quite some time; on the European continent, ownership has been concentrated, with even the largest firms privately-owned or, if their stock traded publicly, with a single owner controlling a big block of stock. In the United States, labor rarely participates in the core institutions of the firm's governance at the top, rarely owns significant stock directly, and even more rarely participates on the board. In France, a dynamic family and entrepreneurial sector challenged a government-dominated sector, public policy favored employees with jobs in place, and diffusely-owned firms were rare. In Germany labor still takes half of the seats of the supervisory board, in the most explicit manifestation of a political determinant of corporate governance. In Italy in the decades ending the twentieth century there were few public firms, social conflict in the largest firms spilled over into politics when the communist party in Italy was strong, and nominally conservative governments both denigrated the profit-oriented culture needed to make large firms' managers function well for shareholders and built up small businesses at the expense of large ones to deny fertile fields to the communist unions. In Japan, the firm was typically run at the top by a large board of insiders assured of lifetime employment. Banks have also been shareholders, and their loans induced them not to seek to maximize their wealth as shareholders. Some of these structures arose and prospered in Japan during times of intense social conflict. Similarly, the incidence of hostile takeovers, proxy fights, and incentive compensation mechanisms varies greatly around the world; sometimes used not at all, sometimes becoming central to corporate governance.

Those are nation-by-nation specifics. But we can generalize into a theory with predictions. Social democracies favor employees with jobs in place. They wedge open the gap between shareholders and managers by pressing managers to expand, to avoid downsizing, and to go slow in taking risks that would affect the work place. These are just the kinds of managerial agency costs that have been common at times in the large American firm: American managers when not strongly tied to shareholders' interests have *also* tended to expand, avoid, and go slow, despite the weaker political pressures here on managers to expand, avoid, and go slow. Moreover, social democracies denigrate the modern pro-shareholder tools—such as incentive compensation, hostile takeovers, shareholder wealth maximization norms, etc.—because it is *not* their policy to promote purely shareholder values.

* * *

Non-political explanations abound for why some nations have concentrated ownership and some do not. Different levels of economic development, technology, culture, or tax and legal structures have all been invoked. Specific structures in one nation or another influence the ownership result: Germany's tax rules favored block ownership. Italy's weak courts made diffusely-owned corporate legal structures hard to maintain. French statist institutions weakened securities markets. British pension funds facilitated diffuse ownership. Banks in Germany, and incumbents more generally, have tried to block securities market development.

Each local institutional structure surely explains some variation. And for some nations at some times a specific structure could explain much variation. But each local explanation is compatible with there *also* being a political explanation that runs across national boundaries. No one single explanation determines ownership and corporate governance.

And each local explanation fails to fully explain the ownership and governance results around the world, leading us to need more to explain the differences. For example, while many developing nations have weak securities markets, there are also several wealthy nations in the West whose securities markets are shallow. Differences in the quality of technical institutions surely explain some of the variation, especially when we compare the wealthy West with the developing East. But too many rich nations have very good institutional structures and strong institutions—corporate, legal, and otherwise—but *nevertheless* have concentrated ownership. Something else is at work promoting concentration and impeding diffusion, and to understand why securities markets and ownership separation do or do not develop, we need to find a better explanation.

We can do so, with a powerful political story, by relating a nation's macro-politics to the firm's micro-structure. Begin by abstracting the firm into three basic parts: ownership, management, and employment. Social conflict, often among owners, managers, and employees, leads to political settlements—indeed, for a nation to be one of the world's richest, social conflict must somehow have been kept from getting out of hand—and these settlements can determine the structure of one of these pieces of the firm.

By determining one of the three basic pieces, politics can thereby often determine the others as well, because the pieces fit together—like pieces of a jigsaw puzzle—as complements. That is, some politically required employment pieces fit well with only a few types of management pieces. Hence, politics could, say, determine a particular labor structure, which might call forth only one type of ownership or management structure. For example, German codetermination—by which labor takes half of the board seats—demands concentrated ownership, because shareholders would do poorly if they failed to meet the boardroom's labor block with their own block. Which came first is not important to the analysis. (And, since concentrated ownership came first, the political complementarity between labor voice and ownership concentration has not been seen clearly.) But once one insti-tution is locked into place, the other is called forth, and *neither* can change easily without the other changing as well. Co-ordinating change of multiple institutions simultaneously is hard, and that is one major reason why many of the differing corporate structures around the world have thus far persisted, resisting full con-vergence despite the post-war convergence of living standards and productivity.

I proceed in this book by telling a few quick stories for national systems and then, in this book's mid-section, I generalize the inquiry. Social democracy fits badly with the diffusely owned public firm. Social democracies fray the ties between shareholders and managers, and ownership thereby seeks a better way to control management, with the best alternative in a social democracy being a concentrated ownership structure. The correlation between a nation's political orientation and its corporate ownership structure is powerful.

Other economic and political elements fit together as well. One can see two packages of industrial organization, democratic macro-politics and corporate ownership structure. One has weakly competitive markets fitting with social demo-cratic politics and concentrated ownership. The other matches fiercely competit-ive markets, conservative almost *laissez-faire* politics, and diffuse ownership. Many of the social democracies have had weakly competitive product markets. Weak product markets weaken one important constraint on managerial agency costs, making diffuse ownership more costly for shareholders. This tends to induce more concentrated ownership, all else equal.

Moreover, contests over how to split the monopoly corporate profits can spill over into democratic politics in ways that are harder to politicize if competitive markets limit the firm to competitive profits: the cupboard is too easily bare, leaving less to contest. Globalization, for example, is said to press firms to do less for employees. Part of the globalization pressure we see around the world is due to the shrinking of local monopolies as product market competition intensifies. True, employees may do better overall when globalization improves their welfare as consumers even if it squeezes them as employees. But the corporate governance implication here is that globalization presses firms to match pay closely to pro-ductivity: managers have less discretion over wages than when they faced less competitive product markets. That shrinking of local monopolies weakens stake-holder pressures on the firm's managers—because there is less available over which managers have discretion to share—and as those internal pressures to share diminish, this source of the demand for concentrated ownership might diminish as well, opening the way for a nation to develop deeper and wider securities markets.

While we examine the rest of the developed world in this book's mid-section, the theory here is one about the United States as well. And that is where we shall conclude: there was a powerful political pre-condition to ownership separating from control in the United States, to the rise and persistent dominance of the American large public firm with diffuse ownership, and to the eventual disap-pearance of block and family ownership, namely *the absence in the U.S. of a strong social democracy.* Where social democracy was strong, the public firm was unstable, weak, and unable to dominate without difficulty; where social democracy was weak, ownership diffusion of the large firm could, if other economic and institutional conditions prevailed, begin.

* * *

The argument here is not normative: it is *not* that strong social democracies do not deliver the goods in a utilitarian sense. There is tension between large diffusely-owned firms and strong social democratic polities, and, hence, one might, by showing this relationship, be taken to suggest that this strain of politics short-changes its citizens. But that is not the argument. Indeed, one might intuitively think the contrary: by providing *more* for a *wider* base of people, those governments may achieve a utilitarian goal of the greatest good for the greatest number more effectively than other polities.

But I do not evaluate this utilitarian possibility—that these arrangements could be more than just a second-best accommodation but a first-best result—one way or the other. Moreover, the argument I present suggests the possibility of *several* roads to utilitarian goals: peace is predicate to production. If substantial social peace is achieved in different ways in different nations, then there were several historical routes to achieve a modern economy.

* * *

Today's policy-makers have reasons to come to grips with these political reflections inside the large firm. International agencies seek to change corporate governance systems in developing and transition nations. But corporate governance is not just mechanical rules and basic institutional capacities (such as good corporate law, good courts, and so on). The corporation ties, sometimes tightly, to national politics, and plunking down modern (usually read as American) rules and business institutions would be unlikely to produce the reformers' desired results if the institutions badly match the politics. The mechanical rules and institutions could be the same, but if politics sharply differs, so might the corporate results.

True, reformers can change business practices and legal rules more easily than they can change a nation's deep political and social structure. So, if one approaches corporate governance from a law reform perspective, it usually is correct to analyse the business firm as it has conventionally been analysed, as an economic, financial, and technological organization: we, or the reform agencies, assume the political and social predicates of the society as given, and look at the 'marginal' institutions susceptible of immediate change. If one seeks to improve business results, it is best to focus first on what can be changed and not what, at least in the short run, will resist change. No need to examine political bedrock, if drilling through it in the short run is impossible.

Yet we cannot always avoid examining it: if the mechanical institutions just do not mesh with the underlying political foundations, fixing the mechanics will be harder than the reformers anticipate. And if our goal is to explain which institutions prevailed in the wealthy West, we cannot avoid looking at the firm's political environment.

* * *

The task here lies across several disciplines, including law, political science, and economics. And the methodologies needed are several as well—the logical analysis of incentives and institutions from law and economics, the statistics and modeling (simple though they may be here) of financial economics, and the historical/political scrutiny of comparative politics. I do not purport to be sufficiently expert to catch every nuance in each field or method, but I hope that by combining them, we gain deeper insights.

* * *

A road map for this book: in Part I, I set out the general theory that peace must precede production and how the terms of peace can affect corporate governance. I also set out the core differences in corporate governance around the world.

In Part II, I set out the theory that social democracy and the diffusely owned firm are in tension. I link a nation's political orientation to the micro-structure of the firm, by showing how social democracies press managers to coalesce with employees, not with distant shareholders, and how the means that tie managers to shareholders in American public firms fray in strong social democracies. Owners must consequently seek other means to control managers, and the best alternative is close ownership or block ownership of the equity. Whether life is better for more people is hard to know, but public firms would be fewer and ownership separation narrower.

In Part III, I test the political hypothesis with a simple statistical inquiry: if we array nations on a left-to-right political scale, and then array them on a highly-concentrated to highly diffuse ownership scale, the two scales correlate powerfully. The political explanation, in statistical terms, does as well, or better, at explaining variation in ownership concentration in the world's richest nations as do competing theories, such as a currently-popular one based on the strength of technical corporate law.

In Part IV, I narrate relationships between social politics and corporate governance in seven of the world's richer nations. France has a long history of statist economic policy. Before the First World War, when the overall tenor of its statism was *conservative*, securities markets were developing strongly; in modern times its leftward bent precluded sharp ownership separation. German codetermination is the clearest institutional manifestation of the social democratic thesis. Labor takes half of the board seats in large firms, inducing shareholders to be better off with a counter-coalition. Italy for a quarter of a century had a communist party on the verge of political power; ownership concentration helped to make deals stick inside the big firms and facilitated a counter-coalition inside the firm and inside the polity. Japanese lifetime employment is another way to achieve social peace. Japanese firms' insider-dominated boards and their history of strong bank-creditor influence—both being risk-avoiding players—fit with lifetime employment. Sweden also exemplifies the thesis: the world's first social democracy, it had strong minority stock issuance, but very little ownership separation. The United Kingdom's securities markets first developed during its first strong *laissez-faire* period and seemed to stagnate mid-century when its political economy changed. And the United States has had one of the world's weakest social democratic influences and one of its strongest securities markets, with much ownership separation.

In Part V, I deepen the inquiry by examining the direction of causality. In the first four Parts I take politics as given and examine its consequences for the firm. In Part V, I inquire into how corporate and economic structures can induce political backlash. Not all efficient structures are politically stable. Some structures induce political backlash, inducing corporate structures to bend to survive, or to crack and fail. I offer some generalized instances of each and show some corporate governance implications. I also in Part V link the political story to product markets: there are complementary fits of ownership structure, politics, and industrial organization. One can in theory take the same agency cost-driven political story of Part I and, by beginning with the severity of market-place product competition, derive the same corporate governance (and, surprisingly, political) results. Separation fits with conservative democratic politics and fierce product market competition. Some of the social tensions around the world today are due to one piece of the package changing quickly without the others yet changing as quickly.

In Part VI, I discuss the fit between the political theory and a leading academic theory, that the quality of technical corporate law determines whether securities markets will arise, whether ownership will separate from control, and whether the modern corporation will prosper. The theory has been used convincingly to explain why we see weak corporate structures in transition and developing nations, less convincingly to explain why concentrated ownership persists in continental Europe, and probably incorrectly to explain why ownership separated from control in the United States. Surely, when an economically weak society lacks regularity—a gap that may be manifested by weak or poorly enforced corporate law—that lack of regularity and economic strength precludes complex institutions like securities markets and diffusely owned public firms. But the converse is not true: when we see ownership concentration we cannot be sure whether distant stockholders fear the rapacity of insiders—who could, if corporate law is weak, divert value to themselves—or the disloyalty of managers, who might fail to get good shareholder profits. Corporate law deals with rapacity and self-dealing, *not* with managerial mistake. But the latter can impede diffuse ownership as easily as the first, and via America's elaborate business judgment rule the latter *is immune from corporate law inquiry*. Indeed, even in nations with good legal structures generally and, by measurement, good shareholder protection—such as in Germany and Scandinavia—ownership *did not* separate from control. Something more than just weak corporate law impeded securities markets from flourishing in such nations. The political theory I offer here tells us what that something else was.

The analysis in Part VI is quite relevant to today's policy-making corporate bodies, such as the international agencies that are promoting corporate governance institutions in Third World and transition nations that would mimic American institutions. Their goals are worthy, but even if they succeed in building the mechanical institutions they are after, the corporate structures might persist if the nations' underlying politics is not conducive to the policy-makers' goals.

In Part VII I unify two political theories: a democratic polity does not easily accept powerful pro-shareholder institutions. In the United States, this unease once manifested itself in a populism that historically kept financial institutions small, denied them strong stock-based portfolios, and took away their authority to act directly inside the firm. In more modern times, this popular force manifested itself in laws that dampened hostile takeovers in many states, without eliminating them. By taming the strongest shareholder institutions such as concentrated financial power, the American polity more willingly, albeit perhaps grudgingly, accepted other pro-shareholder institutions. In Europe, this political force sought to tame capital directly, by constricting its range of motion in the firm: employees with jobs got both protection from being laid off and voice inside the firm, pro-shareholder institutions were denigrated, and owners reacted to maximize their value in that kind of polity. If one fails to understand these political impulses, one cannot fully understand the world's, or any single nation's, corporate governance institutions.

I

POLITICAL CONFLICT AND THE CORPORATION

The corporation is an economic and legal institution and its determinants are usually seen as economic and legal as well, with its principal economic determinants arising from the needs of the engineers for large-scale production, of the financiers for diversification, and of the managers for discretion. These determinants are central, but so are the political predicates to large-scale production, which are rarely examined.

The critical political predicate is simple: sufficient social peace inside the corporation so that it can produce and sell its products. Many means of making social peace diminish shareholder wealth. But the specifics are many, and different nations have reduced social conflict differently, often adopting institutions that affect the structure of the large-scale firm. Japan achieved industrial peace after the Second World War with promises of lifetime employment to many employees. Germany built labor codetermination into its boardrooms. France had a strong state voice in the corporation, a voice that typically has taken labor's side when there was conflict. The United States had little of these, because it had little of the same kind of industrial conflict; but historically similar forces fragmented finance, thereby hastening the development of the diffusely held public firm (because American politics precluded strong financial institutions, thus pushing finance more heavily into other channels).

We can generalize. One persistent contrast in corporate ownership around the world is concentrated versus diffuse ownership. In many continental European nations, families or financial institutions have owned the largest business firms. In the United States for quite some time, and more recently in Great Britain, stock ownership is more diffuse. Some nations achieved economic peace by becoming social democracies, where the state regularly sided with employees. In such social democracies, the diffusely-owned public firm did not fit well with the political institutions. For diffuse ownership to prevail, managers must be tied to shareholders, but social democracies did not allow these ties to be tight. When the ties cannot be tight, the public firm is unstable, unlikely to arise, and unlikely to dominate and spread further if it had already arisen.

More abstractly: pure shareholder wealth maximization fits poorly with a modern democracy. Everywhere democracies put distance between strong shareholder control and the day-to-day operation of the firm, shielding employees from tight shareholder control. But the means and degree differ around the world. Some nations fragment financial institutions, lower shareholder voice, and keep the ownership interests distant from the firm; others allow ownership interests to be close to the firm, but reduce the range of their activities inside the firm. How a nation settles social conflict and distances shareholders from the firm's day-to-day operation— how a nation achieves social peace—can thereafter deeply affect that nation's institutions of corporate governance.

Peace as Predicate

Before a nation can produce, it must achieve social peace. The proposition is obvious, but has thus far not been widely used to understand corporate institutions. To build large enterprises, particularly those in which ownership separates from control, a society must achieve not only key economic, legal, and technological pre-conditions, but political pre-conditions as well, namely, a particular kind of social peace, one in which managers if freed from direct shareholder control would still be largely loyal to distant, non-controlling shareholders. Some ways by which modern societies achieved social peace made it harder for the public firm to emerge and prosper, because they made a diffusely owned firm's managers less loyal to share-holders. Hence, public firms were less valuable to shareholders in those environments. And hence there were fewer of them.

1.1. The Political Foundations to the Firm
1.2. Variety and Persistence in Distancing Shareholders from Employees

1.1. THE POLITICAL FOUNDATIONS TO THE FIRM

The large-scale public firm is typically seen as a purely economic institution, one that solves the economic problem of mobilizing capital from financiers and of organizing large-scale production by managers. Its economic and technical pre-conditions are well-recognized—a transparent accounting system, a good legal system, technologies that are best effectuated via large-scale organization, a cadre of trained managers, a capacity to mobilize finance, etc.

Recognized less well, or not at all, are two political foundations to the public cor-poration: first, before serious economic activity can take place, social and economic conflict must be minimized, and the ways modern societies have minimized it can affect, and have affected, the structure of the modern corporation. All societies have put distance between shareholders and the firm, but they have done so differently, and these differences often determined the institutions of corporate governance.

Second, under one modern and widespread political condition, ownership could not easily separate from control, and the truly public firm could not dominate business. Strong social democracies pressed firms to favor employees over invested capital, but shareholders resisted this, and their best way to resist was often to build or to keep concentrated, and often private, ownership. Moreover, social democracies also frayed the kinds of ties that today bind managers to diffuse shareholders in the American public firm and, with the ties between the two frayed, shareholders had another reason to concentrate their ownership.

Strong social democracies and the public firm have mixed badly. This oil-and-water-mix not only strongly explains why ownership and control have not yet widely separated in European social democracies but also identifies a critical pre-condition to the rise and dominance of the public firm in the United States, namely a political environment that did not tie managers to employees, one that more easily permitted tying managers to shareholders, a political environment not present in every advanced industrial nation.

1.2. VARIETY AND PERSISTENCE IN DISTANCING SHAREHOLDERS FROM EMPLOYEES

The ways to produce social peace in the corporate context are many. All have the common effect of distancing shareholders from the day-to-day operation of the firm. Employees can be guaranteed representation on the firm's board of directors, a solution that still prevails in Germany. Or, some of them may be guaranteed lifetime employment, a solution that benefited large firms' core employees in Japan. Or, the largest industrial firms can be run by the government, and then run in a way that favors incumbent employees, a result common until recently in France. Or, key visible purveyors of shareholder wealth—large, private, salient financial institutions—could attract political attention, and the polity could then fragment them or deny them authority either to own stock or to play a major role in industry, a result historically common in the United States. Or, a social democracy could through rules and norms limit the actions that firms can take *vis-à-vis* incumbent employees.

Dismissing these institutions as inefficient is too easy, especially for a market-oriented American analyst. Understanding them is harder. One can begin by understanding the obvious, that politics can affect, and even disrupt, markets. Voters may see market arrangements as unfair, leading them to lash back and disrupt otherwise efficient arrangements. To quell this backlash, legal and insti-tutional structures may arise and survive, despite that they could not withstand a normal efficiency critique. They may be politically necessary for production, and, were they absent, the social turmoil might be economically unbearable. The prospect of a severe backlash, one that would destroy efficient institutions and drive a society into impoverished turmoil, or of co-optation, in which politicians strategically temper otherwise efficient rules and institutions to finesse away a more destructive backlash, complicates a standard efficiency analysis.

This kind of backlash is usually ignored in American law and economics inquiries, often I believe for good reason. Its absence in American analysis is not so much due to logic, but to American exceptionalism: this kind of backlash and this need to temper social conflict have been much less severe historically in the United States than in the other rich nations, as we shall examine later in Chapter 16. But ignoring it can leave the analysis of why an institution looks the way it does incomplete. Its absence in American analyses opens up two gaps in understanding corporate institutions: first, in nations where stronger means of settling social conflict were needed, we must understand these stronger means and their consequences in order to understand their corporate institutions. Second, in the United States, we must understand that several of our institutions—including, I shall argue in Part III, the diffuse ownership of the public firm itself—rest on the relative absence of such severe social conflict.

2

The Wealthy West's Differing Corporate Governance Structures

What are the major differences in corporate ownership and governance in the developed nations? Differences can be categorized roughly into those affecting ownership, those affecting management, and those affecting employment. One major corporate governance difference to explain is the degree of block ownership and the extent of ownership separation. Another is the degree of managerial control over day-to-day operations. Yet another is the degree of labor influence on the firm. There is reason to think that each can affect the others. Determining one can affect, or determine, the others.

2.1. Diffuse versus Block Ownership
2.2. Managerial Compensation and Labor Influence
2.3. Can a Nations's Size, Development Level, or Corporate Legal Institutions Alone Explain the Differences?

2.1. DIFFUSE VERSUS BLOCK OWNERSHIP

In the United States for quite some time distant, diffuse stockholders have owned the largest firms. In contrast, in continental Europe even the largest firms have been closely held, because many never went public and big blockholders persisted even in those that did. In Germany at the end of the twentieth century, nearly every large firm still had a large blockholder, usually from a family, but for some firms from a bank, insurance company, or another corporation.[1] In France, the family sector in recent decades was large, growing, and highly competitive.[2] In Italy family firms still persist and there are few fully public firms.[3] Firms in continental Europe are owned less by diffuse stock markets and more

[1] Julian Franks and Colin Mayer, 'Ownership and Control of German Corporations', 14 *Rev. Fin. Stud.* 943, 944 (2001).

[2] Paul Windolf, 'The Governance Structure of Large French Corporations', in *Corporate Governance Today* 705 (1998) (Columbia Sloan Project on Corporate Governance).

[3] Alessandro Portolano, 'The decision to adopt defensive tactics', 20 *Int'l Rev. L & Econ.* 425, 427 (2000); cf. Eugenio Ruggiero, *Italy*, in *The Legal Basis of Corporate Governance in Publicly Held Corporations: A Comparative Approach* 79, 82, (ed. by Arthur R. Pinto and Gustavo Visentini 1998) (declining number of listings in 1990s on Italy's leading stock exchange).

by concentrated blockholders than in the United States, with the blocks usually owned by families or, particularly in Germany, financial institutions. Some of this is an artifact of the post-Second World War family-founders of some large firms. But ownership concentration has persisted longer than a generation, and thus far *even* when a family sells out, it typically sells to another, new blockholder, *not* to dispersed stockholders via, say, an initial public offer followed by a relentless sell-off of the family's holdings.[4] Perhaps family-owners will someday prefer this American-style method of exit, but thus far they have not had that opportunity, even in many of the world's wealthier nations.

A few ownership contrasts: in the twenty firms in Germany that have just over $500 million in stock market capitalization (to keep the size comparison across borders constant), *eighteen* have blockholders owning 20 per cent or more of the stock. In France and Italy, *every* one of these mid-sized firms has a 20 per cent + blockholder. In Sweden, eighteen do. In the United States, only *two* do.[5] In Germany, financial institutions have fifty ownership blocks of 5 per cent or more of the stock in the 100 largest German firms;[6] in the United States such institutional blocks are few, at about zero.

One could make the case that the difference is becoming more one of degree than of kind. Not only are large European firms seeking capital from new sources, but institutional investors in the United States are no longer the 100-share individuals of the standard model. They own bigger slices of a company's stock. They are informed about corporate governance trends. And some of them are informed enough about a firm's operations and business to give serious feedback to directors and managers.

But differences remain even today. The data shows that even the new American institutional investors tend to own smaller blocks of stock than institutions, families, and individuals outside the United States.[7] And the European firms may be seeking new sources of capital, but their ownership has not yet diffused as widely as has that of American firms.

2.2. MANAGERIAL COMPENSATION AND LABOR INFLUENCE

Management and managerial control structures tend to differ as well. In the United States, powerful incentive pay goes to American managers, directors are often outsiders, and takeovers and proxy fights occur often enough that they affect managerial motivation. Incentive compensation, takeovers, and proxy fights have all historically been less important in continental Europe and Japan.

---

[4] Franks and Mayer, supra, note 1 at 955.   [5] Table 2.1.
[6] 13 *Monopolkommission Hauptgutachten* 1998/1999, *Wettbewerbspolitik in Netzstrukturen* 251–56 (2000); *Monopolkommission Hauptgutachten* 1996/1997, *Marktoffnung Umfassend Verwirklichen* 187–92 (1998).   [7] See Tables 2.1 and 6.1.

Labor's role also differs. In Germany labor participates directly in the core governance institutions: as is well known, the largest German firms must have half of the board members from labor. Sometimes labor's effect on the core governance institutions is indirect: in Japan, lifetime employment is a basic institution in the largest firms, and corporate governance structures have had to adapt to this. Two adaptations are the inside-board and the prevalence of shareholder-creditors. Each suppresses pure shareholder goals. And in France and Italy, corporate governance structures have had to adapt to the power of labor in the political arena, usually inducing the firms to be smaller and private, or, if large and public but not government-owned, at least with a concentrated ownership block.

And in the United States, in contrast, labor rarely participates in the board or in high-level management. Labor markets are fluid and employment flexible. Labor's absence and the fluid labor market permit corporate governance institutions that the United States could not have developed easily had its labor market been fixed and rigid.

2.3. CAN A NATION'S SIZE, DEVELOPMENT LEVEL, OR CORPORATE LEGAL INSTITUTIONS ALONE EXPLAIN THE DIFFERENCES?

Analysts might once have dismissed the contrast in ownership as a function of economic development. Right after the Second World War, American business and living standards were so far ahead that this alone might have explained the different ownership structures then. But standards of living have converged in the past half-century, yet the ownership structures have not. Our primary task will be to explain why. True, corporate ownership and governance structures change more slowly than the outside environment, but this lag, although important, is not the only basis for differences.

And analysts might once have dismissed the contrasting ownership structures as due to size, in that firms in the United States were larger, and one might then have thought that only the largest firms become truly public firms. Even today, the largest American firms tend to be much larger than the largest firms in Europe and Japan. But we now know enough to reject size as explaining the ownership differences. Even among *similarly sized* large firms around the world today, the public firm is *still* more widespread in the United States than in continental Europe. These differences thus far have persisted, despite converging living standards and business technology.

Technical corporate law institutions, especially those that protect distant minority stockholders from the rapacity of controlling insiders, could in theory be determinative. If outside stockholders do not feel protected, they will not invest. But although the technical institutions are important, building them is not rocket science for societies that already have some of them, like courts that can enforce a contract or regulators who are effective. When the political conditions for stock

Table 2.1. *Ownership Separation:*
Portion of Mid-Sized Firms without a 20
per cent Blockholder in 1995 (From
the 20 Public Firms with a Capitalization
just over $500 Million)[8]

Austria	0.00
Italy	0.00
France	0.00
Germany	0.10
Netherlands	0.10
Sweden	0.10
Belgium	0.20
Finland	0.20
Norway	0.20
Australia	0.30
Denmark	0.30
Japan	0.30
Switzerland	0.50
Canada	0.60
United Kingdom	0.60
United States	0.90

markets and diffuse ownership are there in an economically-ripe rich nation, supporting institutions should not be that hard to build so that ownership can separate. That is, they can be built, if the political will to build them is there. In modern times, in the modern rich democracies, that lack of political will is manifested in social democracy. And in fact, in some nations the technical institutions *are* there in rudimentary form, as we shall see in Part VI, Corporate Law's Limits. But if the political configuration was not conducive to separation, ownership still did not separate from control.

Academic theorists and policymakers have recently turned to technical corporate law as the foundation for ownership separation. But suffice it to say for now that corporate law's scope is too narrow to be critically central to organizing an economy: American corporate law, for example, often seen as exemplary nowadays, leaves a huge surface area of corporate action untouched: the American business judgment rule has judges *refusing* to review and regulate managers' unconflicted acts. Managerial mistakes, disloyalty to shareholders (as long as the managers' hands are not in the cookie jar), over-investment, under-investment, and so on, are just *not* subject to corporate law review. And these possibilities of systematic managerial mistake can easily destabilize diffuse ownership. More on this gap—and how the political theory explains much of what is going on in this gap—below, in Part VI, Corporate Law's Limits. So, our working hypothesis is that political

[8] Adapted from Rafael La Porta, Florencio Lopez-de-Silanes, and Andrei Shleifer, 'Corporate Ownership Around the World', 54 *J. Fin.* 471, 492 (1999).

differences explain much here. Some of these differences arose nation-by-nation, and some of these differences can be generalized and tested across the developed world: social democracies fit badly with the diffusely-owned public firm, and one would predict fewer public firms in the stronger social democracies.

* * *

The public firm is not a *necessary*, inevitable organizational evolution. It has important strengths, as well as critical weaknesses. The strengths are that it provides a means of raising (or for many firms, holding) capital beyond that which a single family or small group of individuals could handle: it facilitates economies of scale and scope. It helps to separate the second or third generation after a firm's founding from control of the firm, an important task when that second or third generation lacks the skill or interest to run the firm. And, conversely, it lets managers with administrative talent but little capital run the firm. And that specialization has its capital market correlate: it enables owners uninterested in managing to diversify and gain liquidity.

These advantages are commonly known. Emphasized less often is the interaction between capital markets and product markets. The possibility of easy separation and easy raising of equity capital facilitates product market competition in one important dimension: an incumbent can often find itself facing a competitor who can compete more quickly and more effectively because it has good access to equity markets. Securities markets, just by providing a means of quickly raising capital and the possibility of separation, can enhance product market competition. The possibility of an entrepreneur eventually exiting via a public offering of his or her stock can motivate new players to enter and compete. A potential competitor, especially if an individual, is more likely to jump in if it knows it can exit if successful. Selling out via the stock market and full separation is an important means of exit, one that helps motivate players to enter. It's probably an under-rated reason why public firms can promote economic well-being.

The public firm's principal weakness on which we will focus is the frequently fragile ties between managers and shareholders. A firm's capabilities may become misaligned with its product market, but it might respond slowly because managers are used to the old routines. The managerial agents may react too slowly for shareholders' tastes. Or managers may be unwilling to take astute risks that shareholders would consider good bets, because managers might not want to rock the boat while diversified shareholders want to maximize value. Or managers may build empires for prestige and power. All of these are the costs to shareholders of running their firm through managerial agents. If owners, potential and actual, worry too much that their managerial agents will not do shareholders' bidding, then founding owners are reluctant to sell, distant investors are reluctant to buy, and ownership does not separate from control.

3

....

A General Theory

One way to achieve social peace is for labor to get a strong voice inside the firm. When labor influence is high, the pressure increases on managers to be less loyal to shareholders.[1] This amplified labor voice can come via codetermination, via lifetime employment, or via state action that favors employees when conflict arises.

3.1. OWNERS, MANAGERS, AND EMPLOYEES

The firm can be abstracted into three simple, broad parts: ownership, management, and employment. Much that is important can be said by keeping the firm's abstract parts simplified. Keeping them simple lets us see how they must fit together and what forces can upset their fit.

Owners, usually from the richest strata in the society, cannot be seen to have acquired their wealth too unjustly; otherwise neither managers nor employees will work well for the owners. Managers must be motivated to do their jobs. They cannot run their firms into the ground or divert its wealth to themselves; otherwise owners will not invest and employees will be too uncertain of long-term prospects to work hard for the firm that would soon be run into the ground. And employees must be motivated to work and be unable to appropriate owners' investments; otherwise owners will not invest. Nor can the employees be positioned to prevent managers from running the firm; otherwise managers cannot effectively induce the firm to produce.

---

[1] Mark J. Roe, *Strong Managers, Weak Owners: The Political Roots of American Corporate Finance* (1994). See infra, Chapter 27, 'Populism and Socialism in Corporate Governance', in Part VI: 'Unifying Two Political Theories'.

These conflicts inside the firm either map onto broader social conflicts in a society, or can spill over from firms into political and social conflict. If the society cannot minimize these conflicts, it cannot produce. One or another of these inputs could withdraw, or sulk, denying the firm a critical input.

Politics often determines the structure of one of these broad parts of the firm. And by determining one part, politics could thereby determine the others, because sometimes only a few forms of the others fit well with the fixed institution.

3.2. CODETERMINATION AND LIFETIME EMPLOYMENT

A few brief examples, to be detailed in Part II: Germany settled upon codetermination, with labor getting half of the seats on the boards of large firms. This brought about labor peace, but then the other pieces, management and ownership, reacted. For managers to have the freedom that they either needed or wanted, German boards were kept, or made, weaker than they otherwise would have been. Powerful boards, one common tool of owners elsewhere, were not available to German owners. But owners must oversee managers from time-to-time. Block ownership provides owners such a means when boards are weak and, hence, codetermination may explain why block ownership persists in Germany.

Similarly, one way for owners to motivate senior managers is via stock options and other incentive compensation that tie them more directly to stockholders. Even if owners do not monitor managers regularly, stock-based incentive compensation can make managers think like owners. But that kind of incentive compensation may not fit well with a codetermined board, one that is leery of compensating managers highly and uncomfortable with seeing managers tied more tightly to owners. More generally, high managerial compensation, whether of the incentive variety or not, might make managers more loyal to shareholders but it can in some environments exacerbate tensions inside the firm, tensions that can reduce the firm's productivity. A cost-benefit trade-off (better motivated managers, but more demoralized employees) could make distant owners pay a price whichever way they go.

In Japan, social conflict not too different from that in Germany led to a social compact with many large firms promising lifetime employment to their core employees. Lifetime employment helped to bring about social peace, but it is not always the best way to motivate employees. Internal promotional tournaments developed, with the last tournament having favored managerial employees promoted to a large board of other honored insiders.

3.3. POSITIVE AND NORMATIVE THEORY

The argument here is positive not normative. My point is not that societies short-change themselves when they demean one organizational form or another (although they may), but that before production can roll, social peace must be achieved. To achieve it, compromises must be made, politics must become stable, social conflict minimized. The forces that stabilize a society inevitably affect the corporation, sometimes directly, sometimes indirectly.

In a sense, one cannot normatively criticize on utilitarian grounds a means of achieving peace if, were that peace not attained, the alternative of turmoil would have been worse. (Nor should one think that the United States has always been immune to the need to settle such conflict. It has not been. It just settled what conflict it had differently, historically by keeping financial intermediaries small and without a sustained powerful voice inside the large firms.)

3.4. EFFICIENCY IMPLICATIONS?

Any efficiency implications here are attenuated. While right now these economies are not performing as well as the American, the contrary was so in the 1980s, especially if we contrasted Germany and Japan with the United States. Differing corporate governance structures generate differing advantages and disadvantages. Sometimes these net out to zero, sometimes these favor one economy over another when the production task is geared to the type of corporate governance they have. Perhaps one system is overall better and will in the long-run dominate, or perhaps a system that could mix and match would be better overall, by allowing for more variety and competition.

Relative efficiency is not the main story here. What is striking is that the corporate governance systems historically have been national, without a strong mix in each nation. The United States has had diffuse ownership, Germany has had bank voice and family ownership, Japan has had bank blocks in the largest firms, France and Italy still have few fully public firms, etc. The fact that variation has tended to be national, and not across industries or tailored to specific firms inside a nation, makes one think that key explanations are likely to be national as well.

3.5. SOCIAL DEMOCRACY

Social peace in many nations has been an ongoing issue in the post-Second World War world. In social democracies, employees were often systematically protected from actions that owners (and managers) might otherwise have liked to take. Lay-offs have been harder than they might otherwise have been, the range of managerial discretion on the shop floor more limited than it was elsewhere, and unemployment benefits were high and easy to obtain. Social peace in strong social democracies also disfavored the core means by which owners tie managers to ownership interests—high incentive compensation via stock options, shareholder wealth maximization norms, and hostile takeovers. Social peace in the strongest social democracies demeaned high incentive compensation (at least if publicly known) because the resulting envy would have weakened employee motivation, weakened or obliterated shareholder wealth maximization norms, or made hostile takeovers illegal or easy to disrupt by those whom such takeovers would have hurt. Social democracies thereby made diffuse ownership harder for the owners, who would have found that managers were harder to monitor, motivate, and keep loyal; and owners accordingly were more likely than otherwise to own big blocks of stock in private or near-private companies.

I treat politics as fixed, for the most part, so that we can analyze political differences carefully. But although treating it as fixed is plausible—basic politics often only changes slowly—it is just a useful working assumption. Later, principally in Chapter 21, Political Change in Continental Europe, I discuss political change, especially the modern political shift to the right (and toward greater acceptance of markets) in Europe, and how it could be affecting corporate governance and ownership.

* * *

Social democracy is not a precise term. I use it in part due to want of a better term. In social democracies—nations committed to private property but whose governments play a large role in the economy, emphasize distributional considerations, and favor employees over capital-owners when the two conflict[2]— public policy emphasizes managers' natural agenda and demeans shareholders' natural agenda. Perhaps a better operational phrase than social democracy would be the less-common 'stakeholder society', or simply a nation in which employee pressures are strong. Italy, for example, is not usually thought of as a strong social democracy—it does not have a cradle-to-grave state support system as has Sweden nor a socially supportive state bureaucracy as France has nor a corporate-law mandated corporate compromise as German codetermination reflects—but stakeholder pressures are high in Italy, and those pressures would affect shareholder interests in large firms, were there many of them.

So we use the phrase social democracy, recognizing its limits. It describes those nations in which the pressure on the firm for low-risk expansion is high, the pressure to avoid risky organizational change is substantial, and the tools that would induce managers to work in favor of invested capital—such as high incentive compensation, hostile takeovers, transparent accounting, and acculturation to shareholder-wealth maximization norms—are weak. Life may well be better for more people in the strongest social democracies, but the internal structure of public firms must necessarily be weaker for shareholders.

* * *

[2] See Adam Przeworski, 'Socialism and Social Democracy', in *The Oxford Companion to Politics of the World* 832, 835 (ed. by Joel Krieger *et al.*, 1993) (social democracies seek 'to implement "functional socialism", even if ownership of productive resources remains private'); S.C. Stimson, 'Social Democracy', in 4 *The New Palgrave: A Dictionary of Economics* 395, 396 (ed. by John Eatwell, Murray Milgate, and Peter Newman, 1987) (European social democracy seeks not to end private ownership, but to improve material conditions for the many).

I next in Part II illustrate how social democracy could affect corporate governance structures. We could instead have begun illustrating the thesis with, say, Japanese lifetime employment and traced its effects on the large Japanese firm. Or we could have begun with the effects of a French élite that aimed to reduce lay-offs and downsizings inside large firms. Or we could have begun with Italy's 1969 'hot autumn', as they called it—of militant labor actions, strikes, factory occupations, and mass demonstrations—and then thought through how revolutionary pressures could have affected ownership structures there.

We could have started elsewhere, but we begin with German codetermination because it vividly shows social democracy affecting corporate governance. The others would also illustrate how political pressures can affect the firm's ownership and governance, but codetermination paints that picture more quickly, more starkly, and more clearly.

II

SOCIAL CONFLICT AND THE
INSTITUTIONS OF CORPORATE
GOVERNANCE

Here we illustrate the peace-as-predicate principle.

Social conflict led Germany to seek a 'middle way' between unbridled capitalism and strong socialism. Inside the large business firm, employees got half the seats in the boardroom. This affected corporate governance directly, by giving German firms a distinctive employee voice in the boardroom. And social conflict affected corporate governance indirectly but powerfully, because managers and shareholders preferred that the boardroom not become powerful and well informed. Board meetings historically were infrequent, information flow to the board poor, and the board often too big and unwieldy to be effective. Instead, out-of-the-boardroom shareholder caucuses and meetings between managers and large shareholders substituted for effective boards. Moreover, diffuse ownership would have ended these informal channels of shareholder control and information flow. Diffuse stockholders would have had to choose between strengthening the board (and hence further empowering the board's employee-half) or keeping it weak and thus living with sub-standard (by current world criteria) boardroom governance. Strong labor voice, one can plausibly speculate, called forth concentrated ownership.

This effect has been more general. Social democracies demeaned shareholder primacy, pushing firms to stabilize employment, to expand whether or not expansion was profitable for shareholders, and to avoid change that would disrupt the quality of the work place. These democratic goals map right to the typical goals of unconstrained managers, typically labelled as agency costs. Social democratic pressures increased managerial agency costs for shareholders and thus decreased the firm's value to diffuse shareholders. Owners presumably sought alternatives that reduced those agency costs, such as close ownership.

Because these social democratic pressures were weaker in the United States, managerial agency costs were smaller here. Despite being smaller, institutions still arose to tie managers to shareholders, institutions such as shareholder wealth maximization norms, transparent accounting, high incentive compensation, and hostile takeovers. Each can fall short, as recent American corporate failures like

Enron and WorldCom show. But overall each tool narrows the gap between American managers and shareholders. And each gap-reducing tool has tended to be weakened, often deliberately so, in the world's stronger social democracies.

Social democracies pressured firms in ways that increased managerial agency costs to shareholders, thereby widening the gap between managers and any diffuse shareholders. Moreover, social democracies weakened the tools that in the United States closed up much of the American firms' smaller gap between the firm and its diffuse shareholders.

4

Social Democracies and Agency Costs: Raising the Stakes

Social democracies raised agency costs for shareholders in the public firm, and shareholders' natural reaction would have been to use an alternative organizational form that kept those costs down. German codetermination—by which labor gets one-half of the supervisory board of Germany's largest firms—is an explicit manifestation of social democracy, one that well illustrates the effects on corporate organization of social democracy. We first look at social democracy's effects through codetermination, by imagining the dilemma that a family-owned firm faced when considering whether to take their firm public. Then we generalize by looking at social democracy's effects on agency costs and ownership structure without codetermination. The formal social-democratic institution of codetermination is not needed for social democracy to affect the public firm's internal workings, but the formal institution boldly illustrates the political effects.

4.1. SOCIAL DEMOCRACY'S EFFECTS THROUGH CODETERMINATION

Germany's long ideological and political encounter with codetermination began just after the First World War when revolutionary leaders established workers' councils (counterparts to the better-known soviets arising elsewhere), which evolved into employee representation on the supervisory council of the larger firms.[1] After

---

[1] Charles S. Maier, *Recasting Bourgeois Europe: Stabilization in France, Germany, and Italy in the Decade After World War I* 59–60, 138, 141–44 (1975).

the Second World War, labor leaders sought to be represented on the boards, partly to convince the Allies not to dismantle Germany's coal and steel industry, by asserting that they, labor, would constrain the wartime industrialists via positions on the firms' supervisory boards. From this 'deal' came full-parity codetermination of labor and shareholders in the coal and steel industry. Later political events expanded this codetermination to one-third of the supervisory boards of most other industrial firms, and in 1976 to one-half of the boards of Germany's larger firms.[2]

Codetermination also had its capitalist promoters, who sought a 'middle way' between the raw capitalism of the market-place and the extreme socialism of state ownership. Industrial leaders sought to co-opt revolutionary ideals,[3] and reformers 'envisioned a gradual dissolution of central state authority and the growth of works councils and industrial self-government.... [W]orkers and entrepreneurs of a given industry could [and should] be seated at the same table to hammer out common policy....'[4]

Business and political leaders such as Walter Rathenau promoted this idea of a corporate middle way between raw market-place capitalism and socialism,[5] and the institution of codetermination has grown into one that many Germans have been proud of.[6]

Consider how codetermination affects agency costs, and thereby should have affected German corporate ownership structure and securities markets, by imagining how a successful family firm, thinking about making an initial public offering and in time withdrawing from managing and owning the company, might have reacted to codetermination. Their supervisory board was never strong. It has met for the statutory minimum of twice annually.[7] The meetings in the 1990s, when we imagine the family owners inquiring whether or not to go public, are formal, without serious give and take. The accounting reports that the board gets are not very good. The reports are given to the board at the very beginning of a

---

[2] Katharina Pistor, 'Codetermination: A Sociopolitical Model with Governance Externalities', in *Employees and Corporate Governance* 163, 167–69 (ed. by Margaret M. Blair and Mark J. Roe, 1999).   [3] Charles S. Maier, *In Search of Stability* 165 (1987).

[4] Maier, supra, note 1, at 12.

[5] Maier, supra, note 1, at 142. More precisely, Rathenau sought to make business property something intermediate between a private possession and a socialized asset. Maier, supra, note 3, at 40 (1987); Walter Rathenau, *Die Neue Wirtschaft* (1918); Walter Rathenau, *Vom Aktienwesen* (1922). Rathenau, a leading thinker and political leader, was from the family that founded Germany's leading electrical company; he ran wartime production and later became Germany's foreign minister.

[6] See Jean-Marie Colombani, Eric Le Boucher, and Arnaud Leparmentier, [Interview with] Gerhard Schröder, '*Je ne pense plus souhaitable une société sans inégalités*', *Le Monde*, 20 Nov. 1999, at 3 (quoting German Chancellor Schröder's belief that, in contrast to the American model, Germany's 'is founded on the participation of workers not just in our prosperity but also in decision-making, notably via codetermination').

[7] Until recently, German boards needed to meet only twice annually, and they often kept to the limit. Well-publicized corporate governance failures in a few public firms induced business pressures and legal changes that pushed supervisory boards to meet three or four times a year. Compare Aktiengesellschaft § 110, in Hannes Schneider and Martin Heidenhain, *The German Stock Corporation Act* 115 (2000) (four) with Uwe Huffer, *Aktiengesetz* § 110, at 440 (1995) (two). See Thomas J. André, Jr, 'Some Reflections on German Corporate Governance: A Glimpse at German Supervisory Boards', 70 *Tul. L. Rev.* 1819, 1825 n.21 (1996).

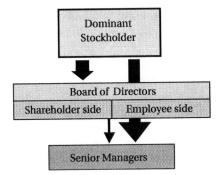

Fig. 4.1. German firm's dominant stockholder, by-passing the codetermined board

semiannual meeting, and are then whisked away at its end. The board has not been a serious monitoring mechanism inside the firm. This until recently has been the typical picture painted of the German boardroom.[8]

Board-level monitoring has not thus far been critical to the firm for two reasons. First, many family owners have also been the firm's managers; hence, the disjunction between ownership and management was weaker than in the fully public firm, and managerial agency costs were lower. Second, even if the family did not manage the firm directly but instead hired professional managers, the family members met regularly with managers to review results and performance, as illustrated in Figure 4.1. In effect, the monitoring role of an active board was fulfilled apart from the supervisory board, whose meetings were stale, formal, and ineffective.

The family may have considered moving more of the monitoring into the boardroom, partly to get ready for a public offering, partly to formalize the informal monthly meetings with managers. But they decided not to move it inside the boardroom because they preferred not to give more information and authority to the labor members of the supervisory board. (Codetermination requirements, which are based on the number of employees, apply to both public and private firms. But the private company's owners can by-pass the board more easily than diffuse shareholders of the public company can.)

The family is hoping to leave the firm. They want to sell their stock and diversify their investments. The firm has been returning $50 million in earnings to them annually, and they accord a capitalization rate of ten to those earnings, valuing the firm at $500 million.

The underwriters with whom they speak confirm that the firm would be worth $500 million if the average annual earnings of $50 million were expected to persist. But the underwriters, hoping to sell the stock to potential diffuse public

[8] See Pistor, supra, note, 2, at 191; see also Jeremy Edwards and Klaus Fischer, *Banks, Finance and Investment in Germany* 213 (1994) ('Supervisory boards...receive relatively little detailed information about the firm's operations.'); Wulf von Schimmelmann, 'Unternehmenskontrolle in Deutschland', in *Finanzmärkte* 7 (ed. by Bernhard Gahlen, Helmut Hesse, and Hans Jürgen Ramser, 1997); Florian Schilling, 'Der Aufsichtsrat ist für die Katz', *Frankfurter Allgemeine Zeitung*, 27 Aug. 1994, at 11 (German survey of business leaders concludes that the supervisory board is weak and that, as a result of codetermination, it avoids controversial topics).

stockholders, say that they fear the earnings will not persist if the board remains weak, meeting only twice annually and receiving such poor information. Eventually there will be an external crisis in the firm's markets, or an internal one in the firm's organization, and a weak, poorly informed board is likely to respond more slowly and less effectively than a stronger one. Eventually current managers will retire or be unable to manage the firm well, and a weak board will resolve a succession crisis less effectively than a strong one. Thus far, the underwriters say, the family fulfilled the role that a strong board would play. But if the family leaves, the firm will at times be rudderless.

The underwriters consider this potential lack of direction when they value the firm, estimating that over time earnings will be $40 million, rather than $50 million, if the board is weak and ineffective. They accord those earnings the same capitalization rate of ten, valuing the firm at $400 million, not $500 million.

The family and underwriters then consider strengthening the board, by changing the by-laws to have the board meet monthly, by improving the information flow to the board, by adopting transparent, understandable accounting with statements going to the board well before the meetings, by instilling in the board an ethic of involvement, and by building aggressive audit, executive, and compensation committees. These improvements to the board, the family tells the underwriters, will improve monitoring and reduce the weak board problems. As a result the expected earnings should be re-pegged to $50 million, and the firm should be valued at the original $500 million in the initial public offer, not $400 million. (Up to here the story would not be much different in the United States prior to an initial public offering.)

The underwriters though respond that, yes, the board will be better. But, they ask, in whose interest will the board run the firm? With the supervisory board codetermined, a charged-up board would tilt more to labor when labor's and shareholders' interests conflict than does a purely shareholder-dominated board. Managers would be monitored more, but not necessarily more in shareholders' interests. The enhanced board would create value, but some of that value would go to labor, not to stockholders. The underwriters conclude that the firm would indeed be worth $500 million, but they believe $100 million of that value would go to labor.

These numbers are not out of line with current empirical work on the effect of the 1976 codetermination law, which expanded labor's representation from one-third of the supervisory boards of large firms to one-half. The data available suggest that the increase had a 10 to 20 per cent negative effect on shareholder value.[9]

But the family wants to keep that $100 million. How can they keep it? They can revisit whether they should sell out completely. They may decide to keep the firm

---

[9] Felix R. FitzRoy and Kornelius Kraft, 'Economic Effects of Codetermination', 95 *Scandinavian J. Econ.* 365, 374 n.6 (1993) (the 1976 change resulted in a productivity loss of '13%–14% of value added'); Frank A. Schmid and Frank Seger, 'Arbeitnehmermitbestimmung, Allokation von Entscheidungsrechten und Shareholder Value', 5 *Zeitschrift für Betriebswirtschaft* 453 (1998); Gary Gorton and Frank A. Schmid, 'Class Struggle Inside the Firm: A Study of German Codetermination' 25 (National Bureau of Economic Research Working Paper, Oct. 2000) (codetermination reduces market-to-book ratio of equity by 27%). Contra Theodor Baums and Bernd Frick, 'The Market Value of the Codetermined Firm', in *Employees and Corporate Governance*, supra, note 2, at 206, 232

private and to re-examine whether they can find an heir who will run it. Or they may hire professional managers to run the firm, if they have not done so already. Or they may sell the firm, but sell it not to diffuse stockholders who will discount the price because they would fear agency costs, but to another dominant owner, who need not discount the price because he or she can overcome those costs. Such block sales are common in Germany.[10] To keep that $100 million difference, the family does *not* launch an initial public offer; as a consequence, there is one less public firm in Germany and one less family interested in seeing Germany develop a strong securities market.

Hence, German social democracy, institutionalized in corporate governance via codetermination, plausibly induces this firm to stay private, so as to avoid the costs to shareholders of an enhanced labor voice inside the firm. Social democracy in the form of supervisory board codetermination mixes badly with the public firm.

4.2. SOCIAL DEMOCRACY'S EFFECTS WITHOUT CODETERMINATION

Codetermination illustrates the thesis crisply, but social democracy even without codetermination has the same effect in inducing concentrated ownership. Social democracy's pressure on the public firm persists even if we remove the formal institution of German supervisory board codetermination. Social democracies press firms and managers from many sides to favor employees with jobs in place.

A simple countervailing coalition image helps to explain why ownership concentration has persisted so long. If employees are favored through private organization, formal representation, or state action, owners will be induced, all else equal, to coalesce to reduce their internal conflicts and face employees more cohesively.

4.3. GENERAL EFFECTS: FAVORING EMPLOYEES OVER SHAREHOLDERS

The effects political pressures can have on the firm can be seen by thinking through the consequences to shareholders of increased managerial agency costs.

Recall the basic agency costs to shareholders: unconstrained managers, unlike shareholders, prefer to expand their firms for more satisfaction, power, prestige, and pay. Managers want to avoid many profit-maximizing risks that would risk

---

(finding no financial loss to stockholders from court decisions extending codetermination rights); see also Bernd Frick, Gerhard Speckbacher, and Paul Wentges, 'Arbeitnehmermitbestimmung und moderne Theorie der Unternehmung', *Zeitschrift für Betriebswirtschaft* 745–63 (1999) (critiquing studies that showed codetermination as negatively affecting stock price).

[10] See Julian Franks and Colin Mayer, 'Ownership and Control of German Corporations', 14 *Rev. Fin. Stud.* 943, 955 (2001).

their careers. Managers prefer to use up capital in place rather than to restructure a firm, because restructuring is painful. And managers may be more willing to tolerate slack than would shareholders.

These basic agency costs are well understood. But less well discerned is that these managerial tendencies fit well with employees' goals, and that a second basic corporate governance problem for employees and capital providers has been the persistent tension between invested capital and current employees, a tension muted in the United States, but historically not muted everywhere else. Employees *also* are averse to risks to the firm, as their human capital is tied up in the firm and they are not fully diversified. Employees *also* prefer that the firm expand, not downsize, because expanding often yields them promotion opportunities, while downsizing risks leaving them unemployed. (Likewise, institutional creditors, who loomed larger in European firms than in their American counterparts, preferred to avoid risk and to maintain stability. And incompletely diversified family stockholders, the last key player in large continental European firms, also preferred stability more strongly than diversified American public firm stockholders. The key risk-avoiding pieces all fit together in continental Europe.)

On a simple level, employees prefer higher wages, and shareholders prefer lower wages (at the same level of productivity). Because wages are not precisely determined, managers hold some discretion in setting wages,[11] and weakly monitored managers ordinarily would not fight as strongly for shareholders as would strongly monitored managers. Even in the United States, slight differences in shareholder control of managers affect wage rates, with less-monitored managers in states where anti-takeover laws are strong conceding higher salaries to employees than similar managers in states where anti-takeover laws are weak.[12] On a more complex level, American managers of firms in declining industries tended in the 1980s to use up their equity capital before shrinking their firms unless corporate governance controls induced them not to use up equity first;[13] this is the strategy that incumbent employees would prefer.

Even today in the United States these stakeholder effects, although much weaker than the pressures abroad, can be detected. Delaware law seems to have increased a firm's value in 1990s data,[14] and the reason seems to be its more expansive takeover law. Although Delaware law is moderately anti-takeover, it obstructs the offeror less than other states do. This extra room for offering companies to maneuver may account for the noticeable increase in value in Delaware firms in the 1990s, of about 2 to 5 per cent over similar firms incorporated elsewhere. Although stakeholder pressure is weaker in American states than it was in most

---

[11] Lloyd G. Reynolds, *The Structure of Labor Markets: Wages and Labor Mobility in Theory and Practice* 156 (1951); Richard A. Lester, 'A Range Theory of Wage Differentials', 5 *Indus. & Lab. Rel. Rev.* 483, 500 (1952).

[12] Marianne Bertrand and Sendhil Mullainathan, 'Is There Discretion in Wage Setting? A Test Using Takeover Legislation', 30 *Rand J. Econ.* 535, 537 (1999).

[13] Cf. Michael C. Jensen, 'Agency Costs of Free Cash Flow, Corporate Finance, and Takeovers', 76 *Am. Econ. Rev.* 323, 324–25 (1986).

[14] Robert Daines, 'Does Delaware Law Improve Firm Value?' 62 *J. Fin. Econ.* 525 (2001).

continental European nations, such pressure in Delaware was even weaker than that in its sister states.[15] Weaker stakeholder pressure—Delaware is small and the weight of the local bar and other professionals is heavier than more traditional stakeholder interest groups—translated into less pressure to impede takeovers.

4.4. DIRECT EFFECTS: SOFTENING CHANGE AND RAISING AGENCY COSTS

Social democracies historically favored incumbent employees. They favored them directly by insisting that firms not lay off employees; when managers are not tied tightly to shareholders, they would not strongly resist such pressures. Managers in the social democratic environment would usually not be paid much for defying the authorities, would prefer the result themselves anyway, and would suffer by taking the heat if they resisted. Hence, agency costs have been higher, as government policy wedged open the gap between managers and employees on one side and shareholders on the other.

True, such governments also sought to stabilize employment in firms *with* dominant stockholders. But dominant stockholders, with their own money on the line, can oftentimes resist the government's actions more vigorously or more surreptitiously. And, next seen, strong owners could avoid getting the firm into a position where those costs from government pressure would be high.

4.5. INDIRECT EFFECTS: RIGID LABOR MARKETS AS RAISING AGENCY COSTS

Even when social democratic employment policies affect diffusely-held and closely-held firms equally, they still affect ownership structure and should still induce close ownership by dominant stockholders.

Social democratic policies often make it hard to lay off workers, even during economic adversity.[16] True, *when* the firm actually faces adversity and seeks to downsize, each ownership structure, whether concentrated or diffuse, faces similar constraints. Hence, one might mistakenly conclude that social democracies should not affect the choice between ownership structures. But dominant stockholders would be more averse to expanding *ex ante* where labor markets were rigid than where employment rules were looser.

---

[15] Mark J. Roe, 'Takeover Politics', in *The Deal Decade* 321 (ed. by Margaret Blair 1993).

[16] 'Des réactions politiques et syndicales sévères', *Le Monde*, 11 Sept. 1999, at 16 (leader of the governing French party says '[i]t's unacceptable that a large firm can decide to reduce employment...simply to enhance shareholder profits').

Unconstrained managers often prefer to expand their firms, as is well developed in the managerial literature. Since they gain prestige, pay, and power as the firm expands, but do not always pay the price if expansion turns out to be unprofitable, they tend (unless constrained) to expand, and their firms' value to stockholders would deteriorate. When initial owners and potential investors anticipate this risk, stock diffuses into public markets less in social democracies than in more conservative nations, because in a social democracy the stock would be worth less to diffuse stockholders than to close owners.

Competitive capital, product, and labor markets can grind away at these political efforts. Thus political constraints were easier for the political players to implement when European international product and capital markets were less integrated than they are today, back when polities and economies were more or less coextensive with a single nation.

Social democratic government policies wedged open the gap between shareholders and employees by creating laws and a social climate that made it harder for managers to downsize when technology demanded it, or harder for managers to take risks with the enterprise when markets warranted it from the shareholders' perspective. They gave employees more rights to resist change.[17] They constructed nationwide bargaining platforms that favored employees, platforms in which employees coalesced and so shareholders sought to lower their own 'coalition costs', seeking to be more effective by acting cohesively. To be cohesive, shareholders needed to be identifiable—not anonymous, diffuse, and distant.

Such societies also often saw managers and employees as allied with one another, but opposed to distant institutional shareholders, who, because they merely seek financial gain, must be constrained.[18] Consider, for example, this passage from a book by a manager and public figure, a book well known in European business circles: 'Is the firm a simple piece of merchandise...? Or is it...a community *in which the stockholders' power is balanced by managerial power, which is in turn...co-opted...by the employees...?*'[19] Managers, already disposed for their own reasons to expand unnecessarily, to go slow when revamping the firm, to avoid risk, and to refuse to downsize, felt pressured to slow down further and faced social opprobrium if they moved too quickly. Managers who excessively expanded their enterprises in a strong social democracy would

---

[17] Gerhard Schröder, when minister of Lower Saxony—he later became the German Prime Minister—had a steel mill nationalized rather than see it taken over by a foreign firm, because he did not want a restructuring that would affect the German employees. Arnaud Leparmentier, 'L'Allemagne industrielle de nouveau conquérante', *Le Monde*, 28 Nov. 1998, at 1.

[18] Frédéric Lemaître, 'Le succès de l'actionnariat salarié bouleverse le capitalisme français', *Le Monde—Enterprises*, 2 Mar. 1999, at 15; see also Alain Faujas, 'Français, Allemands et Italiens n'attendent rien de bon des entreprises', *Le Monde—Economie*, 1 June 1999, at IV ('60% [of the French] feel that government regulation and taxes handicap French firms, but [they applaud this result] as 51% also say the State must more severely control firms to prevent them from degrading social conditions'); id. (a majority in each of Germany, Italy, and France believe 'the firms' interests and the people's interest are not the same', while in Britain a majority thought the contrary).

[19] Michel Albert, *Capitalisme contre Capitalisme* 19 (1991) (translated from the French) (emphasis added).

especially burden their shareholders, since reversing a mistaken expansion is hard in a social democracy. The agency cost issue is not that managers there are lazy, less effective, or more prone to error, but that they are pushed away from dependably acting for shareholders.

Strong social democracies raised the pressures on managers to abandon their shareholders and side with employees to do what managers want to do all along: expand, avoid risk, and avoid rapid change.

Strong social democracies, in short, raised managerial agency costs.

5

Reducing Shareholders' Power to Control Managers

Social democracies do more than wedge open the gap between managers and stock-holders. They also hinder or break the mechanisms that could control managerial agency costs. When the gap separating managers from shareholders is small, some of the tools may not be worth their cost. Nations with lower agency costs do not need all of them. But as agency costs rise—as the gap between managers and shareholders widens—or as intense competition makes even a moderate gap harder to tolerate, the demand for gap-closing tools will rise. Social democracies, as we see next, make the gap-closing tools—shareholder value norms, transparent accounting, incentive compensation, and hostile takeovers and proxy fights—harder to employ.

5.1. Shareholder Wealth Maximization
5.2. Transparent Accounting
5.3. Incentive Compensation
5.4. Hostile Takeovers and Proxy Contests

In the United States, much corporate governance has the effect, and often the inten-tion, of breaking managers' preference for continuance, excessive risk reduction, and over-expansion, the goals employees also prefer. When these governance devices succeed, they align managers more closely with shareholders than they would otherwise be aligned. They reduce the overlap between managers' goals and employees' goals, and enhance the overlap between managers' goals and distant stockholders' goals. Managers become stockholders themselves and get stock options that are valuable if their firm's stock price rises. Managers see their results 'posted' daily in liquid stock markets. Managers are monitored by outside directors, whose lawyers tell them that they, the directors, work primarily for shareholders.[1] Managers know that hostile takeovers are possible and that a sagging stock price can attract one. And managers and directors are socialized in business school and at work to believe that shareholder wealth maximization is a valid norm, one that

---

[1] In one well-known story, directors asked their attorney, a leading merger adviser, to what extent they could consider other constituencies when evaluating offers. 'A buck a share', the adviser is said to have replied.

they should pursue. (The United States historically lacked some, but not all, of these tools; however, the gap between managers and owners was historically smaller than elsewhere because American firms felt only weak social democratic pressures. In recent decades, intensified competition and technological change called forth stronger tools than American shareholders previously needed.)[2]

These then are the modern tools of, roughly, the past quarter century in the United States that tie managers more tightly to shareholders—shareholder primacy norms and practices in the boardroom and the executive suite, takeovers, and incentive compensation. Each is subtle and can go awry for shareholders. Each can be seen as arising from an increasing shareholder desire to increase their managers' loyalty. Each is harder to develop in a social democratic polity.

5.1. SHAREHOLDER WEALTH MAXIMIZATION

Consider first a soft control on managers for shareholders: a managerial belief in shareholder-wealth maximization. This norm, widespread in American business circles, surely affects what managers think about their tasks.[3] But it is not self-evident outside American business circles that business should be organized around a shareholder-wealth maximization norm, a norm that does not inherently derive from even utilitarian principles: why maximize *shareholders'* wealth, when shareholders make up such a small and already-favored part of society?[4] One answer is that this is the distributional 'price' for getting good capital allocation. Another is that shareholder wealth roughly proxies for total wealth and no other norm is, right now, plausible to implement in diffusely-owned firms. Managers need, in this analysis, a measurable guide, and *total* wealth maximization is too hard to measure and implement.

But this 'proxy' justification is theoretically contestable and widely disbelieved in social democracies. Managers there see more newscasts, read more articles, and have more conversations disparaging shareholder-wealth maximization than their

---

[2] And, when American industries were less competitive, large-firm oligopolies lost something from managerial agency costs but gained oligopoly profits to spread around to shareholders, managers, and employees. Mark J. Roe, 'From Antitrust to Corporate Governance? The Corporation and the Law: 1959–1994', in *The American Corporation Today* 102, 105, 111–13 (ed. by Carl Kaysen, 1996). (Only the New Deal era had a flavor vaguely similar to that of European social democracy; however, even the New Deal, one must remember, was designed to save American capitalism. Moreover, one wonders whether the number of public firms then increased, stayed level, or declined.)

[3] See, e.g., the famous essay by Milton Friedman, 'The Social Responsibility of Business Is to Increase its Profits', *N.Y. Times Mag.*, 13 Sept. 1970, at 32. Although aggressive when it appeared, Friedman's perspective is now mainstream in American business circles and not unthinkable then, as it may have been in some social democracies. Cf. Andrew Graham, 'The UK 1979–95: Myths and Realities of Conservative Capitalism': in *Political Economy of Modern Capitalism: Mapping Convergence and Diversity* 117, 119 (ed. by Colin Crouch and Wolfgang Streeck, 1997) (describing the cultural primacy of profit in Margaret Thatcher's Britain); Michael E. Porter, 'The Microeconomic Foundations of Economic Development', in *World Econ. Forum, The Global Competitiveness Report* 1999, at 30, 38, 42 ('In western Europe . . . the inability to place profitability as the central goal is . . . the greatest constraint to economic development.')

[4] Cf. Robert Kuttner, 'Soaring Stocks: Are Only the Rich Getting Richer?', *Bus. Wk.*, 22 Apr. 1996, at 28 (the wealthiest 20% of American households own over 98% of American investments in stocks).

counterparts see, read, and have in a non-social democracy. Political leaders sympathize with employees more there than elsewhere. An American union officer involved in the Chrysler-Daimler merger said: 'It is amazing to me that in Europe the corporations . . . feel that they have [an ethical] obligation to their employees. . . . Th[is] come[s] naturally in the European culture, while here in America we work hard to establish this and in a lot of instances have failed miserably'.[5] American labor has tolerated a corporate focus on profitability more willingly than has labor abroad.

Social atmosphere is important when managers have discretion, as they must have in public firms; the social pressures they feel affect how they exercise that discretion. Weakly monitored public firm managers in social democracies found it psychologically hard to work primarily for shareholders. They would have believed themselves to be somewhat evil, or at least not wholly good, if they maximized shareholder value and tightened up the work place.[6] Hence, they would do so only reluctantly, and sometimes not at all.

5.2. TRANSPARENT ACCOUNTING

Policymakers and academics in continental European nations complained that accounting there was not transparent enough. Distant shareholders could not fully understand their firm, stock could not be quickly priced accurately, and insiders with better information could make out like bandits via insider trading. The headlines from recent American accounting failures like Enron tell us that the contrast is hardly black and white, but the usual view has been, and may still be, that American financial information delivery was good overall and that in other nations it was not as good. (These scandals, which highlight both the importance of transparency and how easily it can be undermined, can be seen against the background rate of many more fully public American firms, inviting a higher absolute number of accounting failures.)

Opaque accounting in Europe could historically have been due to technical failings, as it usually is seen to have been. But the failures may have been more than technical. Business owners in social democracies may have *preferred* that employees *not* know how well the firm was doing, fearing that when profits were high employees would demand higher pay. They may accordingly have *preferred* that the publicly available information be opaque. But when information is poor, the demand rises to have owners closer to the enterprise, owners who can see through the smoke and monitor managers well. Hence, it is plausible that continental Europe's accounting owed its opacity (or the low demand to clear it up) partly to social democracy and not just to technical failure.

Improving accounting would have had two offsetting effects on distant stockholders in the social democracies: strengthening them against insiders, but

---

[5] Timothy W. Ryback, 'The Man Who Swallowed Chrysler', *The New Yorker*, 16 Nov. 1998, at 80, 83.

[6] This anti-shareholder sentiment is hardly absent in the United States. It ebbs and flows, stronger during Ralph Nader's 'Campaign GM' in the 1970s, say, and weaker during the Reagan 1980s, but surely it has been much weaker in the United States than in continental Europe.

weakening them *vis-à-vis* labor. Which effect would be stronger cannot be predicted a priori.[7] (Social democratic governments, facing a similar trade-off—fostering labor power via transparency would promote pro-shareholder culture—would cross public-firm transparency off from the top of their policy agenda. That is, if business players were leery of transparency because of social democratic pressures, one might wonder why socialist governments did not force more transparency. First, the *primary* social democratic goal for the larger firms for several decades was not to facilitate labor interests against private capital inside public firms. Rather, it was to *nationalize* the large firms in heavy industry, which many of the social democracies did. Second, because fewer firms were fully public in their nation, the transparency sought would be for the many *privately* held firms, and the focused players there would resist. Thirdly, as I noted above, transparency is a two-edged sword for a social democratic government: it can promote a shareholder culture (a negative) and facilitate labor power (a positive); hence, the social democratic program might better focus on other non-ambiguously pro-employee goals. Or, when they focus on transparency, they focus not on the ambiguous overall firm results—on product line results or factory-by-factory results—but on employee and popular interests, such as executive pay. And indeed illuminating executive compensation has been the French socialist governments' disclosure initiative, not generally improving reports to shareholders. Social democratic politicians have little interest in promoting shareholder wealth-maximizing transparency: they would not want to make the accounts sufficiently transparent, such that distant shareholders could better understand the firm and thereby be equipped to press managers to re-position non-performing factories.)

5.3. INCENTIVE COMPENSATION

Incentive compensation helps to align managers with shareholders. But stockholders need to oversee managers' compensation to prevent a complete disconnect between pay and performance; and, weak as this connection can be in the United States, making compensation details known to public stockholders better aligns pay and performance than otherwise. But in social democracies, making high compensation publicly known would have exacerbated tensions with employees. Surely that tension arises in the United States, but because the United States is less of a social democracy—or not one at all—the resulting tension is less strong. (I hardly mean that all American incentive compensation rigorously pays managers for good results: options are re-scaled when a stock's price falls and many managers are richly rewarded even if the firm's results are mediocre.[8] The question though is whether some significant portion of the compensation motivates them, and

---

[7] This is not the only reason for opacity: players with informational advantages prefer to keep the firm opaque to others. Banks, if satisfied with the information they get, may not want to increase transparency and thereby lower the costs of the banks' financial competitors.

[8] Lucian Bebchuk, Jesse Fried, and David Walker, 'Executive Compensation in America: Optimal Contracting or Extraction of Rents?' (Harvard Law School Working Paper, 2001). Compensation

whether there is a similarly sized portion of motivating incentive compensation in other nations.)

Continental firms could use incentive compensation. But it worked better for European shareholders if kept secret from employees—opaque accounting again—and if offered by a controlling shareholder, who monitored what public markets did not see. It is no accident that it is the French socialist government that sought to make managerial compensation more transparent and French owners who 'fear[ed] that [more] information about individual salaries [would] induce more... social tensions'.[9] In social democracies with greater employee tensions and demands, public knowledge of a specific firm's high managerial compensation would have heightened employee demands, delegitimated that firm's owners and managers, and, hence, raised the costs to shareholders of this means of controlling agency costs in the public firm. Compensation consultants' survey data show long-term incentive pay to have been low in large firms in Europe (other than in Britain); indeed, it was at zero for several nations.[10]

Firms knew that heavy incentive stock options for managers would raise tensions with employees. When Daimler-Benz sought them, union officials opposed them because they feared the firm's objectives would change and jobs would be lost. This led to a rare contested supervisory board vote, with labor voting against the stock options. The option plan, though passed, stayed small:

The divided vote on Daimler-Benz's supervisory board has shown that there is no consensus in Germany about... shareholder value as it is widely understood in the US or the UK....

[E]ither the option element... will remain small and thus symbolic... or, if... substantial, the relationship between industry and trade unions may become more confrontational, especially when the same managers lay off thousands of employees.[11]

Moreover, governments in the social democracies have often been hostile to stock options.[12] Governments of the left in France have been unhappy about a

---

over the long run seems to correlate with results, even if it does not correlate over the short run. Brian J. Hall and Jeffrey B. Liebman, 'Are CEOs Really Paid Like Bureaucrats'?, 113 *Q.J. Econ.* 653 (1998).

[9] Philippe Mabille, 'Stock-Options: Vers des Prélèvements Allégés et une Transparence Accrue', *Les Echos*, 9 Dec. 1998, at 2; Isabelle Mandraud and Caroline Monnot [interview with Guillaume Sarkozy, a leader of the French entrepreneurs' lobbying association], 'Toute ces dispositions vont nuire aux négociations sociales d'entreprise. . .', *Le Monde—Economie*, 19 June 2001, at iii; cf. Gail Edmondson, 'France: A CEO's Pay Shouldn't Be a Secret', *Bus. Wk.*, 9 Aug. 1999, at 47 (Viénot corporate governance committee, a French blue-ribbon panel, did not recommend disclosure of CEO pay); 'Les Stock-options seraient moins imposées et plus 'transparentes', *Le Monde*, 10 Dec. 1998, at 9 (the governing French socialist party sought rules to have total managerial compensation publicly known). I suspect the socialist government sought not to facilitate shareholder monitoring but to expose high managerial salaries.

[10] Martin J. Conyon and Joachim Schwalbach, 'Corporate Governance, Executive Pay and Performance in Europe', in *Executive Compensation and Shareholder Value* 13, 25 (ed. by Jennifer Carpenter and David Yermack, 1999).

[11] Wolfgang Münchau, 'German Executives Discover a Nice Little Extra: Moves Towards Share Options for Top Managers are Likely to Provoke Controversy', *Fin. Times*, 24 Apr. 1996, at 23.

[12] See Virginie Malingre, 'Les Députés PS Acceptent le Dispositif Stock-Options Préconisé par M. Fabius', *Le Monde*, 28 Apr. 2000, at 9; Virginie Malingre and Michel Noblecourt, 'Les Députés PS Veulent Taxer Davantage les Stock-options', *Le Monde*, 15 Oct. 1999, at 8 (key players in governing party wanted to tax stock options more heavily); Laurent Mauduit, 'Le Gouvernement Diffère la

mechanism that would make the well-to-do better off,[13] and it is plausible that they also did not want a corporate tool that would bind senior managers to stockholders. Even when the technical tools for options were available, their visible use would have exacerbated tensions inside the firm. In Germany and Sweden, stock 'options are not considered entirely ethical',[14] presumably because managers there were expected to represent all of the firm's constituencies, and stock options would bind them tightly to one of them.[15]

5.4. HOSTILE TAKEOVERS AND PROXY CONTESTS

Hostile takeovers can reduce managerial agency costs in public firms. The stock price of mismanaged firms will sag, and takeover entrepreneurs or managers at other firms will buy up the stock cheaply, improve the target firms' operations, and thereby profit. While the debate in the 1980s in the United States was wide as to whether this was the primary goal and effect, surely it was one effect, and a shareholder-oriented takeover policy would cull out the extraneous causes and effects. In prior decades, intermittent proxy fights played a similar role.

Hostile takeovers have been notoriously harder in continental Europe than in the United States and Britain. True, there are fewer fully public European firms, making the background rate necessarily low. But although a few hostile takeovers were attempted in Germany, they usually foundered due to the political pressure one would expect in a social democracy, as workers campaigned to block the takeovers and politicians sided with employees and against the capital owners.[16]

Réforme Fiscale des Stock-Options', *Le Monde*, 9 Jan. 1999, at 7 (left pulled reform to lower high taxes on stock options out of a 'pro-innovation' package); David I. Oyama, 'French Socialists Back Steeper Taxes on Options Gains', *Wall St. J.*, 27 Apr. 2000, at A17; cf. Christopher J. Mesnooh, 'Stock Options in the United States and France: A Comparative Regard', *MTF—L'AGEFI*, No. 102, Nov./Dec. 1998 (arguing that French stock options are taxed unfavorably).

[13] Mabille, supra note 9, at 2 ('The pill [(the subsequently withdrawn proposal to facilitate stock options)] is not an easy one to swallow for the left, which highly distrusts a tool that they see as a means for managers to give themselves a super-bonus').

[14] Peter Goldstein, 'Managers and Managing: Compensation Packages for Executives Aren't All Alike—Base Pay Converges in Europe, but Bonuses and Stock Options Vary', *Wall St. J. Eur.*, 22 Dec. 1998, at 4.

[15] See Graham Bowley, 'Hoechst Launches Stock Option Scheme', *Fin. Times* (London), 13 Sept. 1997, at 19 ('Only a handful of Germany's biggest companies have adopted share option schemes . . . because of strict German regulations on employee share ownership.').

[16] See, e.g., Michael Woodhead, 'A Pyrrhic Victory for Germany', *Sunday Times* (London), 30 Mar. 1997, § 3, at 7 ('The foiling of Krupp's bid for Thyssen is a victory for the social consensus.'); Frederick Stüdemann, 'Steeled for a Battle', *Fin. Times* (London), 22 Mar. 1997, at 9 (a mainstream German newspaper printed a headline asking if an executive seeking a takeover wanted to set Germany on fire). German politicians brokered a partial merger on terms favorable to incumbent employees. See Richard Halstead, 'Steel is Put to the Sword', *Independent* (London), 23 Mar. 1997, at 3 ('The combined forces of federal economics minister Guenter Rexrodt and Johannes Rau, premier of North Rhein Westphalia, Germany's biggest state, bounced Germany's virtually sole corporate raider into "negotiations" with Thyssen.'); Greg Steinmetz and Matt Marshall, 'Krupp Suspends Hostile Bid for Thyssen', *Wall. St. J.*, 20 Mar. 1997, at A13 ('[T]he steel merger is less attractive than a full merger. But the smaller merger is politically more acceptable . . . ').

In a major attempted takeover in the steel industry, the nominally conservative German chancellor said he was 'deep[ly] concern[ed]' over it, asking the firms and players to 'live up to their social responsibilities'.[17] They substantially cut back their planned restructuring. Until 1999, '[n]o hostile takeover . . . ha[d] ever succeeded in Germany'.[18] Takeovers may someday be a normal part of the corporate landscape, and Vodafone's takeover of Germany's Mannesmann has been seen by many as a harbinger, but the history of their long desert-like absence is again clear. Had takeovers been easier, diffusely owned firms might have been more attractive for shareholders.

(The takeover of Mannesmann might have effects other than opening up the market, as the current conventional wisdom suggests: it might instead induce German managers, labor, and political players tied to both to *redouble* their efforts to *stymie* takeovers from rapidly growing. Germany's new opposition to the European Union's effort to ease takeovers—an effort once seen as a done deal—manifests this reaction.[19])

Takeovers occurred from time to time even in a socialist France. But Ministry approval historically had usually been necessary, sometimes as a formal requirement, sometimes as an informal understanding. Moreover, the Ministry rarely approved a takeover without a social plan in place, one that had the offeror renouncing laying off employees at the target for two to five years.[20] If a no-layoff policy was the price for a takeover, as it usually had been, an offeror would have seen a takeover as less valuable because restructuring would have been harder (as restructurings often lead to lay-offs) and because employees' motivation after the takeover might have changed for the worse.[21]

---

[17] William R. Emmons and Frank A. Schmid, 'Universal Banking, Control Rights, and Corporate Finance in Germany', *Fed. Res. Bank St. Louis Rev.*, July/Aug. 1998, at 19, 22.

[18] William Boston, 'Hostile Deal Could Breach German Resistance', *Wall St. J.*, 17 Nov. 1999, at A17. Vodafone's takeover of Mannesmann changed this.

[19] Paul Meller, 'European Parliament Rejects Measure to Ease Takeovers', *N.Y. Times*, 5 July 2001, at C1; 'Europe's Capital Markets: Takeover Troubles', *The Economist*, 12 May 2001, at 14–15. Germany tentatively agreed to pro-takeover rules coming into effect but only after a long delay, during which perhaps there would be either adaptation and acceptance, or another method found to stymie growth in takeovers. But, when the proposal came before the European Parliament, German representatives voted overwhelmingly against the pro-takeover bill, thereby defeating it. Jacques Docquiert, 'En raison de l'opposition des Allemands—Le Parlement européen rejette l'harmonisation des OPA', *Les Echos*, 5 July 2001, at 1, 10.

[20] Cf. *Banque*: 'Le Coup de Poker de la BNP', *Le Monde*, 11 Mar. 1999, at 1 (in a huge French hostile offer to build the world's largest bank, the offeror's CEO immediately promised not to lay off anyone in France). Ministry approval was mandatory for takeovers that foreign firms initiated and typically but less formally required for takeovers that domestic firms initiated. The French government could assert authority through financial institutions, which for a time were government-owned and, even when not, subject to government influence.

[21] Cf. Edmund L. Andrews, 'A French Concoction', *N.Y. Times*, 21 Sept. 1999, at C1 (indicating that after TotalFina bought Elf Aquitaine, most experts assumed that TotalFina would have to close at least one French refinery and perhaps others in Europe, and would thereby ignite protest given that Elf already had strikes that year). A J.P. Morgan oil analyst said it was widely believed that 'the potential savings are well above two billion euros. . . [But the] difficulty is knowing how long it would take to deliver those savings.' Id.

The French Minister of Finance was suspicious of high-priced takeovers because, as he said when deterring one such high-price offer in 1998, the 'high price means the buyer would have to look immediately at higher profits to pay for the acquisition, which could be negative...for jobs'.[22] Until 1999 the state often decided takeover results and, even when it withdrew from overall control, it continued to seek to avoid takeovers that would yield 'a social massacre' with 'massive layoff[s]'.[23] Only recently, as governments in Europe have moved toward the right economically, have hostile offers appeared; historically they were rarer in continental Europe than in the United States. And not all of the movement is economically toward the right: the French ministers proposed a takeover law in March 2000 that would require an offering company to agree on some terms with the *employees* of the target. 'A takeover [should] not succeed without taking into account employees' views', said the French Finance Minister, seeking to formalize what had been an informal policy.[24]

These forces are present in the United States. Labor unions campaigned for anti-takeover laws, and labor can influence politicians' votes.[25] But labor unions and labor-oriented political parties are not as powerful in the United States as they have been in continental nations. Many American politicians ignore them and survive, and American corporate law is made in contexts (such as in Delaware's legislature and courts) where labor's influence is indirect and weak. This weakness helps to explain why constituency laws, which allow boards to consider players other than shareholders, have hardly affected the firm on labor's behalf. One might cynically see these laws as made by and for managers, who wanted freedom to oppose hostile takeovers and, once they had it, offered employees little more. America's underlying political reality did not give managers any further reason to tie themselves to employees on a day-to-day basis.

American constituency statutes in theory released managers from unswerving loyalty to shareholders. Managers can take employees, communities, and the like into account in their decisions. (Through the business judgment rule perhaps American *law* never linked managers tightly to shareholders.) But other powerful means—compensation, shareholder-wealth norms, takeovers, transparent securities markets, etc.—make managers sufficiently loyal to shareholders to keep agency costs low enough. Because the underlying American social reality does not

---

[22] Alan Katz, 'Shareholders Gain Voice in France, but Socialist Tradition Talks Back', *Wall St. J.*, 13 Feb. 1998, at B7E (quoting French Finance Minister Dominique Strauss-Kahn).

[23] Martine Orange, 'La Fin de l'Exception Française?', *Le Monde*, 30 Mar. 1999, at 19.

[24] Frédéric Pons, 'Un Brin d'Éthique dans les Fusions', *Liberation*, 16 Mar. 2000, at 25; *see also* Thomas Kamm, 'French Bill Takes Aim at Takeovers in Wake of Recent Merger Battles', *Wall St. J. Eur.*, 16 Mar. 2000, at 2 (proposed law would require 'a company launching a bid to meet with representatives of its target's staff to discuss its projects in detail').

[25] Samuel H. Szewczyk and George P. Tsetsekos, 'State Intervention in the Market for Corporate Control: The Case of Pennsylvania Senate Bill 1310', 31 *J. Fin. Econ.* 3, 5 (1992); 'Management and Labor Join Forces to Stiff-Arm Raiders in Pennsylvania', *Corp. Control Alert*, Jan. 1990, at 1, 8; Leslie Wayne, 'Takeovers Face New Obstacles', *N.Y. Times*, 19 Apr. 1990 at D1.

continually press managers to side with employees, the long-run effects of constituency statutes have been limited.

Why would the social democracies not *promote* diffuse ownership to facilitate better their political program?[26] If the only means for social democracies to effectuate their program were through the public firm, and if they could simply do so by promoting transparency, then one might expect them to promote public firms and ownership separation. But the social democracies effectuated their program in large firms not by encouraging transparency, but by nationalizing those that they found most important for their program. For those that remained, they preferred labor rules, tax rules, and the like, not a promoting of the public firm. After all, several foundations for the public firm—shareholder primacy norms, high-powered incentive compensation, hostile takeovers with easy lay-offs, etc.—are not goals the social democracies would readily seek. One would not expect social democracies to promote executive profit-based compensation, shareholder primacy norms, and hostile takeovers-cum-downsizings so that the polity could thereafter more readily influence the resulting shareholder-oriented firms. Nor is it assured that a social democratic polity could commit itself to such pro-capital institutions if it were temporarily so inclined. Realistically, the polity would have to shift rightward—away from social democracy—for that commitment to be credible.

* * *

Hence, managerial agency costs in social democracies have been higher than elsewhere. Political pressures induced unrestrained managers to coalesce with employees more than otherwise, and incentives and techniques that would otherwise control and align managers with public shareholders were weak and used only sporadically. The tools that would have aligned managers with shareholders were not publicly provided; and more generally the institutions that would have helped shareholders—securities laws, corporate laws, and stock exchanges—did not command such governments' attention as being important to strengthen. Labor market rigidities have been more costly to shareholders of diffusely-owned firms than closely-owned firms, because there was no easy going back once the firm expanded. Downsizing was not an easy option. The diffusely-owned firm's higher relative cost to shareholders in social democracies reduced its incidence, and shareholders sought another means of control, namely, direct control via block ownership.

---

[26] E.g., John C. Coffee, 'The Rise of Dispersed Ownership: The Roles of Law and the State in the Separation of Ownership and Control', 111 *Yale L. J.* 1, 74 (2001).

III

LEFT–RIGHT POLITICS AND OWNERSHIP SEPARATION: DATA

Social democracies align managers with employees more than do less socially responsive nations, and in parallel, they align managers less tautly with shareholders; hence, social democracies, all else equal, have had higher managerial agency costs to shareholders. Managers there, if left to their own devices, would have been less loyal to diffuse shareholders, and large-block shareholding persisted as shareholders' best remaining way to control managers. Moreover, the modern means that align managers with diffuse stockholders in the United States—incentive compensation, transparent accounting, hostile takeovers, and strong shareholder-wealth maximization norms—have been harder to implement in continental social democracies. The theory here is that social democracies, by fraying the ties between managers and shareholders, made distant and diffuse shareholding difficult or impossible for investors. The prediction would be that the more strongly social democratic a nation, the less, all else equal, ownership would have separated from control.

Empirical tests are consistent with this incompatibility of strong social democracy and ownership separation. When we line up the world's richest nations on a left–right continuum and then line them up on a close ownership–diffuse ownership continuum, the two correlate powerfully.

6

....

Data and Confirmation

Here we take a left–right index from the political science literature, lay it next to a nation-by-nation ownership concentration index from the finance literature, and see if the two correlate. They do. We then find other measures of left–right politics, such as the strength of employment protection, the GINI index of income inequality, and the size of the government sector in the economy. We see whether these correlate with ownership concentration. They do. Then we find an alternative measure of stock market development, the size of a nation's stock market in relation to its GNP. We see whether this measure correlates with the various political measures. It does.

6.1. Regressing Ownership Concentration on Politics
6.2. Tables and Correlations
6.3. Discussion of Data

6.1. REGRESSING OWNERSHIP CONCENTRATION ON POLITICS

We now have a simple, powerful theory: strong social democracies widen the natural gap between managers and distant stockholders, and impede firms from developing the tools that would close up that gap. What correlations should flow from the theory, and do the data confirm or contradict the predictions? We could compare political orientation with ownership structure nation-by-nation, expecting that left nations would have less diffuse ownership and right nations would have more diffuse ownership.

So they do. Table 6.1 lists nations' politics from most left to most right in the 1980s, based on a poll of political scientists from around the world.[1] Table 6.2 lists the incidence of block ownership in the 1980s in a sample of each nation's firms; those with the higher scores have the highest percentage of diffusely-owned firms.[2] Graph 6.1 plots the two and illustrates the tight correlation between politics and separation.

[1] The political data are from Thomas R. Cusack, 'Partisan Politics and Public Finance: Changes in Public Spending in the Industrialized Democracies, 1955–1989', 91 *Pub. Choice* 375, 383–84 (1997), which arrays a survey from Francis G. Castles and Peter Mair, 'Left–Right Political Scales: Some "Expert" Judgements', 12 *Eur. J. Pol. Sci.* 73 (1984).

[2] The ownership data and judgment are from Rafael La Porta, Florencio Lopez-de-Silanes, and Andrei Shleifer, 'Corporate Ownership Around the World', 54 *J. Fin.* 471, 492 (1999), who sought to

Table 6.1. *Political Placement of Richest Nations' Governments in 1980–1991 (Left is 2; Right 4)*

Sweden	2.22
Austria	2.37
Australia	2.50
Norway	2.63
Finland	2.68
Italy	2.76
France	2.83
Netherlands	3.14
Belgium	3.16
Denmark	3.40
Switzerland	3.43
Canada	3.67
Germany	3.82
United States	3.92
Japan	4.00
United Kingdom	4.00

Table 6.2. *Ownership Separation: Portion of Mid-Sized Firms without a 20 per cent Blockholder in 1995 (From the 20 Public Firms with a Capitalization just over $500 Million)*

Austria	0.00
France	0.00
Italy	0.00
Germany	0.10
Sweden	0.10
Netherlands	0.10
Belgium	0.20
Finland	0.20
Norway	0.20
Denmark	0.30
Australia	0.30
Japan	0.30
Switzerland	0.50
Canada	0.60
United Kingdom	0.60
United States	0.90

show something else: that failure to protect minority stockholders primarily determines a nation's inability to get diffusely held firms. The simplest of the concentration indices looks at twenty firms in each nation and sees what percentage of them lack an owner with more than 20% of the stock. If not one of the twenty has such an owner, the county scores a 1.00 for diffuse ownership; if each of the twenty has such a blockholder, the country scores a zero.

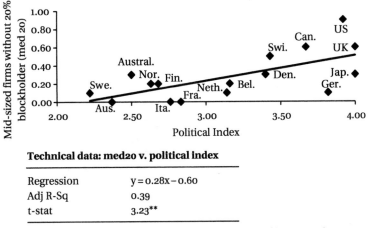

Technical data: med20 v. political index

Regression	y = 0.28x − 0.60
Adj R-Sq	0.39
t-stat	3.23**

** Significant at the 0.005 level (one chance in 200 of being random)

Graph 6.1. Left–right politics as predicting ownership concentration

6.2. TABLES AND CORRELATIONS

An explanation of the data at the end of Graph 6.1: the 'R-squared' tells us that, if we take the data at face value, politics explains 39 per cent of the variation in owner-ship concentration. Other institutions, or random variation, explain the other 61 per cent. The regression co-efficient (0.28) tells us that if a nation moves rightward one unit on the political index, an additional 28 per cent of its firms are diffusely held. The 't-statistic' measures the power of the correlation, telling us that the relationship has less than a 1 per cent chance of being random. (It is an important number, but it is not dispositive: a third feature that is the core determinant could induce the two features that we see correlating. Correlation tells us neither whether the theory of causation (politics affects diffusion) is correct nor whether the measures used accurately reflect politics and dispersion. Correlating the two does give us an opportunity to refute the idea that the two features in fact do fit together.)

6.3. DISCUSSION OF DATA

The political scientists' index is not the only way to measure national political orientation. The strength of employment security is central to the thesis here: if a polity gives employees strong 'property' rights in their own jobs, and reduces firms' authority there, then we should, if the theory is right, expect greater ownership concentration than in nations where employees lack that security. And so it is: the OECD has indexed the world's richest nations' employment laws, ranking nations by how well they protect employees from being fired. The United States is the weakest; Italy the strongest. Draw a graph of the protection against diffusion, and

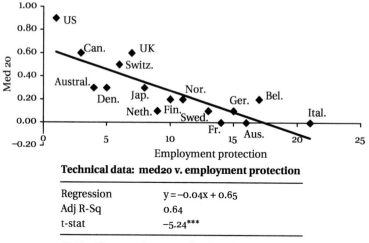

Technical data: med20 v. employment protection

Regression	$y = -0.04x + 0.65$
Adj R-Sq	0.64
t-stat	-5.24***

*** Significant at the 0.0005 level.

Graph 6.2. Employment protection as predicting mid-sized firms' separation

one sees the nearly straight line emerging from the data, a line that shows the tight fit between employment protection and ownership concentration on one end of the graph, and weak labor laws and ownership diffusion on the other. Employment protection and ownership separation have a remarkable correlation: if one goes up, the other goes down in the world's richest nations.

Again, these results are statistically significant, suggesting that political orientation could explain quite a bit of the variation. Although the reader need not be reminded that correlation need not imply causation, the facts here comport with the theory that strong social democracies drive a wedge between shareholders and managers, thereby raising agency costs.

One should be cautious in interpreting these statistical results. True, the correlation of the political line-up with the ownership concentration is strikingly strong despite the fact that the political indices are only partly tuned to the political hypothesis I have set out here. But with only sixteen rich nations to work with, one cannot immediately compare alternative explanations that might trump (or be explained by) the political theory.

And, second, the ownership index does not include privately held firms that have never gone public. There are many of these, but systematic, comparable data for these nations are unavailable. (It is unsurprising, based on the political thesis here, that such financial data for the strongest social democracies is obscure; some owners keep their firms private to keep their profile low.) The theory here would predict that some of those large firms would never go public in the first place in a very strong social democracy (and would retain block ownership if they did). If so, better data here should strengthen the political hypothesis.[3]

---

[3] The financial researchers building the concentration index classified government-owned blocks as if they were privately owned blocks. La Porta *et al.*, supra note 2, at 476. But

Table 6.3. *Income Inequality and Ownership Separation*

Country	Gini	Ownership separation: Portion of mid-sized firms without a 20 per cent blockholder
Finland	22.3	0.20
Austria	22.7	0.00
Belgium	23.0	0.20
Sweden	23.3	0.10
Norway	23.3	0.20
Denmark	24.3	0.30
Germany	25.0	0.10
Italy	25.5	0.00
Netherlands	27.6	0.10
Canada	28.6	0.60
France	29.9	0.00
United Kingdom	30.9	0.60
Australia	30.9	0.30
Switzerland	32.9	0.50
United States	34.3	0.90

Third, the ownership index uses each nation's twenty largest firms above a $500 million capitalization. If only the U.S. economy had historically been big enough to generate enough very big firms, then size—not politics—might be the underlying determinant. By correcting for size, as the correlation in Table 6.3 does, we avoid so skewing the results. But some readers might prefer to see the results for the twenty largest firms anyway, because there is a size beyond which *only* public firms can exist easily, and that size might vary from nation to nation. So, just to be sure, we can focus on the largest firms and see that the correlation between politics and ownership concentration persists, as Graph 6.4 and Table 6.4 in this chapter's appendix show.

Fourth, one might believe that politics affects corporate structures over the long-run, not just on current tendencies. The political index measures leftness versus rightness for the 1980–1991 period; the concentration index measures ownership separation in 1995 (with a trickle of data from 1996). Since the political scientists also provided a 4-decade political index, ending in 1991, we could measure long-term political effects on ownership structure. So I ran the same concentration index against the four-decade average. The correlation persisted. (A better longitudinal look would correlate ownership concentration in each decade with the political index in each decade. But that data is unavailable. And, on the other hand, political coalitions come and go; corporate structures are the result of long-term expectations of governmental orientation.)

government-owned blocks do not at first reflect the owners' decision that concentration will promote shareholder wealth better than would dispersion. Still, governments often take blocks if social pressures deter private players from investing, and the firm can continue, or arise, only if the government invests. Thus linkage is plausible.

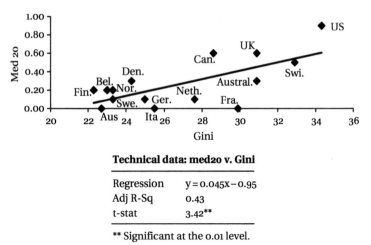

Technical data: med20 v. Gini

Regression	$y = 0.045x - 0.95$
Adj R-Sq	0.43
t-stat	3.42**

** Significant at the 0.01 level.

Graph 6.3. Income inequality as predicting ownership separation

Fifth, the political index is based on a polling of political scientists who rated political parties from left to right on a numerical scale;[4] characteristics beyond economic issues, such as nuclear disarmament, race, and other non-economic concerns surely figured into the ratings. These characteristics will only roughly correlate with the economic left–right scale that would be the best foundation for this study. For example, the French conservative parties were consistently rated as more conservative than the American Democratic Party,[5] although on economic issues I see them as to the left of the Democratic Party. Despite the 'noise', politics correlates with ownership concentration.[6]

The employment protection index though is more attuned to the political thesis and, sure enough, it shows an even tighter relationship between left politics (via protecting employees with jobs) and weak ownership separation. And we can also turn to two additional measures of the strength of a nation's social democracy: the degree of inequality a nation tolerates; and government spending as a percentage of gross domestic product. The Gini coefficient of national income inequality roughly quantifies the richest nations' relative tolerance for inequality and, hence, the relative strength of social democracy. (Inequality does not directly weaken the foundations for separation, but it proxies for general social democratic political orientation.) Table 6.3 shows income inequality and ownership separation. Graph 6.3 shows that the first predicts the second: nations that refuse to tolerate much inequality have a weaker stock market. (The Gini table is also satisfying in moving some nations closer to where one would intuit should be their political

---

[4] Castles and Mair, supra, note 1, at 75.   [5] Id. at 78, 83.

[6] A few general notes on the data: countries are in the sample if and only if they were in the Castles-Mair political index. The time periods for the political side and the concentration side are not identical, but because both politics and ownership structure tend to persist, this mismatch may not be important. Indeed, persisting political foundations (and expectations of future politics) should influence ownership structure.

position: Germany is further left in the Gini table than in the political table; Australia is further right.)

A second rough measure of social democracy is government spending as a percentage of gross domestic product. Activist governments gather in more resources for public use than do less active, more conservative governments. This measure *also* strongly correlates with ownership concentration.

On the ownership side, one would want an alternative to the concentration indices prevailing in the finance literature, because these indices include government ownership blocks (a social democratic factor to be sure, but not one that is this book's focus) and do not include privately held firms that have never gone public. An alternative index measures the size of each nation's stock market in proportion to the size of its economy, and one might suppose that, if many firms in a nation stay private, that nation's stock market capitalization will be smaller than another's in which firms rush to go public and sell stock.[7] I substituted the OECD's measure of stock market capitalization for the concentration index, reran the regressions, and the statistical strength generally persisted, as the tables and graphs in the appendix show.

We thus have several measures of concentration and several proxies for social democracy; all the correlations between social democracy and ownership concentration, as well as between social democracies and weak securities markets overall, are strong.

While the correlations are strong, a sample of the world's sixteen richest nations is not big enough to readily test out the comparative power of *other* explanations. But we cannot extend the sample, because the poorer nations are not economically 'ripe' for large public firms. So, the nature of legal systems (common law versus civil law) has been advanced as helping to explain ownership concentration, with the French and German systems said to protect minority stockholders badly.[8] (We examine this theory, and its limits, in Part VI. We examine data suggesting that Germany and a few other purportedly weak-law nations may in fact protect minority stockholders almost as well as American law in Chapter 25.) We would want to test out the comparative explanatory power of politics and law by, say, finding those nations that protect minority stockholders well but are strong social democracies, and then see the density of public firms there. If such nations regularly had diffuse ownership, the legal theory would seem stronger; but if they had concentrated ownership, the political explanation would seem to trump the law-based one.

Sweden and Germany fit the latter category:[9] minority stockholders by measurement are protected, they are strong social democracies, and they have few public

---

[7] This index has its own imperfection in that it measures stock-market capitalization without accounting for how much of that stock is in public hands and how much of it is in a controller's portfolio.

[8] See Rafael La Porta, Florencio Lopez-de-Silanes, Andrei Shleifer, and Robert W. Vishny, 'Law and Finance', 106 *J. Pol. Econ.* 1113, 1145–51 (1998) (arguing that civil law countries give investors less legal protection than common law countries, inducing higher ownership concentration in civil law countries). [9] See Part IV, Nation by Nation.

firms. If this result were generalized, it would support the political thesis over a legal thesis, but there are not enough such examples, one way or the other, to generalize. (The theory is not that law is unimportant: transition economies that fail to produce satisfactory legal institutions may never get public firms, regardless of whether social democratic policies are strong; rather the argument here is that *in Europe and the wealthy West*, legal differences are joined, and often over-shadowed, by political differences.)

I also ran pair-wise comparisons of politics against each of relative wealth, size of the economy, and an index of legal protection of minority stockholders. The pair-wise comparisons indicated that politics correlates more strongly with ownership concentration than does wealth and size of the economy. The legal index is the only one that survives as a plausible determinant. These results do not mean that per capita wealth and size of the economy are irrelevant as prerequisites to public firms and securities markets. Rather, it is again that *at the economic levels prevailing in Europe and the wealthy West*, disparities in wealth and economic size among *these* nations do not explain the relative strength of their securities markets, whereas political differences among them do.

The correlations here make for, in a lawyer's rhetoric, a prima-facie case that political placement affects ownership structure. But the correlations do not give us a clear sense of how heavily to weigh the political explanation against the more orthodox ones, and, although the data shows a persisting political explanation even when one tests it against alternative theories, the observations are few and the measures crude, making the tests, shown in Chapter 25, useful but not dispositive.

Hence, the discussion of competing theories must also be qualitative, not quantitative, and I offer that discussion next, by looking briefly behind the numbers in several of the nations, with a view toward understanding whether this stakeholder-oriented, political economy theory plays a role in structuring large business enterprises in the wealthy West. Such a qualitative, nation-by-nation, look buttresses the political theory.

APPENDIX

I primarily used two measures of the separation of ownership from control: the incidence of dispersion among mid-sized firms in a nation and size of the stock market as a percentage of gross domestic product in a nation.

One might believe that the best focus for separation would be on a nation's largest firms, because, say, it is the largest in each nation that would be most likely to go public. Politics predicts ownership dispersion for the largest firms as well as for mid-sized firms. In fact, politics more strongly predicts ownership concentration for the wealthiest nations' largest firms.

Or, one might think that the correlations are artifacts of the large block needed to classify a firm as not fully diffuse. But using a 10 per cent cut-off instead of

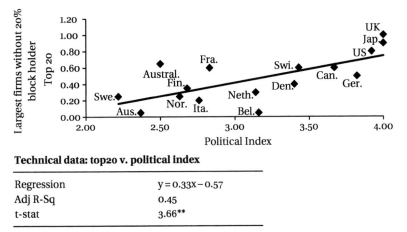

Technical data: top20 v. political index

Regression	$y = 0.33x - 0.57$
Adj R-Sq	0.45
t-stat	3.66**

**Significant at the 0.01 level.

Ownership separation for 'top 20' was measured among the 20 largest public firms. If the firm had a blockholder owning 20% or more of the firm's stock, it was classified as not fully public.

Graph 6.4. Left–right politics as predicting largest firms' separation: I

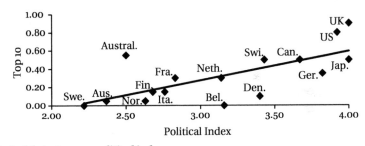

Technical data: top10 v. political index

Regression	$y = 0.32x - 0.69$
Adj R-Sq	0.45
t-stat	3.62**

**Significant at the 0.01 level.

Ownership separation for 'top 10' was measured among the 20 largest public firms. If the firm had a blockholder owning 10% or more of the firm's stock, it was classified as not fully public.

Graph 6.5. Left–right politics as predicting largest firms' separation: II

20 per cent yields similarly strong results, both for the mid-sized and for the largest firms.

We also have several measures of politics. We have primarily focused on the political scientists' index, and secondarily on the GINI index of income inequality. Data for two other measures are available: one could measure a nation's 'leftness'

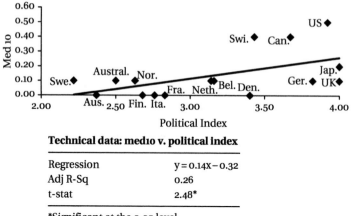

Technical data: medio v. political index

Regression	$y = 0.14x - 0.32$
Adj R-Sq	0.26
t-stat	2.48*

*Significant at the 0.05 level.

Here the cut-off for the blockholder was 10%, not 20%.

Graph 6.6. Left–right politics as predicting mid-sized firms' separation

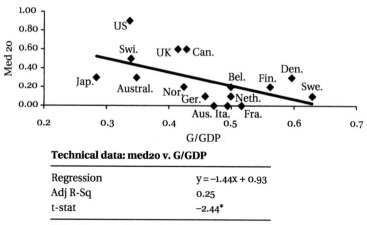

Technical data: med20 v. G/GDP

Regression	$y = -1.44x + 0.93$
Adj R-Sq	0.25
t-stat	-2.44^*

* Significant at the 0.05 level.

Graph 6.7. Government's role in the economy (G/GDP) as predicting mid-sized firms' separation

by the degree to which it protects employees with jobs. The OECD has such an index. Another measure might be the degree to which the government plays a role in the economy. This measure, the ratio of government spending to gross domestic product (G/GDP) also nicely predicts ownership separation. Graphs 6.2 and 6.7 illustrate these relations, using the 20 per cent cut-off for mid-sized firms as the measure of dispersion. Both employment protection and government role in the economy predict ownership dispersion.

Thus we have five measures of politics and five of ownership dispersion. The graphs depict the relationship; the following table shows the relationship's

Table 6.4. *Political Measures as Predicting Ownership Separation*

Explanatory Power of Political Index (1980–91)	Coefficient	Adj R-sq	t-stat
top20	0.33	0.45	3.66**
top10	0.32	0.45	3.62**
med20	0.28	0.39	3.23**
med10	0.14	0.26	2.48*
Dom Stock Market Cap/GDP	0.27	0.40	3.29**
Explanatory Power of Four-Decade Political Index			
top20	0.45	0.63	5.20***
top10	0.42	0.58	4.61***
med20	0.24	0.18	2.06
med10	0.15	0.20	2.19*
Dom Stock Market Cap/GDP	0.30	0.36	3.05**
Explanatory Power of Gini Coefficient (usually 1991)			
top20	0.06	0.55	5.27***
top10	0.06	0.75	6.61***
med20	0.05	0.43	3.42**
med10	0.03	0.41	3.29**
Dom Stock Market Cap/GDP	0.04	0.47	3.65**
Explanatory Power of Employment Protection			
top20	−0.03	0.40	−3.31**
top10	−0.03	0.39	−3.25**
med20	−0.04	0.64	−5.24***
med10	−0.02	0.38	−3.18**
Dom Stock Market Cap/GDP	−0.02	0.22	−2.29*
Explanatory Power of G/GDP			
top20	−1.84	0.35	−3.00**
top10	−2.00	0.45	−3.65**
med20	−1.44	0.25	−2.44*
med10	−1.01	0.34	−2.98*
Dom Stock Market Cap/GDP	−1.61	0.35	−2.98*

* Significant at the 0.05 level.
** Significant at the 0.01 level.
*** Significant at the 0.001 level.

persistence. Below, in Tables 22.1, 22.2, and 22.3 and the surrounding discussion, I statistically compare the political explanation to other plausible explanations to assess their relative and cumulative strength.

* * *

The following two tables show the raw data and describe their sources. The first table shows the five political indices. The second shows the five dispersion measures.

Table 6.5. *Political Measures*

Country	(1) Political Place (1980–1991)	(2) Political Place (1960–1991)	(3) Gini Coefficient	(4) Employment Protection	(5) G/GDP (1996)
Australia	2.50	3.48	30.9	4	0.348
Austria	2.37	2.39	22.7	16	0.472
Belgium	3.16	2.93	23.0	17	0.499
Canada	3.67	3.34	28.6	3	0.428
Denmark	3.40	2.78	24.3	5	0.596
Finland	2.68	2.61	22.3	10	0.562
France	2.83	3.62	29.9	14	0.516
Germany	3.82	3.36	25.0	15	0.458
Italy	2.76	2.90	25.5	21	0.494
Japan	4.00	3.99	Not comparable	8	0.284
Netherlands	3.14	2.99	27.6	9	0.499
Norway	2.63	2.41	23.3	11	0.424
Sweden	2.22	2.22	23.3	13	0.629
Switzerland	3.43	3.55	32.9	6	0.339
United Kingdom	4.00	3.40	30.9	7	0.414
United States	3.92	3.63	34.3	1	0.337

Sources: (1) and (2): Thomas R. Cusack, 'Partisan Politics and Public Finance: Changes in Public Spending in the Industrialized Democracies, 1955–1989'. 91 *Pub. Choice* 375, 383–84 (1997), which arrays a survey from Francis G. Castles and Peter Mair, 'Left–Right Political Scales: Some 'Expert' Judgements', 12 *Eur. J. Pol. Sci.* 73 (1984).

(3) GINI came from the Deininger-Squire OECD on-line compilation. They describe their data in Klaus Deininger and Lyn Squire, 'A New Data Set Measuring Income Inequality', 10 *World Bank Econ. Rev.* 565 (1996). The data measures income inequality after taxes, for each individual (as opposed to each household). A GINI number depends on assumptions and methodology. From the compilation I used, if possible, the 1991 Luxembourg Income Study data. For Austria, Australia, France, Switzerland, and the U.K., no 1991 data was available, so I used the latest Luxembourg 1980s data. For Japan no comparable data was available: no Luxembourg calculation was in the compilation, nor was there an alternative net, after-tax calculation.

(4) The OECD index of employment protection comes from its 1994 jobs study. OECD, *The OECD Jobs Study: Evidence and Explanations—Part II—The Adjustment Potential of the Labour Market*, at 74 (1994).

(5) G/GDP comes from: *OECD In Figures: Statistics on the Member Countries* 36–37 (2000).

Table 6.6. *Separation Measures*

Country	(1) Widely-held at 20% for Top Corps (top 20)	(2) Widely-held at 20% for Med Corps (med 20)	(3) Widely-held at 10% for Top Corps (top 10)	(4) Widely-held at 10% for Med Corps (med 20)	(5) Domestic Stock Market Cap/GDP (1990)
Australia	0.65	0.30	0.55	0.10	0.37
Austria	0.05	0.00	0.05	0.00	0.17
Belgium	0.05	0.20	0.00	0.10	0.33
Canada	0.60	0.60	0.50	0.40	0.43
Denmark	0.40	0.30	0.10	0.00	0.30
Finland	0.35	0.20	0.15	0.00	0.17
France	0.60	0.00	0.30	0.00	0.26
Germany	0.50	0.10	0.35	0.10	0.22
Italy	0.20	0.00	0.15	0.00	0.14
Japan	0.90	0.30	0.50	0.20	0.99
Netherlands	0.30	0.10	0.30	0.10	0.42
Norway	0.25	0.20	0.05	0.10	0.23
Sweden	0.25	0.10	0.00	0.10	0.40
Switzerland	0.60	0.50	0.50	0.40	0.69
United Kingdom	1.00	0.60	0.90	0.10	0.87
United States	0.80	0.90	0.80	0.50	0.56

Sources: Columns (1)–(4) come from Rafael La Porta, Florencio Lopez-de-Silanes, and Andrei Shleifer, 'Corporate Ownership Around the World', 54 *J. Fin.* 471, 492 (1999). The data principally come from 1995 or 1996; column (5) comes from OECD, *Financial Market Trends* 18, tbl. 2 (Feb. 1998).

IV

NATION BY NATION

In this Part IV we examine the world's richest nations in light of the main thesis. Each illustrates variants on the concept. In France a socialist elite for decades pressed firms to stabilize employment. Shareholder wealth maximization was denigrated and the family firm persisted with few truly public companies until recently, when French politics moved rightwards. Germany's codetermination institutionalized social democracy and demeaned strong securities markets in the world's third largest economy. Italy's features, although they nicely support a contrasting, law-centered thesis, display aspects of the political thesis—a strong communist party, ideologies even on the right that were hostile to markets, and concentrated ownership. In Japan, lifetime employment settled social conflict, and financial institutions played a strong role in firms in ways that complemented Japan's post-Second World War social understandings. Sweden, the world's first social democracy, has protected minority stockholders well, but strong ownership concentration persists and owner-ship has not yet separated from control; the social democracy thesis better explains Swedish results than alternative theories. The United Kingdom was on both sides of the political spectrum in the twentieth century. But Britain's socialist interludes did not overturn the stock market institutions it had previously developed during its laissez-faire era. Many firms were public and stock markets persisted, but family and block ownership in public companies persisted in Britain much longer than it did in the United States. And in the United States, the absence of social democracy made ownership separation easier than it was anywhere else, as pro-shareholder institutions, while not every bit as strong as shareholders would always have wanted, had an easier time forming. Political pressures were not absent, but mani-fested themselves via controls on financial institutions' role inside the firm historically and, in recent decades, in dampening the frequency and ease of hostile takeovers that could disrupt employment relationships. Lastly, one might like to look at many more nations, but we cannot, because most are not yet at an economic and technological level where the public firm would play a large role. Someday soon, perhaps, but not yet.

7

France

In France a socialist elite, as well as its political competitors, pressed firms for decades to stabilize employment inside the firm. Shareholder wealth maximization was denigrated, and the family firm persisted with few truly public companies until recently, when French politics moved rightwards. France, a more conservative nation at the very beginning of the twentieth century, then had incipient securities markets that were about as strong as those in the United States. But the twentieth century wars and economic havoc 'reset' the French corporate agenda, and, by the time it was reset, French politics had moved to the left and was no longer conducive to separating ownership from control. French statism did not bar the initial rise of a strong French securities market a century ago, when France was conservative, because conservative statism propped up the capital-owning side of the firm. But when French politics moved leftward later in the twentieth century, French statism impeded securities markets from recovering from the mid-century devastation in continental Europe, and ownership did not widely separate from control.

Qualitative French business histories are consistent with the social democracy thesis. Consider Charles Kindleberger's perhaps hyperbolic description in a standard work of European economic history:

[The French family firm] is said to have sinned against economic efficiency . . . [by] failing . . . to extend into new markets. . . . Public sale of stock was avoided. . . . Recruiting was undertaken from within the family, except for faithful retainers who assisted the firm against the revolutionary working force.[1]

Political leaders excoriated profitable French firms seeking to downsize, threatening to deny them discretionary government benefits if they persisted. The press today reports popular animus against such firms,[2] American institutional

---

[1] Charles P. Kindleberger, *Economic Growth in France and Britain: 1851–1950*, at 115 (1964).

[2] David Owen, 'Michelin Slips after Provisions', *Fin. Times* (London), 15 Mar. 2000, at 32 (reporting that the French Prime Minister's 'remarks were seen as a warning that there were limits to the extent to which big French companies should adopt aggressive Anglo-American profits-oriented tactics').

investors feel compelled to deny that they instigated the downsizings,[3] and even distant French stockholders are said to be unreconciled with downsizings.[4] Managers presumably have been yet more reluctant to downsize.

Nominally conservative or middle-of-the-road political parties have pursued the core social democratic policies:

[The] Giscard [government, a nominally conservative one, under attack from, and eventually displaced, by the socialists] protected workers from layoffs and firms from bankruptcy.... A 1975 law required firms seeking to make more than 10 layoffs for economic reasons to obtain permission from a local ministry of labor inspector. Approval was by no means granted automatically, particularly in the case of the high-profile, often heavily unionized national champions.... [Economic modernization was] subordinated to the imperatives of preserving the social peace, not to mention the electoral prospects of the right.[5]

Although takeovers have happened in France, as I noted in Chapter 5, Ministry approval historically had usually been necessary, sometimes as a formal require-ment, sometimes as an informal understanding, and the Ministry rarely approved a takeover without a social plan in place, one that had the offeror appropriately renouncing laying off employees.[6] A no lay-off policy as the price for a takeover made a takeover less valuable because restructuring would have been harder (as restructurings often lead to layoffs) and, as I mentioned in Chapter 5, because employees' motivation after the takeover could change for the worse.[7]

The Minister of Finance has been suspicious of high-priced takeovers because, as he said when deterring one such high-price offer in 1998, the 'high price means the buyer would have to look immediately at higher profits to pay for the acquisition, which could be negative ... for jobs.'[8] Even when the state withdrew

---

[3] Cécile Prudhomme, '[Interview with] Bill Crist, président de CalPERS: "Danone n'a pas réduit ses effectifs en réponse a une demande d'un fonds de pension"', *Le Monde*, 7 May 2001, at 15.

[4] Joël Morio, 'Comment démarrer en Bourse', *Le Monde—Argent*, 7 May 2001, at 1.

[5] Jonah D. Levy, *Tocqueville's Revenge: State, Society, and Economy in Contemporary France* 41–42 (1999).

[6] Cf. 'Banque: Le Coup de Poker de la BNP', *Le Monde*, 11 Mar. 1999, at 1 (in a huge French (unsuc-cessful) hostile offer to build the world's largest bank, the offeror's CEO immediately promised not to lay off anyone in France). Ministry approval was mandatory for takeovers that foreign firms initiated and typically but less formally required for takeovers that domestic firms initiated. The informal web of control was easiest to implement when the state owned the leading financial institutions. Rules were less needed if the Minister's will could work its way through the state's financial arms.

[7] Cf. Edmund L. Andrews, 'A French Concoction', *N.Y. Times*, 21 Sept. 1999, at C1 (after TotalFina bought Elf Aquitaine, most experts assumed that TotalFina would have to close at least one French refinery and perhaps others in Europe, thereby igniting protest given that Elf had already had strikes that year). A J.P. Morgan oil analyst said it was widely believed that 'the potential savings are well above two billion euros.... [But the] difficulty is knowing how long it would take to deliver those savings.' Id.

[8] Alan Katz, 'Shareholders Gain a Voice in France, but the Socialist Tradition Talks Back', *Wall St. J.*, 13 Feb. 1998, at B7E (quoting French Finance Minister Dominique Strauss-Kahn). A high price might indicate high inefficiencies, including perhaps redundancies in the work force. In contrast, consider what an American analyst deems to be the critical social issues to negotiate in a takeover: 'A critical part of the negotiation of large merger transactions is the resolution of such social issues as the location of the headquarters for the combined entity and the determination of who will lead the "new" company, [a Goldman, Sachs managing director] explained.' Eileen J. Williams, 'Focus: Mergers and Consolidations', *BNA's Corp. Couns. Wkly.*, 24 Mar. 1999, at 8.

from active involvement in takeovers in 1999, it continued to condemn those takeovers that would yield 'a social massacre' with 'massive layoff[s]'.[9]

French corporate events of 2001 reflect continuing, albeit weaker, pressures of the type that hinders ownership separation. Several firms not near bankruptcy restructured, by downsizing and laying off employees: most notably Marks and Spencer, the British-headquartered department store; and Danone, the French food-products company. Media and political publicity and pressure brought on a government backlash, with the government passing new laws to impede lay-offs in financially healthy firms.[10]

And AOM-Air Liberté, a secondary airline with two large investors, one French and one Swiss, sought to downsize its operations and lay off some employees when it began to fail in 2001. Strikes ensued. The combination of poor profits, perhaps due to poor management, and poor labor relations induced the airline's bankruptcy. All along, government officials excoriated the airline's owners, attacking the large French investor for not pumping in more cash to keep the firm aloft and the jobs intact.[11]

Thus the potential gap between French managers and stockholders in the diffuse firm would seem wide, and investors would have reason to avoid ownership structures with that gap.

* * *

And incentive compensation has been harder to use in France than in the United States because it would, if publicly-known, exacerbate tensions inside the firm between line-workers and senior managers. The French socialist government sought to make managerial compensation more transparent, and French owners 'fear[ed] that [more] information about individual salaries [would] induce more... social tensions'.[12] High managerial compensation, one surmises, would have heightened employee demands and weakened their motivation to work for the

---

[9] Martine Orange, 'La Fin de l'Exception Française?', *Le Monde*, 30 Mar. 1999, at 19; see also Frédéric Pons, 'Un Brin d'Éthique dans les Fusions', *Liberation*, 16 Mar. 2000, at 25; Thomas Kamm, 'French Bill Takes Aim at Takeovers in Wake of Recent Merger Battles', *Wall St. J. Eur.*, 16 Mar. 2000, at 2 (the proposed law would require 'a company launching a bid to meet with representatives of its target's staff to discuss its projects in detail').

[10] Françoise Fressoz and Jean-Francis Pécresse, 'Licenciements: Jospin évite la crise mais mécontente les partenaires sociaux', *Les Echos*, 14 June 2001, at 4–5.

[11] François Bostnavaron, 'Le PDG d'AOM-Air Liberté décide de déposer le bilan de la compagnie aérienne', *Le Monde*, 17–18 June 2001, at 16; Marc Lomazzi, 'Polémiques sur la débâcle d'AOM-Air Liberté', *La Tribune*, 18 June 2001, at 2; François Bostnavaron, 'Le dépôt de bilan de la compagnie AOM-Air Liberté paraît imminent', *Le Monde*, 16 June 2001, at 19 (French Minister of Transportation demands that the jobs be saved and that, since the firm is rich in human capital, the owners pump in more cash).

[12] Philippe Mabille, 'Stock-Options: Vers des Prélèvements Allégés et une Transparence Accrue', *Les Echos*, 9 Dec. 1998, at 2; cf. Gail Edmondson, 'France: A CEO's Pay Shouldn't Be a Secret', *Bus. Wk.*, 9 Aug. 1999, at 47 (Viénot corporate governance committee, a French blue-ribbon panel, did not recommend disclosure of CEO pay); 'Les Stock-Options Seraient Moins Imposées et Plus "Transparentes,"' *Le Monde*, 10 Dec. 1998, at 9 (the governing French socialist party seeks rules to have total managerial compensation publicly known). I suspect the socialist government sought not to facilitate shareholder monitoring but to expose high managerial salaries.

well-paid managers, delegitimated that firm's owners and managers in the workers' eyes, and, hence, raised the costs to shareholders of this means of controlling agency costs in the public firm.

Employee stock ownership was promoted as a means to resist takeovers,[13] presumably especially those that would lead to lay-offs and downsizing. Reports to the French Prime Minister extolled employee stock ownership not for the perhaps denigrated Anglo-Saxon reasons of promoting employee loyalty and motivation, but to shift the balance of power inside the firm away from owners and to employees.[14]

Nor has the French corporate law demanded shareholder-wealth maximization; indeed, it is said to encourage managers to run the firm in the general social interest, for all the players in the firm.[15] Modern French managers have been socialized in two elite schools—which account for half of the managers and directors of France's leading firms[16]—to think more of national progress than of shareholder-profit maximization.[17]

France's modern corporate form with strong family, individual, government, and financial ownership can be linked to other French institutions. If France had deficient securities and corporate laws (and enforcement)—a common American assumption—then one must ask how this came about. The task of writing a passable law and getting a plausible enforcement agency in place is not insurmountable, and France is not incapable of good government administration. Indeed, to the extent American securities law is Code and regulatory-based, France might have a legal leg up on institutional capacity here.

Public choice forces could help explain the perceived deficiency. Securities markets and securities laws may have been weak because the demand for them was weak. And that demand may have been weak because founders would not readily sell into the securities market if the firm would be worth much less to scattered outside owners.

French political traditions have been more statist than American traditions, with government directives extending into the operation of the stock exchange. One might mistakenly think that this statism in itself is a strong impediment to

---

[13] Laurent Mauduit, 'M. Jospin Ouvre avec Précaution le Dossier de l'Épargne Salariale', *Le Monde*, 29 Jan. 2000, at 6.

[14] Ministère de l'Economie, des Finances et de L'Industrie, *Rapport au Premier Ministre sur l'Epargne Salariale*, Jan. 2000, at 2, Pt II, at 8–10, 15.

[15] See James A. Fanto, 'The Role of Corporate Law in French Corporate Governance', 31 *Cornell Int'l L.J.* 31, 47 (1998) ('The concept of the intérêt social, which permeates the French corporate code, permits directors to consider the interests of all constituencies when deciding upon corporate strategy. This concept allowed the state-owner to use controlled corporations for purposes other than profit-making.') (Citation omitted).

[16] Cf. Michel Bauer and Benedicte Bertin-Mourot *Administrateurs et Dirigeants du CAC 40* (Report of CNRS Observatoire des Dirigeants, Oct. 1997). The two schools are the Ecole Nationale d'Administraion and the Ecole Polytechnique.

[17] Cf. Michel Noblecourt, 'Pour une Extension des Stock-Options à l'Ensemble du Personnel', *Le Monde*, 7 Oct. 1999, at 6 (the leader of France's governing socialist party asserted that 'although our goal is not to socialize the means of production, one can neither leave the private sector without rules . . . nor allow stockholders alone to decide, without any input from employees, what to do solely due to shareholders' purely financial interests').

Table 7.1. *Domestic Stock Market Capitalization as a Percentage of GDP: 1913 and 1990**

France	0.78	0.24
Germany	0.44	0.20
Italy	0.17	0.13
United States	0.39	0.54

*Drawn from Raghuram G. Rajan and Luigi Zingales, The Great Reversals: 'The Politics of Financial Development' at 61, tbl.3 (Working Paper, Feb. 2001).

securities markets and ownership separation. In theory it could have been; in practice it was not. At some level of extreme statism, yes, the state obliterates private activity. Strongly statist France has been, but its nineteenth- and early twentieth-century statism was not insurmountable for nascent securities markets when it was more conservative. Earlier in the twentieth century, when France was a more conservative nation, its securities markets were developing nicely, on a par with America's. (See Table 7.1, which lays out the numbers, for France and the United States.[18]) Wars and collapse reset the economic agenda, and by mid-century France, still statist but by then on the left, did not provide the political milieu in which securities markets could further develop. True, self-governing bodies (analogous to the New York Stock Exchange) could not prosper in a left-oriented statist environment, but this impediment did not stop securities markets from starting when France was conservative and more market-friendly.[19]

[18] Vintage data such as the 1913 column, although the best available, may be off, or not comparable from one country to another. Nor does the data tell us the quality of these securities markets: their liquidity, the equity float, the types of firms that got to the market, etc.

[19] John Coffee makes this argument (from French and German statism), but for the reasons stated in the text, relies much too heavily on it. The facts of French twentieth-century economic and political history—good securities market development when the government was statist and conservative but weak securities market when the government, although still statist, had turned leftward—make the pure French statist argument incorrect. John C. Coffee, 'The Rise of Dispersed Ownership: The Roles of Law and the State in the Separation of Ownership and Control', 111 *Yale L. J.* 1, 9, 45 (2001). France's conservative, anti-labor statism of the end of the nineteenth and the early twentieth centuries was compatible with incipient securities markets.

The problem is not theoretical, but factual: even modern authoritarian states worked satisfactorily with securities markets, if their politics was economically on the right. One has to go quite a ways down the authoritarian dimension before pure statism (not *left* statism) thwarts securities markets: even Mussolini's fascism saw a *rise* in stock market capitalization in the 1920s.

The central problem with this effort is that to make the French and German nineteenth-century examples into counter-examples to the social democracy thesis, one would have to show that securities markets were noticeably weaker then in those conservative but statist nations than they were in contemporary but conservative nations. The data though argues the contrary. (And the claim in this book is: if social democracy, then demeaned stock markets and poor separation. The syllogism here does not require all demeaned stock markets to be demeaned by social democratic politics. There is more than one way to kill a market.)

Both France and Germany at the end of the 19th century were developing stock markets at a level similar to that of the United States. Indeed, qualitatively the German stock market then might have been better: the cost to German firms in selling common stock was *lower* then than it was in the United States. Charles W. Calomiris, 'The Costs of Rejecting University Banking: American Finance in the German Mirror, 1870–1914,' in *Coordination and Information: Historical Perspectives on the Organization of Enterprise 257* (Naomi R. Lamoreaux and Daniel M. Raff, eds., 1995).

Before the First World War the Paris Bourse (not New York's) was the world's second most significant stock exchange, and French securities markets were, as a percentage of French GNP, about the size of America's, and not all that much smaller than Britain's. Politically France was then conservative: '[The b]ackbone of the third Republic was [a] bourgeoisie ... [that] completely dominated the Third Republic from 1875.'[20] 'From 1906 until the eve of the [First World] war France was plagued by a series of strikes ... most of [which were] put down by the government with force. Army troops were often called out to intimidate the strikers. On a few occasions they opened fire and there were casualties . . .'.[21] Even nominally labor-friendly governments arrested union leaders and drafted strikers into the army. 'In no other country of the West [at that time] did the working class become so alienated from society as in France.'[22] Thus, unlike the more modern French regimes, the early twentieth-century French Third Republic was an anti-labor government:

The collapse of the general strike in May 1920 ... almost destroyed the trade-union movement in France. Ruthlessly put down by the government ... with troops, police, and strike-breakers, the work stoppage ended with hundreds of labor leaders in jail, [and] the CGT ([the] General Confederation of Labor) outlawed by the courts. ... [E]mployers[,] ... encouraged by the collapse of the strike, were now determined to eliminate the unions completely ....[23]

True, French statist, *dirigiste* traditions are important in explaining French business structures. But France's earlier statist *conservative* governments did not demean securities markets in the same way that a statist *left* government could have and, later in the twentieth century, did. Indeed, a statist environment can catch up easily by copying rules from another society. France did this when conservative (imitating British corporate limited liability), but by the mid-twentieth century, when securities laws might have been profitably copied to separate ownership from control, France did not take that opportunity. The lurch to the left in France is usually marked by the ascension of the Popular Front in 1935. From then on, its government had little interest in propelling a shareholding society and an equity-based corporate environment. Even when the governments were not formally from the left, their political competition with a powerful left drove them to support stakeholder values strongly.

The French context thus illustrates the basics of the social democracy political thesis: more pressure on managers to defect from shareholder loyalty, and difficulty in using the tools that would close up that widened gap between managers and shareholders.

---

[20] William L. Shirer, *The Collapse of the Third Republic* 85, 192 (1969). And French statism was as anti-labor then as it was pro-labor later.

[21] Id. at 90.   [22] Id. at 90.   [23] Id. at 192.

Germany

German securities markets have historically been weak. A shareholder-driven board-room is impossible in the largest firms, because labor gets half of the German supervisory board. With labor having half of the boardroom, shareholders do better with a counter-coalition than they would in nations where labor is not as well represented in the boardroom. Other indicia of a shareholder-denigrating culture have been present in Germany, with codetermination 'just' formally manifesting the underlying drive for institutions that would keep social peace and, historically, a middle way between harsh capitalism and strong socialism.

Germany lacks good securities markets. Initial public offers until recently have been infrequent, securities trading is still shallow, and even large public firms typically have big blockholders that make the large firms resemble 'semi-private' companies.

8.1. GERMAN CODETERMINATION

German codetermination (by which employees control half of the seats on the German supervisory board) undermines diffuse ownership for two related reasons that we examined in Chapter 4. First, stockholders may wish that the firm's governing institutions have a blockholding 'balance of power' on the supervisory board, a balance that, because German law mandates that half the supervisory board represent employees, diffusely-owned firms may be unable to create. Codetermination in a fully publicly-owned firm should raise managerial agency costs to shareholders, by pushing managers to choose strategies that they and employees, but not shareholders, prefer. Managers have a well-known propensity to expand firms in ways that do not benefit shareholders, but rather favor themselves (and incumbent employees). Blockholders can sometimes mitigate the increased agency costs by either managing the firm directly or by being sufficiently cohesive to align managers with themselves.

Second, managers and stockholders sapped the supervisory board of power (or, more accurately, prevented it from evolving into a serious governance institution in the face of the 1980s and 1990s global competition and technological change), because to have done otherwise would have enhanced employee influence, thereby diminishing managerial autonomy and shareholder value. Board meetings were infrequent, information flow to the board poor, and the board often too big and unwieldy to be effective. Instead of boardroom governance, out-of-the-boardroom shareholder caucuses and meetings between managers and large shareholders substituted for effective boardroom action. But, because diffuse stockholders at key points in a firm's future need a plausible board (due to a succession crisis, a production downfall, or a technological challenge), diffuse ownership for the German firm would deny the firm both strong boardroom and blockholder governance. Blockholder governance would end if the block dissipated into a diffuse securities market, and board-level governance would be unavailable because the shareholders and managers had divested the board of authority beforehand. Stockholders would have had to choose between charging up the board (and hence further empowering the employee-half of the governance structure) and living with substandard boardroom governance. In the face of such choices, German firms (i.e. their managers and blockholders) retained their 'semi-private', blockholding structure, and the German securities market has been slow to develop.

8.2. GERMAN BOARDROOMS

One might begin analyzing the German boardroom with American observations about what makes for a good board:

- small size, with specialized subcommittees
- frequent meetings
- intense information flow
- low conflicts of interest.

The German boardroom historically seemed weak on all four traits. That observation might be taken as advice for German boardroom players. Or, second, it might begin an analysis of German boardroom origins: did shareholder voice in the firm through banks' direct ownership and their control of the proxy system combine to induce a reaction, a backlash, of codetermination legislation to give labor a louder voice in the firm? And once both shareholder voice and labor voice were firmly heard, was it hard for reformers to lower one without lowering the other as well?

I shall focus here on the second inquiry, assuming that these four traits are desirable but historically lacking in German boardrooms. We can help to explain even these mundane boardroom traits, I argue, by linking them up to German social politics. In reaction to German codetermination, players inside the firm, namely managers and shareholders, seem to have kept the supervisory board weaker for longer, despite global business changes that led to its strengthening elsewhere.

Although we focus on political pressure, surely it is not the only basis for understanding Germany's historically weaker securities markets. Standard accounts identify the lack of an equity-holding culture (a demand-side perspective), the lack of an entrepreneurial culture of businesspeople who create new firms (a supply-side perspective), inappropriate corporate and securities laws, opaque accounting, and the influence of the banks (in business and politics) to explain the lack of a vibrant German stock market. One need not reject these to accept the effect of German politics. Even if these other impediments had been overcome earlier, the codetermined structure would have fit poorly with diffuse ownership. This poor fit between codetermination and diffuse ownership historically made firm founders less willing to sell off their blocks of stock to the public, and made distant potential buyers more wary of owning stock in the German firm than they would have been otherwise.

8.3. CODETERMINATION AND BOARDROOM REACTION

Consider information flow, the size of the board, and the frequency of board meetings. American studies find that smaller boards are more effective than big ones; here it is easy to link codetermination with the big board's structure. The codetermination statute mandates that the boards be big, requiring that they range between twelve and twenty members depending on the firm's size.[1]

The statute does not mandate infrequent meetings or a formalized information flow. But each can also be seen as buttressed by codetermination. Begin with the frequency of meetings: American boards tend to meet more frequently, about eight times per year. Many German boards typically met two to four times per year. Although the German statute set the minimum frequency of two meetings annually, the board was free to meet more frequently—but many did not, and those that did typically only met four times a year. (True, some boards now meet more often, and perhaps recent governance problems have induced a trend to more frequent meetings.) Obviously, a board that seldom met would, all else being equal, be less informed and less able to monitor management than one that met frequently.

Moreover, key documents are said to have often been placed in front of the board members only as the meetings began, rendering directors unable to intensely prepare to examine the firm's current operations (if they were so

---

[1] Katharina Pistor, 'Codetermination: A Sociopolitical Model with Governance Externalities', in *Employees and Corporate Governance* 163 (ed. by Margaret Blair and Mark J. Roe, 1999) (discussing Mitbestimmung der Arbeitnehmer, § 7). Companies with more than 20,000 employees must have a 20-person board; those with fewer than 10,000 must have a 12-person board; and those with between 10,000 and 20,000 get a 16-person board.

inclined), or to closely question managers. Directors could not monitor managers effectively if they saw basic information only moments before a formalized meeting began and then watched as the documents were whisked away shortly thereafter. Moreover, it is unclear how motivated the directors were to scrutinize managers: shareholder-side directors are said to have been quite reluctant to criticize management in front of the labor representatives.[2] Reticence hardly makes for a good monitoring board.

Why did evolutionary pressure not lead to a better board?[3] Perhaps increasing its strength also would have brought on costs, either to the firm or to players inside it. Codetermination might have played a role in the internal calculus of the firm's players.

That the German supervisory board was never formally intended to have a hands-on role is not critical. True perhaps, for the German supervisory boards to evolve, the players needed a formal legal mandate even if business pressures pushed it to become more active. But this too begs our question: even if the lack of formal authority blocked evolution (if formalities are important in German institutions), we would still not know why the German corporate players did not ask parliament to grant that formal authority.

Abstract the German firm into three parts: management, labor, and capital. Managers might have performed better if they had faced supervisory board scrutiny. But for a board to scrutinize the managers, it had to meet frequently and be well informed. Capital might have insisted on this scrutiny, if it would not have had to pay for it elsewhere. Normally the board would have been the vehicle for this scrutiny.

Look at capital *vis-à-vis* labor. Assume capital preferred that labor not be well informed. Capital's desire could have been functional, dysfunctional, or neutral, but is easy to understand. Their desire could have been functional in the sense that labor could sometimes damage the firm, especially when labor's representatives pursued the goals of senior employees who had only a few years left to work at the firm.

Capital's desire could here also have been neutral to the total size of the pie. Internal grabs between capital and labor could have been in play; capital might have wanted to keep labor in the dark so that labor would be less effective in internal rent-seeking, and capital more so. Or capital's desire could have been dysfunctional because some labor-management decisions require trust, and well-informed labor that gets good information through the board could enhance that trust in shop-floor activities. But if this enhanced firm performance were offset by

---

[2] Klaus Hopt, 'The German Two-Tier Board: Experience, Theories, Reforms', in *Comparative Corporate Governance: The State of the Art and Emerging Research* 227, 247 (ed. by Klaus Hopt, Hideki Kanda, Mark Roe, Eddy Wymeersch, and Stefan Prigge, 1998).

[3] Thus one would hypothesize that recent boardroom failures in Germany would have increased the pressure on supervisory boards to meet more often. See Gerhard Liener, 'The Future of German Governance', *Corp. Board* 1 (May 1995), cited in Thomas J. André, Jr, 'Some Reflections on German Corporate Governance: A Glimpse at German Supervisory Boards', 70 *Tul. L. Rev.* 1819, 1825 n.21 (1996).

capital's perception that it would lose value because labor would get more (or capital less), or by management's fear that consulting labor would constrict their own autonomy, then capital's (and management's) desire to keep labor in the dark and the boardroom under-informed became dysfunctional.

But if the supervisory board were the smoothest conduit for information to capital as well, then owners, by keeping the board ill informed, would have been constricting the information flow to itself. Constricting the flow to its own people could be rational if the costs to owners from labor being better informed were greater than the gains to capital from better firm performance: i.e. capital might have preferred to take its chance with unmonitored managers than with well-informed labor.

Or owners might have decided that they could get enough information elsewhere through informal discussions, through control of the speaker's seat of the supervisory board (the 'speaker' chairs the board), through separate meetings between management and the shareholder bench of the board, or through bank loan channels. Owners might have known that these channels could have been enhanced with better boardroom information, but if the better boardroom channel came with the price of better informed labor, they may have preferred the co-determined board to be poorly informed. Bankers are said to have believed they got no more information from their seats on the supervisory board than they got as a creditor of the firm, and we may just have found one reason why.[4]

Shareholders and managers may look at meeting frequency similarly. They may believe that more monitoring should somewhat improve operations at critical junctures, and they may believe that more meetings should improve monitoring. But more meetings would enhance labor's voice in the codetermined boardroom, making management and capital shy away from asking the supervisory board to meet more.

The board's large size also increased the inside-the-boardroom free-rider problem. ('Why prepare, if I'm only a small player inside the boardroom?') If free-riding board members did not prepare well anyway, then there was little reason to give them reports to study early; small benefits (like confidentiality) could have justified last-minute distribution.

The evidence available, although indirect, is consistent with this view of codetermination inducing a deliberately-weak supervisory board. Early studies suggested that managers and shareholders sought to weaken the labor side of the codetermined board via, say, equity-dominated subcommittees. More than

---

[4] Peter O. Mülbert, 'Empfehlen sich gesetzliche Regelungen zur Einschränkung des Einflusses der Kreditinstitute auf Aktiengesellschaften?', Gutachten E, zum 61. *Deutschen Juristentag* 49 (1996). Labor could similarly have sought alternative information channels, through the works councils or straightforward union negotiation. Board seats may also have become a patronage item, one that compensated employee-side players who entered the boardroom and became less likely to confront the firm and its managers in other arenas. As such, owners may have had other reasons to keep the meetings few and the work limited, as a means of co-opting some players who could disrupt the firm elsewhere.

half of the German boards adopted one or more of these 'equity-enhancing' characteristics:

(1) additional stockholder vice-chairs of the board (to adjust from German corporate law's default rule that the vice-chair come from the labor side, the chair from the equity side);

(2) equity-controlled subcommittees;

(3) enhanced power of the chair (who typically is from the shareholder side) to control the agenda;

(4) quorum rules that favored equity;

(5) additional authority of the chair to postpone action if he or she could not be present;

(6) requirement that the chair cast the tie-breaking vote if a board vote was tied; or,

(7) restraint on board members from making statements outside of the boardroom.

Data is consistent: one study suggests codetermination brought overall social gains, but decreased firm-level productivity and profitability (without affecting wage rates).[5] These results suggest that internal rent-seeking by labor and shareholder governance counters are plausible. The authors of a more recent study conclude that the law that increased labor representation from one-third of the board to one-half of the board for most large German companies cost shareholders about 15 or 20 per cent of their shares value.[6] (To be sure here, since fully codetermined firms are larger firms, the authors cannot be certain whether they were measuring size effects or codetermination effects.) In brief, shareholders and managers sought to undermine codetermination, and the data suggests why.

8.4. SECURITIES MARKETS AND MONITORING MANAGERS

Corporate governance and securities markets are linked. The usual American perspective is that liquid and diffuse American securities markets induced special governance features, such as the Berle-Means corporation, takeovers, independent boards, and enhanced agency costs. A standard refrain in the American literature is that firms went public because of financing needs, either to finance the firm itself or to finance the owners' diversification out of the firm they founded, and, as the new buying owners diversified into small lots, power shifted from free-riding shareholders with poor information to concentrated inside managers. Structures and practices then evolved to align managers better with shareholders.

---

[5] See Felix R. FitzRoy and Kornelius Kraft, 'Economic Effects of Codetermination', 95 *Scandinavian J. Econ.* 365, 373 (1993).

[6] Frank A. Schmid and Frank Seger, 'Arbeitnehmermitbestimmung, Allokation von entscheidungsrechten und Shareholder Value', 5 *Zeitschrift für Betriebswirtschaft* (ZfB) 453 (1998).

But persistent corporate governance structures can also affect the demand for securities markets, and this view vividly applies to Germany. The codetermined board might have kept corporate issuers' demand for securities markets and their supporting apparatus (like good securities laws and transparent accounting) weak. Family founders in Germany may have wished to cash out and diversify like their Anglo-Saxon counterparts, but if the buyers would not have paid 'full' price for the stock because the buyers would have had to deal either with a weak board or strong labor, then the founders may have retained the block and induced the next generation in the family to enter and run the firm. When they sold, they might have sold a block to new blockholders who could monitor the firm and its managers, and the evidence suggests this was so.[7] Blocks persisted and the demand for better corporate law was low.

This observation helps to explain the relative scarcity of entrepreneurs willing to set up new firms. If the German firm had to be sold intact to a new blockholder for the successful entrepreneur to diversify, then these entrepreneurs may have been unable to find many bidders for their firm. In the United States, in contrast, the bidders for the existing blocks are not just new blockholders but also underwriters who can sell into the securities markets. Competition from the securities markets helps the entrepreneur to get full price for the firm. In Germany, the seller may often have been, and perhaps still is, unable to get 'full' price because buyers were too few and fully selling into the stock market not an option.

8.5. SUBSTITUTES

The point here is not that boardroom monitoring is the *sine qua non* of securities markets. Nor is it that American boardroom monitoring is so superior to Germany's. The point is that securities markets need managers to be monitored from time to time. The principal monitoring mechanisms are market competition (in capital and product markets), takeovers, a good board of directors, and/or a concentrated shareholder. The United States is strong in the first control mechanism (competition) and, even with recent boardroom scandals, thought to be passable in the next two. Germany has historically been weak on competition, lacked takeovers, and was weaker in boardroom governance. All that was left for large German firms has been the fourth—blockholding. Had German firms dismantled blockholding, via diffusion in ownership of their largest firms, shareholders would have been left with no significant internal or external control device. Evidence of this may be the fact that over 85 per cent of Germany's largest firms persist in having a stockholder owning over 25 per cent of the firm's stock. Large blockholders' representatives met informally with managers outside of the formal meetings, and this seems to have been Germany's key means of monitoring. While American firms have substitutes (or improvements), German

---

[7] See Julian Franks and Colin Mayer, 'Ownership and Control of German Corporations', 14 *Rev. Fin. Stud.* 943, 955 (2001).

firms historically had no other method to monitor managers and therefore would have suffered if the blockholders had dissipated their blocks. If the other substitutes for monitoring improve enough, through, say, enhanced European product market competition after implementation of Maastricht or a European Monetary Union, then the German governance trade-off would also change.

8.6. WHICH CAME FIRST?

One might argue that the analysis here gets the structural sequence backwards. *Blockholding* came first and resisted change. Hence, blockholding plausibly induced codetermination, and not codetermination that initially induced blockholders.

That kind of response is just true enough to mislead us in analyzing the German corporation. Blockholding *did* come first, resisted change (in contrast to American direct financial influence, which populist political pressure broke up early), and codetermination then came forth as a political and social *reaction* to blockholding. Certainly the historical sequencing was along those lines: codetermination got its most recent formal push in 1976, *after* blockholding had been around in Germany for quite some time.

But a focus on the historical sequence misses the point. *Once the two were in place*, neither could change easily without changing the other. German blockholding called forth codetermination, *and vice versa*. Evolution was harder, and maybe still is because the two complementary institutions must move in unison.

8.7. BUT CONCENTRATION PREVAILS ELSEWHERE IN CONTINENTAL EUROPE

Most other continental European nations have had concentrated block ownership, but lacked codetermination. Hence, one might argue, German codetermination was not a key fit with blockholding, so something else must have impeded separation.

Two responses make this rebuttal a weak one. First, there are several hurdles to ownership diffusion. Germany would have had an additional hurdle had it sought to evolve away from blockholding and toward American-style diffuse ownership. Even if other roadblocks lifted, the close fit between codetermination and blockholding was there, impeding separation.

Second, German codetermination is just a formal, specific exemplar of why the other continental European nations have not yet, at the end of the twentieth century, had widespread diffuse ownership.

* * *

Germany has several codetermination regimes, each reportedly with similar ownership.[8] Labor gets one-third of the seats in mid-sized firms with more than 500 employees; one-half in large firms with over 2,000 employees (but labor loses if there's a tie vote); and a 'full' one-half in coal and steel firms, like Krupp (originally, until it diversified away from steel) and Thyssen. This might be, and has been, interpreted to mean that codetermination 'doesn't matter',[9] but a more plausible interpretation of ownership not varying as the firms get larger (500 to 2,000 employees; private and closely-held to public) is that it *does* matter. As firms get larger the normal expectation is that ownership would become more diffuse. If it does not, then one might hypothesize that some friction impedes fuller diffusion in the German system.

8.8. LIMITS TO A LEGAL THEORY: CODETERMINATION AFFECTS SHAREHOLDER VALUE MORE THAN DOES CORPORATE LAW

A popular alternative explanation to this political theory is a legal one: if corporate law fails to protect outside stockholders, securities markets will not develop. The two theories are partly consistent and partly in tension, as we shall see in Part VI, 'Corporate Law's Limits'. Here we can preview some of the German data and see how the two could be inconsistent.

For Germany, the political theory trumps the legal one (not so for every country). Two data sets show that the premium blockholders get in control transactions—a rough measure of the value of control and, hence, of how well corporate law protects minority stockholders—is about 5 or 10 per cent.[10] That is not small, but it is not much higher than what blockholders get in the United States.

But the data show codetermination affects stockholder value *more* strongly. The 1976 law that increased the codetermined side from one-third to one-half had a 15 per cent or more negative effect on shareholder value.[11] Obviously, these 15 per cent results *understate* three elements:

(1) the total effect of codetermination (from no board representation to 50 per cent representation);
(2) the total effect of social democratic pressures on the firm from all sources; and

---

[8] John W. Cioffi, 'State of the Art: A Review Essay on Comparative Corporate Governance: The State of the Art and Emerging Research', 48 *Am. J. Comp.* L. 501, 525 (2000).

[9] E.g., id., at 525 & n.6.   [10] See infra, Ch. 25.

[11] See FitzRoy and Kraft, supra note 5; Schmid and Seger, supra note 6. Cf. Gary Gorton and Frank Schmid, 'Class Struggle Inside the Firm: A Study of German Codetermination' 25 (National Bureau of Economic Research working paper, Oct. 2000). Contra Theodor Baums and Bernd Frick, 'The Market Value of the Codetermined Firm', in *Employees and Corporate Governance* 206, 232 (ed. by Margaret Blair and Mark J. Roe, 1999); Bernd Frick, Gerhard Speckbacher, and Paul Wentges, 'Arbeitnehmermitbestimmung und moderne Theorie der Unternehmung', *Zeitschrift für Betriebswirtschaft* 745–63 (1998-V).

(3) the cost to shareholders if they did not have counter-measures—i.e. block ownership—to reduce the social democratic impact.

As measured, the political economy effects on the German boardroom are as strong, or stronger, than the corporate law institutional effects.

8.9 TAXES

Germany plans to roll-back its capital gains tax, which makes blocks, once assembled, illiquid.[12] A bank that invested in a big block of stock and saw its value increase would be heavily taxed when the block was sold. The bank could avoid this tax by not selling the block. Tax law made diffusion harder than it would have been otherwise.

Repeal will allow the banks to get rid of their blocks, thereby inducing a more free-wheeling capitalism that tax law primarily impeded. This may happen, but one might ask why repeal did not happen earlier. Perhaps repeal and a free-wheeling capitalism was something feared, and Germany's shift politically rightward in recent years makes it easier for blocks to dissipate. Headlines such as a recent one in the *Wall Street Journal* proclaimed an end to Germany's stakeholder capitalism,[13] political scientists record a shift rightward,[14] and these shifts facilitate dissipation and dispersion, making German players more comfortable with the consequences of repealing the tax friction.

Moreover, the incentives here are more complex than generally acknowledged. Once a block was acquired, taxation of gains made the blocks, even undesired blocks, illiquid. And, hence, repeal should induce the banks to sell *those* unwanted blocks. But exit barriers such as the tax rule were *entry* barriers as well. The unfavorable tax rules have been in place for quite some time; despite them, banks and others often took big blocks despite the dilemma that the unfavorable tax rule set up: some large block positions fail to be profitable. For those the stock price would decline and the bank would lose. But for those blocks for which the bank, through skill or luck, had a gain, the bank would be stuck with an albatross. It would have enhanced value, but it could not readily cash in. Hence, the banks had a tax reason *not* to take blocks; presumably they accordingly took *fewer* blocks than they otherwise would have taken. To the extent these incentives carry forward, then contrary to the now conventional wisdom, after the initial sell-off of the undesirable blocks, the repeal could induce the banks to be *more* or as willing to take the occasional big block that fits strategic plans, investing, holding, and then later re-positioning it after that tax friction is gone.[15]

---

[12] Eugen Bogenschütz and Kelly Wright, 'A Look at Germany's New Reduction Tax Act 2001', *Tax Notes Int'l*, 31 July 2000, at 499, 502–3.

[13] Christopher Rhoads and Vanessa Fuhrmans, 'Stakeholders Yield to Shareholders in the New Germany', *Wall St. J. Europe*, 21 June 2001, at 1.   [14] See Table 21.1.

[15] Moreover, the German tax package has other provisions that could yield increased inter-corporate holdings: more inter-corporate dividends, for example, will not be taxed at all.

Thus, analyzing incentives yields an ambiguous conclusion: repealing the tax friction could lead to fewer blocks (as pent-up demand to sell is satisfied), more blocks (as a barrier to investment is removed), or no net change. The current conventional wisdom predicts the first result.

8.10. CONCLUSION: THE TENSION BETWEEN CODETERMINATION AND DIFFUSE OWNERSHIP

German supervisory boards have been weak, and they may well have been weak because of codetermination. Stockholders have had mixed incentives to strengthen a labor-oriented boardroom. And weak German securities markets may have been partly due to a weak German supervisory board. Diffuse stockholders would have faced either a labor-dominated board or a weak board. Neither choice would have appealed to potential distant stockholders, so they would not have paid full price to buy from blockholders, and blockholders may have been unwilling to take the loss. Stock persisted in big blocks and fluidity came not from initial public offerings dispersing privately-owned stock, but from private blocks changing hands intact. Thus the demand for good securities market institutions may not have been strong and hence these institutions did not develop.

German codetermination did not *initially* cause a weak securities market, tight family ownership, and bank influence. The historical sequence of first powerful banks (and the family founders), then codetermination, and Germany's prior history of repressing labor, obscured the interdependence of the two. Codetermination and block ownership are complementary, and it is hard for one to exit without the other also exiting, irrespective of which one came first historically.

* * *

I do not wish to paint a portrait of German uniqueness here on all levels of abstraction. *No* nation allows unbridled shareholder control of the firm, and the brakes on full control come into play differently. Japanese lifetime employment, inside boards, and ownership by major creditors break unbridled shareholder control. French and Italian state ownership and state regulation also broke unbridled shareholder control. And even in the United States, one might see the persistence of managerial control as reining in any pure shareholder control of the firm. Nevertheless, some nations put the brakes on harder than others, and these nations tended to have fewer truly public firms, because, unless they maintained blockholding, the distant stockholders would have found themselves with weakly loyal managers.

Nor should we conclude that this undermines the bottom line efficiency of the society. What is lost in shareholder value may be gained on the shop-floor in motivation. And what is not made up in motivation might be made up for in a greater sense of involvement, of a generalized increase in utility. Such value cannot be readily measured, but may still be there. And then there is the political economy issue that, were the institution absent, social tensions might have been great enough to degrade productivity and shareholder wealth more than they were.

Italy

Italy's features, although they nicely support a contrasting, law-centered thesis, also display key aspects of the political thesis. For decades the Communist Party was strong, markets denigrated, and ownership concentrated. Social and economic conflict in large industrial firms was intense, and they were not well-suited to diffuse ownership and managerial control. Governments pressed firms not to restructure. And conservative governments sought to prop up the small firm, in which they believed employees would be less susceptible to appeals from the left.

Italy has many small family-owned firms and few public firms. A simple legal theory, one based solely on whether minority stockholders are well-protected, is plausible for Italy, whose courts, regulators, and practices are reputed thus far to be ineffective in preventing controlling shareholder machinations. Indeed, the statistics suggest a factor beyond politics at play in Italy: its firms are less diffusely owned than political placement alone would predict. Corporate pyramids are common, and controlling insiders can shift value from outsiders to themselves.[1]

Weak corporate law, however, is only part of the story, even in Italy. Italian players dissatisfied with basic corporate law have at times used contract to give themselves the core private law rules that they wanted.[2] *Other* legal weaknesses may be just as important, or even more so: owners of closely-held businesses probably evade the tax collector more effectively (with the owner taking the risks

---

[1] Magda Bianco and Paola Casavola, 'Italian Corporate Governance: Effects on Financial Structure and Firm Performance', 43 *European Econ. Rev.* 1057, 1059–60 (1999); Luca Enriques, 'Off the Books, but on the Record: Evidence from Italy on the Relevance of Judges to the Quality of Corporate Law' (University of Bologna working paper, 2001); Piergaetano Marchetti, 'Diritto societario e disciplina della concorrenza', in *Storia del Capitalismo Italiano* 467 (ed. by Fabrizio Barca, 1997) (an Italian SEC was not founded until 1974 and an anti-trust commission not until 1990). Cf. Lorenzo Stanghellini, 'Corporate Governance in Italy: Strong Owners, Faithful Managers. An Assessment and a Proposal for Reform', 6 *Ind. Int'l & Comp. L. Rev.* 92, 180 (1995) ('[T]he Italian legal framework discourages investors unable to enter in[to] the control group from entering the company at all.')

[2] Minority stockholders in Mediaset, Silvio Berlusconi's principal corporate vehicle—Berlusconi has a wheeler-dealer reputation—insisted on a corporate charter term requiring super-majority board approval for any related party transaction. They expected board representation and, hence, veto power. Board approval for such transactions is not required under Italian corporate law, but

of evasion but getting the gains) than would managers of diffusely-owned public firms. Labor law, which is tighter for large employers than for small ones, should have induced firms to remain small, and, hence, lowered the demand for large-size firms that would need access to securities markets: by the 1970s, larger firms were subject to a labor law that effectively barred the firm from dismissing a worker.[3] Hence, firms had reason not to grow to be big enough to be covered, thereby keeping the demand for large and public firms low.

And economic-based social conflict has been historically high, labor-management co-operation low,[4] labor-influenced political parties powerful, and Italy's Communist Party for several decades supported by a quarter of the Italian electorate. Italian Christian Democratic governments fostered small closely held businesses, and especially co-operatives. One reason they did so was because they thought employees would identify with owners in small firms, but oppose them, especially distant owners, in large firms. Large firms provoked more social tension than smaller closely held ones.[5]

Consider this description:

After 1963, when the Socialist Party entered government... [the] trade unions became more powerful....

[Economic tension] was accentuated by the 'hot autumn' of 1969, a season of strikes, factory occupations, and mass demonstrations throughout northern Italy. Most stoppages were unofficial, led by workers' factory committees or militant leftist groups....Jobs...were virtually guaranteed in the 'official' economy, and trade unions became influential on a host of planning bodies.

Labour militancy continued throughout most of the 1970s, often led by unofficial 'autonomous' unions. Many firms therefore chose to 'restructure' themselves into smaller units employing part-time or 'unofficial' workers on piece rates, who could be dismissed easily and did not enjoy guaranteed wages.[6]

A violent strike at Fiat as recently as 1980 could only be settled after tough bargaining at the political level, in which the players—the communist union and

contract law could fill the gap. See Giovanni Battista Bisogni, 'Autonomia ed eteronomia nella disciplina dei rapporti associativi della publicly held corporation', 42 *Rivista delle Società* 649, 702–03 n.116 (1997). I discuss contract and corporate law in Part VI.

[3] Emilio Reyneri, 'The Italian Labor Market: Between State Control and Social Regulation', in *State, Market, and Social Regulation: New Perspectives on Italy* 167, 180 (ed. by Peter Lange and Marino Regini, 1989); Tiziano Treu, 'Employment Protection and Labor Relations in Italy', in *Employment Security and Labor Market Behavior* 385 (ed. by Christoph F. Buechtemann, 1993) ('legal regulation and collective bargaining...seek to apply rigid measures to protect workers from...employment reduction').

[4] Marco Magnani, 'Alla ricerca di regole nelle relazioni industriali: breve storia di due fallimenti', in *Storia del Capitalismo Italiano* 501 (ed. by Fabrizio Barca, 1997).

[5] Linda Weiss, *Creating Capitalism: The State and Small Business since 1945*, at 104–05, 127–38 (1988) (the small Italian firm provided political stability in the face of strong public support for leftist politics, a mobilized labor movement, and intense capital-labor conflict). Cf. Robert E. Carpenter and Laura Rondi, 'Italian Corporate Governance, Investment, and Finance', 27 *Empirica* 365, 384 (2000): '[Italy's policy of] providing small, mature firms with low-cost government finance, for example, amounts to a redistributive subsidy toward small firms, and not necessarily an effective development policy.'   [6] 'Italy', *Encyclopædia Britannica Online* (accessed 3 Aug. 2001).

the owners—needed political correlates to get their side a plausible result.[7] (Gianni Agnelli was in the 1970s both the head of Fiat and the head of Confindustria, a business lobbying group. He was seen as a tough 'anti-union' Fiat president, striking bargains with the Italian Communist Party when needed for industrial peace.[8]) And Italian governments sought tripartite bargaining among the state, the leading labor unions, and the owners.[9]

Even before then, Fiat had been the focus of worker struggles to establish Italian works-councils, and owner attempts to defeat the communist unions.[10] Fiat's industrial history is described as a continual jockeying for power between the owners and the unions, with each trying to dominate the other internally (via company unions by the owners and radical unions by workers) and externally (through local political influence), and then negotiating an unstable but partial *modus vivendi*.[11] Fiat's owners and managers 'followed a hard [anti-union] line.... Management [held] to a neoliberal philosophy... challeng[ing] the unions politically, play[ing] at exacerbating workers' divisions, refus[ing] to bargain at the shop-floor level... and refus[ing] all government mediation.'[12]

For several decades, *no* major political party's ideology was friendly toward promoting profit-enhancing institutions, legal or otherwise: '[I]n Italy, until [perhaps the mid-1980s], a counter-ideology [to American-style market thinking] prevailed that ... emphasize[d] the market's destabilizing effects and its excessive social and economic costs as compared with other regulatory mechanisms, above all the state.'[13]

This ideological foundation is obvious for Italy's Communist Party, which often got a quarter of the vote. But the Christian Democratic Party did not strongly support profit-based institutions either. Normal political theory would expect it to move close to its principal rival ideologically, to capture as big a chunk of the electorate as possible. And internally as well the Christian Democrats felt uncomfortable with raw profit-making institutions. Unlike 'American-style... capitalism and [its celebration of] money... Italy's traditional right-wing ideology... is statist, Catholic and suspicious of overnight wealth.'[14] Guido Carli, a well-known central

---

[7] Gianprimo Cella, 'Criteria of Regulation in Italian Industrial Relations: A Case of Weak Institutions', in *State, Market, and Social Regulation: New Perspectives on Italy* 167, 180 (ed. by Peter Lange and Marino Regini, 1989).

[8] Paolo Garonna and Elena Pisani, 'Italian Unions in Transition: The Crisis of Political Unionism', in *Unions in Crisis and Beyond: Perspectives from Six Countries* 114, 141 (ed. by Richard Edwards, Paolo Garonna, and Franz Tödtling, 1986).   [9] Cella, supra, note 7, at 173.

[10] Giovanni Contini, 'The Rise and Fall of Shop-Floor Bargaining at Fiat 1945–1980', in *The Automobile Industry and its Workers: Between Fordism and Flexibility* 144, 148 (ed. by Steven Tolliday and Jonathan Zeitlin, 1986).

[11] Richard M. Locke, 'Political Embeddedness of Industrial Change: Corporate Restructuring and Local Politics in Contemporary Italy', in *Transforming Organization* 31–36 (ed. by Thomas A. Kochan and Michael Useem, 1992).   [12] Garonna and Pisani, supra, note 8, at 152.

[13] Antonio Chiesi and Alberto Martinelli, 'The Representation of Business Interests as a Mechanism of Social Regulation', in *State, Market, and Social Regulation: New Perspectives on Italy* 187, 189 (1989), who add: 'In Italy, the low appreciation of market mechanisms is in part due to the relative weakness of the industrial bourgeoisie... which was unable to diffuse a shared market ideology.'

[14] Alessandra Stanley, 'The Power of Celebrity Hits Italian Politics', *N.Y. Times*, 20 May 2001, at WK4. See also Paul Ginsborg, *A History of Contemporary Italy: Society and Politics, 1943–1988*, at

bank governor, quipped that Marxist and Catholic ideology dominated Italian political and social thought, one on the left and the other on the right, and neither much respected the market.[15]

Only by the 1990s, or late 1980s, did the labor market rigidities and the anti-market ideologies soften,[16] and the economy liberalized enough that it became plausible to think about encouraging public firms, securities markets, and ownership dispersion.[17] Then Maastricht and integration into the European Union increased product market competition, thereby tightening the constraints managers faced in running their firms while reducing the government's potential to control labor markets as fully as it had before. It could in 2001 be said that: 'As elsewhere in Europe, Italy's voters and main parties of the right and left have stampeded towards the center ground. They are all for the market now.'[18] And then reform of the corporate law rules and institutions could have impact, so Italian players began that reform, with Italy's 1990s Draghi Commission recommending what to do and subsequent laws beginning the reform.

121, 255 (1990) (Christian Democratic economic policies similar to those of left political parties in other nations); Gian Maria Gros-Pietro, Edoardo Reviglio, and Alfio Torrisi, *Assetti Proprietari e Mercati Finanziari Europei* 208–12 (2001) (strong redistributive policies of Italian government in post-World War II decades).

[15] Guido Carli and Paolo Peluffo, *Cinquant'anni di vita italiana* 14 (1993). Cf. Piero Barucci and Antonio Magliulo, *L'Insegnamento Economico e Sociale della Chiesa (1891–1991)*, 140, 153 (1996), who analyze church economic ideology, which until the 1980s mistrusted the market, sought politics' supremacy over economics, and favored subordinating capital to labor.

[16] See Barucci and Magliulo, supra, note 15, at 153 (grudging 1990s acceptance of capitalism in church ideology).   [17] Reyneri, supra, note 3, at 140–41.

[18] Xan Smiley, 'They're (nearly) all centrists now—Italian Survey Special Section', *The Economist*, 7 July 2001, at 6.

10

Japan

Japanese lifetime employment reflects a political cast to corporate organization, arising during a time of fiery social turmoil, a time not otherwise economically conducive to pro-labor bargains that would yield lifetime employment, because unemployment then was high and the economy weak. Stable employment is, or at least was, a key part of the Japanese peace predicate.

10.1. VIOLENCE AND CONFLICT IN POST-WAR JAPANESE LABOR RELATIONS

After a fifty-day strike at Toshiba in 1946, in a prelude to several years of conflict, labor won power to run the factories, for a time.[1] Throughout Japan in the post-war desolation of a destroyed nation, starvation was not distant, labor strife was common, and the conflict was rough: workers at times took over and ran the factories without the managers, paying themselves, paying the factories' other costs, and depositing any profit in a company bank account. The first such takeover strike hit in the fall of 1945, and during the first six months of 1946, Japanese managers faced 255 of these 'takeover strikes'.[2]

Contrary to conventional wisdom about lifetime employment in Japan, the firm's promise of employment security did not directly induce employees or employers to invest in developing the employees' human capital. Nor has it been a long-standing feature of Japanese business culture. It does not directly induce investment in human capital because the employee could still quit and

---

[1] Kiyoshi Yamamoto, *'Toshiba Rongi—1949' [Toshiba Dispute—1949]* (1983).

[2] Carl Mosk, *Competition and Cooperation in Japanese Labour Markets* 96 (1995); Andrew Gordon, *The Evolution of Labor Relations in Japan: Heavy Industry, 1853–1955*, at 331–32 (1985); Sheldon Garon, *The State and Labor in Modern Japan* 238 (1987); John Price, *Japan Works: Power and Paradox in Postwar Industrial Relations* 54 (1997).

the employer could still reduce wages after the employees invested in human capital, as Ronald Gilson and I have analyzed elsewhere.[3] (Instead, it was principally lifetime employment's complement—the nearly closed external labor market—that induced employers to invest in human capital.)

Nor was lifetime employment a long-standing cultural tradition in Japan: before the Second World War Japanese firms fired excess employees, and ambitious employees jumped to other jobs. Rather, it arose after vicious labor strife—such as the Toshiba dispute—in a post-war, devastated Japan, as part of a package that brought social peace to the large Japanese firm. To maintain morale after the large firms wrested control of the factories back from the workers, firing many of them, and ending much of their influence over factory management, the firms' senior managers promised lifetime jobs to the core of remaining employees. From there, the Japanese system evolved to become as productive as possible. Lifetime employment induced changes in the labor market, including internal promotional tournaments, back-loaded seniority-based wages, large and variable bonuses, early retirement at age 55, and, probably most importantly, a closing of the external labor market; no longer could employees jump from firm to firm easily, or at all. And it fit well with some developing corporate governance institutions, such as the large board of inside managers and limiting stockholder influence to that of banker-creditors who owned the firm's stock.

American occupation authorities initially induced some of this labor strife. Determined to break down Japan's militarist institutions, the occupying authorities, some of them displaced New Dealers, helped unions to organize as a counter-weight to the existing interests. They urged Japanese officials to enact the Trade Union Law of 1945, which guaranteed workers the right to form unions and to strike, both of which the workers did: unions had 381,000 members when the Trade Union Law was passed, more than 3,000,000 a year later, and nearly 5,000,000 by the end of 1946.

But SCAP (the Supreme Command, Allied Powers) later changed its mind about Japanese unions. America acquired a new anti-communist Cold War policy, and SCAP came to see the militant unions as threatening that policy. SCAP abandoned the pro-union policy and prodded Japanese managers to reassert control. In 1947, Japanese unions planned a general strike, but SCAP barred them from striking and then encouraged the Japanese Parliament to ban all public sector employees from striking. Force implicitly lay behind the policy change: once American tanks supported the Japanese police in ousting workers.[4]

In one incident, famous in Japan, Toshiba's managers, encouraged and prodded by American authorities and Japanese officials who wanted an anti-labor example, began an anti-labor offensive in 1948 to regain the full control of their factories, which they had partly lost to labor in that earlier 1946 fifty-day strike. Toshiba's managers in 1948 shut down labor-controlled Toshiba factories by physically retaking control and removing key machines; they dismissed workers (and bought

---

[3] Ronald J. Gilson and Mark J. Roe, 'Lifetime Employment: Labor Peace and the Evolution of Japanese Corporate Governance', 99 *Colum. L. Rev.* 508 (1999).

[4] Gordon, supra, note 2, at 332–33; Mosk, supra, note 2, at 96–97; Price, supra, note 2, at 66.

other workers' voluntary resignation); and they ended labor union authority over basic management of Toshiba factories.[5]

By 1950 the Japanese Red Purge was in force: 12,000 employees said to be Communist Party members were fired from their jobs and barred from union activity. Existing unions, often communist-influenced, were replaced with more co-operative enterprise unions.[6] At the same time, socialists threatened the conservative parties with electoral victories.

10.2. THE RISE OF LIFETIME EMPLOYMENT TO SETTLE CONFLICT

How could firms and senior managers retain the loyalty of the remaining demoralized employees after so many others had been dismissed? Management sought to incorporate remaining workers into the firm by promising employment security.[7] 'In exchange for union acceptance of... [among other things] limited union input in regulation of the workplace, workers received some job security.'[8] When managers sought to rationalize production in a restructured firm after mass lay-offs, they had to deal with the poor morale of the survivors and the prospect of new labor unrest; privileging remaining employees with lifetime employment was one strategy managers used to reduce unrest, raise the morale of the remaining employees, and sever the remaining employees' loyalty to those who had been laid off:

[During the] offensive against labour during 1949,... *state policies (mass lay-offs and the rescinding of union rights in the public sector...)* [induced] major private employers... to assert their authority. Management [won] ... showdowns with militant enterprise unions. At the same time, the big firms accepted union demands for job security and ... [seniority-based] wages....[9]

This genre of trade-off is not alien to American labor history: when Henry Ford announced his famous 5-dollar day for workers whose next best job opportunities paid half as well, he quite plausibly was buying them away from the Wobblies. He feared employees on his new assembly line were susceptible to appeals from, and organization by, the Wobblies; and he paid them well to divert their loyalty away from the Wobblies.[10]

* * *

[5] Yamamoto, supra, note 1.

[6] Gordon, supra, note 2, at 333; Mosk, supra, note 2, at 96; Price, supra, note 2, at 83–97.

[7] Nobuhiro Hiwatari, 'Employment Practices and Enterprise Unionism in Japan', in *Employees and Corporate Governance* 275, 285 (ed. by Margaret Blair and Mark J. Roe, 1999).

[8] Price, supra, note 2, at 253.

[9] *Japanese Models of Conflict Resolution* 71 (ed. by S. N. Eisenstadt and Eyal Ben-Ari, 1990) (emphasis supplied). For similar analyses, see Toshihiro Nishiguchi, *Strategic Industrial Sourcing— The Japanese Advantage* (1994); Takashi Araki, 'Flexibility in Japanese Employment Relations and the Role of the Judiciary', in *Japanese Commercial Law in an Era of Internationalization* 249, 251 (ed. by Hiroshi Oda 1994).

[10] Daniel Raff, 'Wage Determination Theory and the Five-Dollar Day at Ford', 48 *J. Econ. Hist.* 387 (1988). Raff argues that the dominant alternative hypothesis to Ford defeating the Wobblies' union-organizing—that Ford was paying the employees an 'efficiency' wage, to motivate them to be more productive—fails to fit the data nicely.

This Japanese picture is a grim one: workers struggle to survive, workers and managers struggle to control the factories, the American occupation authorities first foster and then seek to crush strong unions, and in the end a deal is cut. Although grim, this picture is realistic. A more positive spin on the same basic facts would see employees as seeking security, community, and dignity, and see managers resisting at first and then acceding to some workers' demands for security, a security that made the favored workers more willing to cede control to management. Whatever spin one prefers, political conflict led large Japanese firms to promise lifetime employment to their core employees. (The grim narrative resembles that of Japanese labor scholars, with the happy view more common in American views of Japanese labor history.[11])

And whatever the 'spin', by the mid-1950s, the central features of lifetime employment were in place: fixed employment for part of the workforce, with the rest of the workforce made up of temporary workers, whose numbers managers could shrink or expand as economic conditions demanded. The favored portion of the workforce and the company were protected from changes in the external labor market by the shock absorption capacity of temporary workers, many of whom were women.

10.3. COMPLEMENTS, INSIDE BOARDS, AND CREDITOR-OWNERS

Once Japanese social peace led firms to promise lifetime jobs to their core employees, the firms faced potential productivity problems. Key employees had lifetime jobs and no reason to fear dismissal even if they were unproductive. So firms and managers had to react to maintain productivity. Most reaction affected the firm's labor institutions, some its corporate governance institutions.

Although lifetime employment could dilute employees' incentives to work well, this job security was offset by the large size of workers' bonuses relative to their fixed wages and by an internal tournament in which better performance has been rewarded by promotion.[12] Security in one area; insecurity in another.

Lifetime employment also fit with the emerging features of Japanese corporate governance. Japanese corporate boards are very large and, except during crises, composed almost entirely of insiders. This contrasts sharply with the prevailing American norm of outsiders dominating the boardroom. But when one realizes that internal labor tournaments facilitated keeping lifetime white-collar employees productive, one sees the fit with inside boards as the honorary and prestigious promotion of first-rate employees after a lifetime of excellent service.[13]

---

[11] See Andrew Gordon, 'Contests for the Workplace', in *Postwar Japan as History* 373, 374 (ed. by Andrew Gordon, 1983).

[12] Eugene Kandel and Neil Pearson, 'The Value of Labor Market Flexibility' (Bradley Center Working Paper FR 95-04, University of Rochester, 1995).

[13] The original lifetime norm helped bring peace to strife involving blue-collar workers, but the norm eventually spread to cover management as well.

Moreover, the lifetime commitments fit with the typical firm's ownership structure. Masahiko Aoki, a leading Japanese business scholar, asserts that in Japan only banker-shareholders, not pure, non-creditor shareholders, influenced managers. This subdued shareholder influence protected workers from the opportunism of pure shareholders who might have wanted to end implicit contracts mid-stream. (Since the firm makes the bulk of the human capital investment, as I outline in the next section, this specific reason for reducing shareholder influence could be disputed.) In Professor Aoki's view, managers are not free from all accountability. If corporate results were bad, the main bank intervened. That contingency, he argues, prevented managers from wandering too far from shareholder profitability.[14] Monitoring from a pure shareholder is absent, but Aoki argues that the bank interfered when the company performed poorly, but not otherwise. This forbearance-unless-performance-is-poor motivated both managers and workers to perform, to maintain their autonomy from banker-shareholders.[15]

The model I offered with Ronald Gilson is analogous: employees won lifetime employment promises after vicious labor strife, but then the firm had to evolve to balance off (1) keeping shareholders from reneging and perhaps reigniting the strife; and (2) putting into place means to monitor managers, even if only lightly, especially if internal labor tournaments led to large insider-dominated boards. Large shareholder-creditors fit the bill. A bank-shareholder who is a lender has incentives differing from a pure shareholder's; its aversion to risk more nearly matches employees' preferences than it does those of pure shareholders.

The full-range of scholarship here shows other, perhaps more important, historical influences that created main bank stockholder-creditors,[16] but the fit between creditor-stockholders and lifetime employment suggests one strong reason why, whatever the origin of the system, the two features—lifetime employment and stockholder-bankers—tended to stabilize one another.

Thus, as elsewhere in the world, shareholder influence on the firm's day-to-day operations was diluted in Japan: core employees could not readily be fired, boards were of insiders only, and the only influential stockholders were also creditors, whose aversion to high risk and rapid change corresponded to the aversion of employees and managers.

---

[14] Masahiko Aoki, 'The Japanese Firm as a System of Attributes: A Survey and Research Agenda', in *The Japanese Firm: The Sources of Competitive Strength* 11, 25–26 (ed. by Masahiko Aoki and Ronald Dore, 1994); Gerald Garvey and Peter Swan, 'The Interaction Between Financial and Employment Contracts: A Formal Model of Japanese Corporate Governance', 6 *J. Japanese & Int'l. Econ.* 249 (1992); Paul Milgrom and John Roberts, 'Complementarities and Systems: Understanding Japanese Economic Organization', 9 *Estudios Económicos* 3, 22–23 (1994).

[15] See Masahiko Aoki, Paul Sheard, and Hugh Patrick, 'The Japanese Main Bank System: An Overview', in *The Japanese Main Bank System: Its Relevance for Developing and Transforming Economies* 1 (ed. by Masahiko Aoki and Hugh Patrick, 1994). Thus, Japanese bank shareholding may partly depend on lifetime employment.

[16] Hoshi shows that post-war main bank relations grew directly out of the authoritative wartime allocation of defense companies to particular banks. Takeo Hoshi, 'Evolution of the Main Bank System in Japan', in *The Structure of the Japanese Economy: Changes on the Domestic and International Fronts* 287 (ed. by Misuaki Okabe, 1995).

10.4. NOTES ON THE DATA

Japan's place in both the political and the ownership indices in Chapter 6 demands comment. The political scientists classified Japan as further to the right than one might think. And the finance economists classified it as having a higher level of diffuse ownership than one might think, despite the common perception of Japan as historically an exemplar of bank influence and ownership.[17]

I did not adjust the indices, taking them as I found them in the political science and finance literatures. But qualitative judgments might well have led us to place Japan differently in each index. The governing political party has been conservative in name, but the public policies have been in many ways social democratic, although with a flavor differing from that of Europe. Lifetime employment has been a key institution, one developed to support social peace. Lifetime employment in some ways has made Japan 'more' socially democratic than the European social democracies.

To view Japanese ownership as only moderately concentrated is also questionable, but understandable once one sees how the indices were constructed. A firm was classified as concentrated if a single shareholder owned 20 per cent or more of the firm's stock.[18] Few big firms in Japan have ownership so concentrated; more but not all medium-sized firms have a 20 per cent owner. But in Japan's main bank system the leading industrial firms' largest four or five owners each own 4.9 per cent of the firm's stock, aggregating often to more than 20 per cent. If we cumulated the bankers' stock because the banks were said to defer to the main bank during corporate crises,[19] *all* of Japan's very large firms would have concentrated ownership, and, although I did not verify the following, one suspects more of its mid-sized firms would be as well. Hence, if we qualitatively adjusted both the political side and the concentration side, lifetime employment and the main bank system would push Japan up on both. The correlation between politics and ownership structure would persist.

10.5. SUMMARY

Lifetime employment arose in Japan after vicious labor strife. Firms in a devastated Japan had fired many employees, and they had to deal with the sinking morale and

---

[17] Masahiko Aoki, 'The Japanese Main Bank System: An Introductory Overview', in *The Japanese Main Bank System*, supra, note 15, at 3–49.

[18] Rafael La Porta, Florencio Lopez-de-Silanes and Andrei Shleifer, 'Corporate Ownership Around the World', 54 *J. Fin.* 471, 476–7, 482, 484 (1999). In addition, institutions that are themselves diffusely owned were made transparent in the ownership index, so even if a firm had a 20% shareholder that was a diffusely owned bank, the firm was classified as diffusely owned. Id., at 477.

[19] Masahiko Aoki, 'Toward an Economic Model of the Japanese Firm', 28 *J. Econ. Literature* 1, 14 (1990).

potential revolutionary potential of those who were left. The firms' promises of lifetime employment quelled tension with those employees who were left, raised their morale, and severed the remaining employees from an alliance—electoral, union, or otherwise—with those who had been fired. But once the strife died down, firms and managers needed to motivate those lifetime employees. Most of the complementary evolution was in labor markets—with early retirement, internal promotional tournaments, and, most importantly, the closing of the external market. (And as the economy grew, stable employment was not sharply at odds with the economic environment.). But *some* of that evolution was in corporate governance. Governance structures adapted to the peace-induced labor structures. Or, once the post-war corporate governance structures emerged for other reasons, they fit snugly with the labor structures, and each reinforced the other.

Promotion to a large board of insiders helped the promotional tournament of managers with a key honor at the end of a successful and hard-working career. American-style shareholders that could disrupt the lifetime employment would have been a bad match, but some means, however weak, to monitor managers was still needed. Banker-shareholders fit the bill: shareholders who are also creditors do not fully maximize shareholder wealth. They tend to avoid some risks (those that threaten their credit position) and are less interested in abruptly changing the firm's business profile (if that brings on risks that threaten their loans). Yet, such shareholders are not oblivious to mismanagement, as they want to be repaid as creditors and they want to get a return as stockholders. Hence the two—creditor-stockholders and lifetime employees—fit together, stabilizing one another. Japanese corporate governance and ownership fit with the way post-war Japan settled social conflict.

11

Sweden

Swedish stock markets are well developed in that there are many public firms. But insider stockholders dominate, and there are few American-style, fully diffusely-owned public firms. Yet, data and opinion say that Sweden, like the other Scandinavian nations, protects minority stockholders well, thus contradicting (for Scandinavia) a law-driven explanation for why ownership separates from control. But Sweden has been one of the world's strongest social democracies, and leading shareholders there often participate in the political-economic settlements that make production run smoothly.

The world's first democratically-elected socialist government took power in Sweden in 1920.[1] It has been for quite some time the paradigm of the social welfare state, with cradle-to-grave social coverage.

Sweden both illustrates the political theory here and displays limits to one competing theory. First, Swedish corporate structures are reputed to protect minority stockholders nicely. That is, a leading explanation for why concentrated ownership persists is that if minority stockholder protection is poor, outsiders will buy stock only reluctantly, or only at a steep discount. This reluctance translates into heavy ownership concentration and few public firms. It can explain results in many nations, especially developing and transition economies with weak institutions. But by conventional measures, Swedish institutions protect minority stockholders well:[2] not only is it hard even to find *anecdotes* of insider blockholders diverting value to themselves,[3] but the premium for voting stock, a measure of the value of control (and the opportunity to divert value into the controllers' pockets), is low, about that of the premium prevailing in the United States.[4]

[1] Adam Przeworski, 'Socialism and Social Democracy', in *The Oxford Companion to Politics of The World* 832, 835 (ed. by Joel Krieger *et al.*, 1993).   [2] See Part VI.
[3] Jonas Agnblad, Erik Berglöf, Peter Högfeldt, and Helena Svancar, 'Ownership and Control in Sweden: Strong Owners, Weak Minorities, and Social Control', in *The Control of Corporate Europe* 228, 229 (edited by Fabrizio Barca and Marco Becht) (2001).
[4] Luigi Zingales, 'The Value of the Voting Right: A Study of the Milan Stock Exchange Experience', 7 *Rev. Fin. Stud.* 125, 146–7 (1994); cf. Clas Bergström and Kristian Rydqvist, 'Ownership of Equity in Dual-Class Firms', 14 *J. Banking & Fin.* 255, 267 (1990) ('[D]ata do not support the argument that dual classes are used [in Sweden] for wealth expropriation by holding control with

The authors of one study conclude: 'the value of control [does not derive] from the possibility to expropriate the fringe of minority shareholders', but rather '*has to be motivated by some other economic motives.*'[5] Other leading Swedish researchers say the same:

Outside shareholders do not refrain f[ro]m investing on the Stockholm Stock Exchange since 55% of the Swedish population own shares... and 33% of outstanding shares are owned by foreign investors.... [T]he ratio of the stock market capitalization held by minority shareholders in relation to GDP... is 0.51 for Sweden compared to 0.58 for the U.S.... *[I]t is not likely that weak investor protection has hampered financial market development in Sweden...*[6]

Law on the surface cannot explain the continuing dominance of blockholders in those public firms, as we saw (and shall see again in Part VI) it cannot for Germany.[7]

The numbers also suggest that blockholders seem *not* to be diverting much more value from minority stockholders in Germany or in Sweden than they do in the United States. Outsider small minority stockholders could buy without gross fear of expropriation from insiders; and insiders could sell and diversify without taking a gross discount. Yet the insiders do not sell out. *Something other than faulty law impedes them.*

Second, closely related to the legal theory is a theory based on trust. In mistrustful cultures, outsiders greatly fear the depredations of insiders. But if trust is high and insiders would no more steal from outside stockholders than would citizens steal an unlocked bicycle, outsiders will entrust their investments to insiders. Sweden is a high trust society. Yet ownership remains concentrated, despite the high level of trust. Although outsiders should feel protected, ownership is concentrated not diffuse, and politics seems better able to explain the concentration than does law or trust.

Third, Swedish ownership has a high disjunction between cash flow rights and control rights, and this could relate to its social democratic politics. The controlling family, often the Wallenberg family, may have, say, 25 per cent of the company's votes, but because much of the stock is non-voting or owned through pyramids,[8] the family receives a smaller fraction of the company's profits.

---

little equity.'). Thus, the quality of corporate law cannot explain the continuing dominance of blockholders in Swedish public firms.

[5] Clas Bergström and Kristian Rydqvist, 'The Determinants of Corporate Ownership: An Empirical Study on Swedish Data', 14 *J. Banking & Fin.* 237, 252 (1990) (emphasis added).

[6] Martin Holmén and Peter Högfeldt, 'Corporate Control and Security Design in Initial Public Offerings' 38 (Stockholm Sch. of Econ. Working Paper, 1999) (emphasis added).

[7] See supra, Ch. 8, section 8.8.

[8] The quintessential pyramid has the controller owning 51% of a holding company, while public stockholders own the non-controlling 49%. The holding company in turn owns 51% of an intermediate company, while public stockholders own the non-controlling 49% of its stock. And the intermediate company owns 51% of the operating company, while public stockholders own the non-controlling 49% stock of the operating company. The controller votes a majority of the operating company's stock although it owns only about 13% of its capital.

Intricate theories have arisen to explain the use of pyramids, dual-class structures, and non-voting stock. The most sophisticated rely on the owner seeking to protect the private benefits it gets from controlling the firm, benefits unshared with minority stockholders and often acquired by diverting value from them to the controller. That is, the controller is reluctant to leave control 'up for grabs' because if the controller dips below 51 per cent control of the operating company, an outsider could grab a majority and then reap the benefits of control.[9] The theory is plausible and is surely important in explaining results in some European nations, such as, say, Italy. However, in its current stark form, it cannot explain the Swedish situation well, or at all, because Sweden is said to protect minority stockholders well. Hence, in Sweden, little value would be left up for grabs by controlling shareholders who exited and diversified.[10]

But a political theory can better explain Swedish concentrated ownership than can a primarily legal theory. By adding employees and social democratic pressures back into the Swedish equation, we get a better idea why ownership has not separated from control. Social democracy affects ownership in two ways here. First, the concentrated owner has stronger incentives than the Berle-Means managers to avoid giving up too much in shareholder value to social pressures. Although an owner whose 25 per cent in control rights corresponded to equal cash flow rights would have even greater incentives to retain shareholder value, the issue here is one of relative strength. The pyramid, dual-class, and non-voting stock structures are less than ideal in providing incentives *to the owners*, but they help to give the owners *authority over the managers*, while still motivating a focused owner to deflect some social pressures: (1) a lot of the controller's wealth is still on the line; and (2) the structure preserves the controller's authority even while its cash flow rights decline. If the controller controlled fewer votes, managers would be freer to ignore that controller.

Second, if the concentrated owner is progressive, has a social conscience, and is not a thirsty shareholder-wealth maximizer, then the political authorities and voters may prefer the incumbent over someone else who might grab control. That is, the authorities may prefer to avoid government ownership for its well-known inefficiencies, but not want the crass, cold market as the alternative. If the Swedish incumbents, such as the Wallenbergs, are 'soft' players, who co-operate with a social democratic ethos, then it may well be the social democratic players who

[9] See Lucian Arye Bebchuk, Reinier Kraakman, and George G. Triantis, 'Stock Pyramids, Cross-Ownership, and Dual Class Equity: The Mechanisms and Agency Costs of Separating Control from Cash-Flow Rights', in *Concentrated Corporate Ownership* 295 (Randall K. Morck ed., 2000); Lucian Arye Bebchuk, 'A Rent-Protection Theory of Corporate Ownership and Control' (Harvard Law & Economics Working Paper No. 260, 1999); Lucian Arye Bebchuk, 'A Theory of the Choice Between Concentrated and Dispersed Ownership of Corporate Shares and Votes' (Harvard Law & Economics Working Paper, 1998); cf. Rafael La Porta, Florencio Lopez-de-Silanes, and Andrei Shleifer, 'Corporate Ownership Around the World', 54 *J. Fin.* 471 (1999).

[10] If the incumbent owners are subject to social controls but if new entrants would not be, then the status quo protects minority stockholders but a change in owner might not. One suspects though that the social controls on the incumbent could be translated into similar social controls or, if necessary, hard controls on a new entrant.

want to stop control from going 'up for grabs'. They prefer partially co-opted owners to pure shareholder primacy. If control were more contestable, an American-style shareholder-wealth maximizer might grab control, tighten the workplace, and undermine the social democratic program.[11]

Thus, one way to look at the Swedish situation is this: corporate control-based benefits are protected. Governmental and social value in the corporation, however, is the protected control benefit, *not* the *ordinary* owner's private benefits from control. The evidence is that private value diversions in Sweden are low. Rather the *political* benefits that a social democracy produces for the firm's employees and for political players are protected via road-blocks to transferring control to pure profit maximizing owners.

(This social control possibility helps to explain how minority stockholders are protected in Sweden. Incumbent controllers could be susceptible to social and political influence, impeding them from diverting value even if the formal corporate institutions do not impede them directly. But others, who could enter if the firm's ownership were diffuse, might be less susceptible to social and political control. *If* the Swedish goal were to diffuse ownership, their informal minority shareholder protections would have to be hardened.)

* * *

Another way to look at the pyramid issue is this: social democracies level wealth and income. They raise the 'incentive' to focus control, but they constrict the 'supply' of rich people with the wealth to own very large industrial companies. *When technology and scale economies demand very large industrial firms, and when social democratic pressures demand focused ownership but reduce the number of wealthy people, then tools that facilitate control without vast wealth will be demanded.* Pyramids, dual-class structures, and non-voting stock are typical such tools. Sweden, like several of the other social democracies, has them.

---

[11] See, e.g., Almar Latour and Greg Steinmetz, 'Swedish Giant: Barnevik Sets about Task of Preserving Wallenberg Empire', *Wall St. J.*, 18 May 1998, at A1 (reporting that Peter Wallenberg, owner of a Swedish business empire, might view short-term goals as not necessarily serving society's best interests).

12

....

United Kingdom

British securities markets developed early, although separation came much later. Combining a law-based and a political theory can best explain the British sequence: securities markets got their start in a conservative era with minority stockholders satisfactorily protected. Some firms' ownership separated, many firms' ownership did not. But by the time more firms were ready for control to separate at, say, mid-century, British politics had lurched leftward. Pre-existing structures stayed in place, although they might not have arisen de novo *in the new political and social milieu: stockholder protection continued but stockholder value would have been compromised if more firms had become fully public managerial firms. Some firms that were already fully public could not survive in the new milieu; several of them were nationalized. Business historians castigate Britain's family owners for staying in place well past the prime of their managerial capabilities; a political theory explains why they might have had little choice until British politics moved rightward.*

The United Kingdom would seem the hardest case for the political theory here, in that by reputation Britain has had a deep securities market for quite some time but has been on both sides of the fence politically, having been a social democracy (Britain's Labour Party controlled politics in eighteen years of the half-century after the Second World War) and having been one of the planet's economically most conservative nations both earlier in the twentieth century and since 1979.

But even for Britain, a political theory helps to explain much that other theories cannot fully. Its securities markets first developed when it had a conservative, *laissez-faire* polity. The market's development path gave Britain its powerful financial 'City', which was simultaneously an interest group that could resist change,[1] a symbol of Britain's global role and imperial grandeur whose luster neither Labour

---

[1] Cf. Lucian A. Bebchuk and Mark J. Roe, 'A Theory of Path Dependence in Corporate Ownership and Governance', 52 *Stan. L. Rev.* 127 (1999) (interest groups slow corporate evolution). Michael Moran, 'Finance Capital and Pressure-Group Politics in Britain', 11 *British J. Pol. Sci.* 381, 384, 387, 396, 398 (1981) (the City was well-organized to press its case through the Bank of England).

nor Tory was eager to tarnish,[2] and a source of international revenue (in securities services). The existing interest group, the enduring international symbol, and the continuing source of revenue gave British securities markets much path dependent power to persist, especially when Britain's social democracy was an on-and-off affair for eighteen of the first fifty post-war years, as Labour won, then lost (winning two consecutive elections only once), then transformed itself, ending its modern life as a militant left-leaning party.

The persistence power of previously-built structures helps to explain why Britain's Labour Party did not attack private corporate structures in general, but instead nationalized those firms whose structures it wanted changed, while leaving the rest intact.[3]

[B]oth [the] right and left... [saw] the company [as] ... a private association that should either be left alone in accordance with laissez-faire principles, or abolished altogether in the name of social justice. Missing... was the idea of the company as an association whose internal structures might be altered in order to pursue pragmatic compromises between capital and labour.[4]

Thus while British history fits awkwardly with a *purely* political theory, social politics still explains much here: securities markets first developed when the nation was *laissez-faire* and, although full separation did not happen early (as it did in the United States), there was some, and some of those separated firms became the nationalized firms of the Labour era.

And Britain also fits awkwardly with a pure law-driven theory. As we have seen, a competing theory to the political theory is that the degree to which minority stockholders are protected determines whether ownership separation will occur, with family founders turning their firms over to professional managers by selling out into the stock market if stockholders would be well protected. British institutions are said to have protected minority stockholders well. Yet leading business historians such as Alfred Chandler say flatly that the largest British firms were family-dominated as late as the Second World War, and that family influence and control persisted well after then.[5] What little data is available seems to confirm Chandler's instinct: 'The separation of ownership and control...had *not*

---

[2] Linda Weiss and John M. Hobson, *States and Economic Development: A Comparative Historical Analysis* 212 (1995).

[3] Ben Clift, Andrew Gamble, and Michael Harris, 'The Labour Party and the Company', in *The Political Economy of the Company* 51, 81 (ed. by John Parkinson, Andrew Gamble, and Gavin Kelly, 2000) ('In the 1940s, [reconstructing the private, non-nationalized corporation] never registered as a significant [Labour Party] priority; in the 1970s, when it did, the Party was too divided internally and too politically weak to find a way to implement it.')

[4] Andrew Gamble, Gavin Kelly, and John Parkinson, 'Introduction: The Political Economy of the Company', in *The Political Economy of the Company* 1, 6–7 (ed. by John Parkinson, Andrew Gamble, and Gavin Kelly, 2000).

[5] Alfred D. Chandler, Jr, *Scale and Scope: The Dynamics of Industrial Capitalism* 240 (1990). See also Alfred D. Chandler, Jr and Herman Daems, 'Introduction', in *Managerial Hierarchies: Comparative Perspectives on the Rise of the Modern Industrial Enterprise* 1, 6 (ed. by Alfred D. Chandler, Jr and Herman Daems, 1980) ('Until World War II, the British economy was for the most part an example of family capitalism.')

progressed [by 1948] far enough to displace founding or family directors from company boards . . . and 119 [out of the 200 largest firms in Britain], or 59.5 per cent, [had founding or family directors].'[6] Another researcher states:

A final characteristic discovered within the sample population [from 1950–1970] was a large number of 'family' companies. Despite substantial share ownership dilution in many British companies, there was a distinct tendency for many of them to continue to be managed by members of the family or families closely associated with their formation or development . . .

[There was a] relatively large number of [single-product, undiversified] family-controlled companies present in the sample in 1950. In total, 50 out of 92 companies were controlled by families at this time.

This number fell progressively *but not substantially* [during the twenty years from 1950 to 1970].[7]

And 'evidence on the extent of ownership control in British industry [in 1975] . . . shows that the extent of managerial control [was then] more limited than has been thought and may not have an inexorable tendency to increase [in light of evidence that at least 40 per cent of the 250 largest firms had a dominant blockholder].'[8] Another authority tells us that 55 per cent of Britain's largest firms were owner-controlled as late as 1980.[9] How one interprets these estimates—55–59 per cent at the beginning of the Labour era, circa 1950, and 40–55 per cent at the end, circa 1970 or 1980—probably ties to one's prior theoretical interpretation. Some might see a trend toward diffusion to confirm their theory and to disconfirm a political theory. Others might see the numbers as close enough, and the data messy enough, that they may indicate no substantial change at all. Certainly the numbers fail to reveal a rush toward ownership separation. And the qualitative assessments from major business historians like Alfred Chandler are consistent with there not having been any such rush.

Chandler blames persistent family control for Britain's industrial decline in the mid-twentieth century.[10] As late as the 1970s, 'British industry was over-financing itself from retained profits. . . . [Financial institutions' unwillingness to provide new

---

[6] Leslie Hannah, 'Visible and Invisible Hands in Great Britain', in *Managerial Hierarchies*, supra note 5, at 41, 53 (emphasis supplied); cf. Leslie Hannah, 'Mergers, Cartels and Concentration: Legal Factors in the U.S. and European Experience', in *Law and the Formation of the Big Enterprises in the 19th and Early 20th Centuries* 306, (ed. by Norbert Horn & Jürgen Kocka, 1979) ('In the period before 1914 . . . it seems that the United States and Germany led the industrial world in introducing large-scale corporate organisation, whereas Britain retained a stronger inherited structure of family enterprise.')

[7] Derek F. Channon, *The Strategy and Structure of British Enterprise* 15–16, 75 (1973) (emphasis added).

[8] Steve Nyman and Aubrey Silberston, 'The Ownership and Control of Industry', 30 *Oxford Econ. Papers* 74, 74, 85–6 (1978).

[9] Arthur Francis, 'Families, Firms and Finance Capital: The Development of UK Industrial Firms with Particular Reference to Their Ownership and Control', 14 *Sociology: J. Brit. Soc. Ass'n* 1, 1 (1980).

[10] See also *The Decline of the British Economy* 5 (ed. by Bernard Elbaum and William Lazonick, 1987) ('British industrialists clung to family control of their firms').

financing] should be attributed to poor productivity performance and [the] lack of profitable investment opportunities in British industry.'[11]

This persistent family ownership during Britain's social democratic era seems consistent with the political theory, but not with a pure-form minority protection theory: *if Britain protected the minority stockholders, why did those families not sell out and diversify quickly?* Many of these families were still block owners in the 1970s: '[The] managerial revolution heralded by Berle and Means in 1932 has probably not yet happened [here:]...over 55 per cent of the largest 250 UK industrial companies [are] under owner control', said one authority *in 1980*, who, not anticipating the results in the subsequent two decades, concluded: 'most [British] firms are unlikely ever to become controlled by their own professional managers...'.[12] But within several years, by the mid-1980s, many of these families were gone from the largest British firms;[13] Britain's revolution from the right in 1979 made, on the theory presented here, the fully public, diffusely owned firm much more viable than it had been during Britain's social democratic era.

All the basic institutions for diffuse ownership save one, namely a non-social democratic economic consensus, were in place in Britain from the nineteenth century onwards. Its economy was industrialized, its firms had a high demand for capital, and it was capable of building complex financial markets. But right after the Second World War, Britain's large firm ownership structure was said to be *closer* to *continental* family ownership structures than to American structures, with family owners as players in many, or most, big firms.[14] But Britain's economic policy moved rightward during the ensuing decades; not only did Margaret Thatcher's 'revolution' overturn British socialism, but Tony Blair's Labour Party of the 1990s was less of a socialist party than was the party of his predecessors.[15] In the 1980s Britain's securities markets increased massively, much more than did such markets in the United States, which at that time had an equally conservative

---

[11] James Foreman-Peck and Leslie Hannah, 'Britain: From Economic Liberalism to Socialism—And Back?', in *European Industrial Policy: the Twentieth-Century Experience* 41 (ed. by James Foreman-Peck and Giovanni Federico, 1999).   [12] Francis, supra, note 9, at 1.

[13] John Scott, 'Corporate Control and Corporate Rule: Britain in an International Perspective', 41 *Brit. J. Soc.* 351, 366–7 (1990) (reporting on the 'decline of family control' from 1976 to 1988).

[14] Chandler, supra note 5, at 240. Even today, Britain's ownership structure is more concentrated than that of the U.S. On average, the largest British firms *do* have a 9.9 per cent blockholder (just below the cutoffs for the concentration data used here and in the underlying database from Rafael La Porta, Florencio Lopez-de-Silanes, and Andrei Shleifer, 'Corporate Ownership Around the World', 54 *J. Fin.* 471, 495 (1999), and it is usually a financial institution. Marco Becht and Ailsa Röell, 'Blockholdings in Europe: An International Comparison', 43 *Eur. Econ. Rev.* 1049, 1053 (1999); Mark Goergen and Luc Renneboog, 'Strong Managers and Passive Institutional Investors in the United Kingdom', in *The Control of Corporate Europe* 259, 271 (ed. by Fabrizio Barca and Marco Becht, 2001).

[15] See Ralf Dahrendorf, 'The Third Way and Liberty: An Authoritarian Streak in Europe's New Center', *Foreign Aff.*, Sept.–Oct. 1999, at 13; Andrew Sullivan, 'The End of Britain', *N.Y. Times Mag.*, 21 Feb. 1999, at 39, 54 ('[Blair] had long since lost faith in the sclerotic European social-democratic model....[H]e made some...Clintonite changes...All were worthy ameliorations of Thatcherism—but no reversal.')

government, but one that did not break with the American past as strongly as did the British government of the time.[16]

Yet, Britain by many measures had deeper securities markets and more public firms than much of the rest of the world *earlier in the twentieth century*, although families held on to blocks and managerial positions until quite late in the century. To explain this pattern, a synthesis of the minority-protection theory and the political theory works well. British institutions protected minority stockholders, so that family owners could sell much stock even in the early twentieth century without too severe a discount. Yet during that time, class conflict was deep, widespread, and severe.[17] The potential for high agency costs in the managerial firm was there and hence at mid-century, many family owners had reason to retain concentrated ownership. This hybrid theory seems to explain the British facts: (1) a long history of firms going public; (2) families retaining control in many public firms until well after the Second World War (because minority stockholders were protected *and* because politics made concentration desirable for shareholders) with only some of those firms' control fully separating from their ownership; and (3) a sell-off by many of the remaining family owners in the late 1970s and in the 1980s (when Britain's lurch to the economic right made diffuse ownership more stable).[18]

Or, stated simply: British history suggests that good corporate law protection for minority stockholders (or a substitute) is a precondition to starting securities markets. But concentrated ownership persisted and separation did not proceed if social democratic pressures (or other pressures) kept managerial agency costs high. With securities markets in place when Labour intermittently took the reins of power, the securities market institutions were not torn down, even though the political consensus would not have built them then. They persisted, and then flourished when Britain moved rightward.

---

[16] Organization for Economic Cooperation and Development, *Financial Market Trends* 18, tbl. 2 (Feb. 1998). In 1985, British domestic stock market as a percentage of gross domestic product more than doubled from that of 1975. In contrast, the American percentage rose only modestly. Id. See Table 12.1, next page. Some of this is just a rise in value. Some of this is due to privatization, which complicates but does not contradict the social democracy thesis. The largest 250 British firms included 13 government corporations in 1976 and still had 11 in 1988. Scott, supra, note 13, at 366. Firms were nationalized either because markets demanded a downsizing that political actors would not permit or because of ideologies of state ownership. When these social democratic, or socialist, sentiments declined, the government began to privatize these firms.

[17] Neville Kirk, *Change, Continuity and Class: Labour in British Society* 159, 169 (1998).

[18] A social democratic Britain might have directly attacked Britain's financial markets. But, again, sequencing was important. British securities market institutions arose early, while it was a non-social democratic nation. Their rise yielded an interest group—the City in London—that could delay its own demise until electoral results changed. Second, London was already an international financial center whose damage would diminish earnings from abroad. Many City institutions were not directly corporate governance related—and hence would not directly raise the social democratic ire: they involved trading in government bonds, both British and foreign, corporate bond trading, and insurance. Social democratic governments would not have sympathized with constructing them, but because they were already in place, they could survive for a few years in the changed political environment, especially while the government pursued policies it valued more highly, such as nationalizing the nation's largest firms.

Table 12.1. *Market Capitalization of U.K. and U.S. Listed Domestic Equity Issues as Percentage of GDP*

	1975	1980	1985	1990
United Kingdom	37	38	77	87
United States (NYSE, Amex, and Nasdaq)	48	50	57	56

This political interaction with ownership structure helps to explain Chandler's conundrum: if the British families held on to control (as Chandler reports), and ran many firms into the ground (as he argues), why did they not sell out when they became bored with running their firms? Many offer cultural reasons to explain the result, but perhaps more was at work. Family owners may have run their firms badly, but when class conflict was rife, the alternative to family control may have been even worse for shareholder-owners.

And thus even for Britain political determinants were probably in play and important.

13

....

United States

Economic-based social conflict has been lower in the United States than elsewhere, keeping the pressures low that would make diffuse shareholders wary of leaving their money in managers' hands. A tradition of low government involvement meant firms were pressed less than they otherwise would have been, even when political pressures simmered. And similar popular pressures were handled otherwise in the United States, by fragmenting financial institutions as the most visible manifestations of shareholder power.

Why has the United States had fewer social conflicts of the type that would debilitate the public firm? The reasons why it has had less conflict, and hence more diffuse ownership, correspond to the reasons why a strong socialist movement did not arise in the United States.

Mobility, both geographic and economic, has been high, or at least the average person has believed it to be high.[1] Dissatisfied people have blamed their local circumstances (which they thought they could change, by heading out West or by getting another job) more than their class position. Hence, class conflict was less likely, and incipient conflicts were violently suppressed.[2]

The United States has also had a long and deep anti-government bias, so citizens have not looked as longingly to government to resolve problems as have Europeans. Economic conflict was not absent in the United States, but manifested itself differently than in Europe, often provoking politicians to break up concentrations of economic power, a result that further propelled the public firm because there were fewer financial institutions capable of controlling large American firms at the end of the nineteenth century than there otherwise would have been.[3]

---

[1] Frederick Jackson Turner, *The Frontier in American History* (1920).

[2] John R. Commons, 'Is Class Conflict in America Growing and Is it Inevitable?', 13 *Am. J. Soc.* 756 (1908), reprinted in *III Classics in Institutional Economics* 112, 120 (ed. by Malcolm Rutherford and Warren J. Samuels, 1997).

[3] Mark J. Roe, *Strong Managers, Weak Owners: The Political Roots of American Corporate Finance* vii–xvi (1994).

In the nineteenth century, America systematically destroyed strong financial institutions: American voters historically tended to be intolerant of big government *and* of big private finance.[4] This fragmenting of finance may also have later diluted other social conflict *by removing the visible targets of a strong social democracy movement*; and, with the visible targets gone, norms like shareholder-wealth maximization flourished more easily than they otherwise would have. (Similarly, destroying family control in continental Europe could reduce subsequent social conflict sufficiently so that agency control institutions could emerge in the newly created public firms.)

Political packages are complementary: American politics tolerates pro-shareholder institutions, partly because the typical shareholder is CalPERS (California's public employees pension fund), not J. P. Morgan. European politics could tolerate large, influential stockholders, banks and families, as long as it also stabilized employment and circumscribed the range of actions of the stockholders, bankers, and the family owners.

Even during the American era closest to a social democratic one—the New Deal—American political institutions did not attack the public firm. Indeed, political leaders said, and acted as though, they were seeking to save American capitalism. The public firm might not have arisen during that era—Berle and Means after all discovered it in 1932 *before* the New Deal began—but the political change was not so severe that it destroyed what already was in place, put there during a more conservative era.[5]

Moreover, ethnic conflict in the United States has been deep, at times vicious. For some of the social conflict that would affect the Berle-Means firm to express itself in the political arena, employees would have had to act together or politicians would have had to appeal to all employees to elect them in order to enact a common program.[6] But ethnic divisions—principally based on race—made it historically hard for American politicians to make an economic appeal across racial lines. As a result, the economic conflict that raised managerial agency costs in public firms on the European continent was rarer in the United States.[7]

---

[4] Id. at 26–36, 48–9.

[5] Cf. Lucian A. Bebchuk and Mark J. Roe, 'A Theory of Path Dependence in Corporate Ownership and Governance', 52 *Stan. L. Rev.* 127 (1999).

[6] John R. Commons, 'History of Labor in the United States: 1896–1932' (1935), reprinted in *Classics in Institutional Economics*, supra, note 2, at 438, 454–5; Commons, supra, note 2, at 118–19.

[7] E. E. Schattschneider, *The Semisovereign People: A Realist's View of Democracy in America* (1960) (politicians seek to divide the electorate on issues in which the divider will be allied with a majority of the division). I hardly mean that only the United States has had ethnic conflict, but rather that America's long-simmering race and ethnic divisions stymied economic-based coalitions that arose in many other nations.

14

Extending the Sample?

Other nations are emerging from economic under-development. Eventually they will yield data for testing the importance of political and other theories in explaining the depth of securities markets and the degree to which ownership separates from control. For now those nations have too low a demand for large fully public firms. Private financing, or bank financing and retained earnings, can implement the technologies available for their largest firms. True, for some of the poorest, the institutional environment is so degraded that whether the political environment favors public firms never enters into the equation because the institutional infrastructure just could not support the fully public firm (or in some instances, even very large organizations).

One could extend the 'sample' to include more nations outside Western Europe, developed Asia, and North America, adding, say, Thailand, Malaysia, Nigeria, Argentina, and the Ukraine. But extending it would reveal little, because too many of these nations have not *yet* arrived economically at the point where their economies demand many large firms. And some lack the basic institutions needed for a very advanced economy, such as a capacity to enforce contract effectively.

One cannot know now how much relative poverty is explained by a nation's inability to enforce basic contract—and hence an inability to build the legal institutions needed for commerce—and how much of its poverty is explained by poor corporate law—and hence weakness in building large public firms. There is a difference: in some European nations there is no problem getting a commercial contract nicely enforced, but corporate and securities law is not as effective, perhaps because the demand for it is low.

That is, even for less-developed and transition nations, their weak institutional structure—including poor property rights, weak contract enforcement, and substandard public administration—is more likely to be the primary reason why they do not have public firms. They do not get to the economic level where they have much demand for them. The vast literature on accounting quality, transparency, and corporate law quality might thus not be uncovering the core bases for their paucity of public firms and securities markets, but instead reading the surface manifestations of weak property rights regimes and poor public administration. These more fundamental institutional gaps are more likely to be the core considerations for economic development.

More telling for the political theory here is to look at those nations that have already developed many of the needed institutions and have a high demand for large economic units, but whose politics makes some institutions either function poorly or not be worth building, because they would not be much used.

But one might extend the political view here beyond today's rich, democratic nations in one dimension. Non-democratic governments might stymie development: extreme statist regimes—like communism and fascism—are historically the most obvious, but other heavy-handed states might disrupt the institutions that would support complex private institutions like the public firm. Much could be said about these, some of it obvious, as to why totalitarian statist regimes of either the left or the right do not facilitate diffusely-held public firms and deep securities markets. But we ignore these regimes because the focus here is on a single question: why, with so much similarity in other business dimensions, do today's rich, democratic nations differ in ownership structure and depth of their securities markets?

V

THE DIRECTION OF CAUSALITY

Thus far I have shown a prime way that politics affects firms. Social democracy, or its absence, affects what kind of ownership structures do better for shareholders. The world of course is more nuanced. In this Part I formulate the thesis otherwise and examine how political backlash and the degree of product market competition affect the firm and its ownership structure.

In Chapter 15, we reformulate the social democracy thesis in several ways: as rent-seeking, as simple labor market micro-foundations interacting with ownership structures, as ownership concentration facilitating and not just originating in social democratic politics, as a craving for stability, or as reflecting differing managerial utility functions.

Markets cannot always produce politically stable arrangements. If economic players persist in pushing them, politics lashes back at them. In Chapters 16 and 17 I examine this problem abstractly, then pursue it closer to home by showing how some American laws that seem unarguably inefficient economically could be re-interpreted in terms of backlash: they were either the backlash itself or the political means to head off more serious backlash, thereby preserving a core of property rights and private incentives. I also speculate that law and economics scholarship has had an easier time in the United States than elsewhere because the range of policies that would produce little backlash is wider here than elsewhere. Pro-shareholder institutions have been more stable in the American environment than they have been elsewhere. And concentrated ownership, even if narrowly efficient abroad, may have helped to propel a backlash there of social democratic politics.

In Chapters 18, 19, and 20, I reformulate in another way: weakly competitive products markets can produce both the political and the corporate social democratic structures. If a nation's product markets are systematically uncompetitive, the monopoly profits seed a fertile field for conflict inside the firm—how should those profits be divided among stockholders, managers, and employees?—and inside the polity. Political parties, I speculate, could reflect the players' positions inside the firm. In nations where monopoly profits are smaller, and product markets more competitive, the political correlates would be weaker, because there is less to contest inside the firm or inside the polity. And indeed as product markets have become more competitive in Western Europe, these political forces have slackened, as

I discuss in Chapter 21. In Chapter 22, I present data showing the relationships between product market competition and securities markets among the world's richest nations. I also show, in preparation for Part VI, the relative strength of the political indicators in predicting ownership concentration. Corporate law quality, product market strength, and politics all predict the degree of ownership separation. Although corporate law indicators predict diffusion, when we control for politics, however crudely, corporate law's predictive power weakens and sometimes even drops out as a significant indicator.

15

....

Alternative Formulations of the Thesis

I have thus far looked at the political players as sincere public-regarding actors seeking to build the good society, and at social democracies as having a vision differing from the one prevailing in the United States. Those holding these ideologies seek to maximize social well-being, and in doing so they reduce the incidence of public firms, securities markets, and diffuse ownership. Life may be better for more people, I have suggested, but public firms are fewer. One can, however, look more crudely at the phenomena as bare power grabs by interest groups, as the predictable result from weak product markets, as a polity craving stability, or as a cultural environment that shapes managers' utility functions.

15.1. SOCIAL DEMOCRACY AS RENT-SEEKING

Interest groups seek laws and structures that benefit them. One could see social democracies as labor's crude but successful rent-seeking, whereby they gain at the expense of others in the political arena. (Or one could see the results in conservative nations as financial interests' successful rent-seeking.) Ideology may help or retard the success of one group or another, or it may make that self-seeking respectable instead of crude, but in this public choice view it is raw self-seeking that determines results. Labor wins in the name of stability in some nations; shareholders win in the name of fluid capital markets in other nations. Concerted arrangements via tripartite bargaining characterize some nations, as the three players—labor, owners, and the government—negotiate corporatist deals. Incumbent owners could ally with other players—their employees, for example—to squelch upstart competitors. This is not exactly social democracy, but it is government often taking labor's or its ally's side in negotiations inside and outside the firm.

15.2. ANTAGONISM, OR BENIGN NEGLECT, FOR SHAREHOLDER INSTITUTIONS

Social democracies may also be unfriendly to institutions that facilitate the public firm. Tax laws may stymie the big public firm. Stock markets, and stock exchanges, may be squelched or subject to benign neglect because political players and voters see them as pernicious institutions that support capital, not people. The source of the disruption of the public firm is the same—a social democratic anti-capitalist impulse—but the mechanisms would be more complex, as governments disrupt the large firm's basic supports.[1]

15.3. SIMPLE MICRO-ECONOMIC FOUNDATIONS

We could begin without using social democracy, by again viewing the firm as having three inputs: capital, management, and labor. We could begin the abstraction with labor institutions determined first, while capital and management vary and adjust to the labor institutions they find. If a nation's labor markets are rigid, with employees 'owning' their jobs, then management and capital structures ought to evolve differently there than in economies with fluid labor markets, where employees have few 'property' rights in their jobs. One would expect managerial agency costs to be higher where employees 'own' their jobs and firm expansion is nearly irreversible: managers when unconstrained like to expand, and when expansion is irreversible, the costs to shareholders of the mistaken expansion can be quite high. One would expect shareholders to prefer structures that would control these managerial agency costs.

15.4. CONCENTRATED OWNERSHIP AS FACILITATING SOCIAL DEMOCRACY

I have thus far relentlessly viewed politics as independent of business structure, with social democracy inducing, or strengthening, concentrated ownership structures. But causation can also run the other way.

German codetermination again provides a concrete example. Early in the twentieth century, the visible power of Germany's large banks, people's envy and

---

[1] Some commentators have argued that a heavy tax rule or hostility to stock markets is the 'real' cause, not political social democracy. But when they do so they largely re-state the social democracy thesis, not contradict it, discovering one of the means by which social democratic governments implement their program.

resentment of rich industrialists, and the disorientation and anomie induced by Germany's rapid transformation from an agricultural nation into an industrial one helped to call forth codetermination to tame the bankers and industrialists, and to give the workers a voice in the strange new industrial enterprises. Corporate structure may have *induced* politics then, as much as it was induced by politics. Not all productive arrangements are equally stable politically; some induce political opposition, while others a democratic polity finds more acceptable.[2] Social democracy and concentrated ownership mutually reinforce one another.

15.5. RENT-SEEKING IN SMALL NATIONAL ECONOMIES

Business structure may induce social democratic politics in another way. Many of the strongest social democracies have been nations in which product markets have been only weakly competitive. Weaker competition produces rents—profits above those needed by capital to invest—and these rents can be captured not just by the capital-owners but shared with managers and employees. There is thus more 'give' and more of a possibility of successful rent-seeking through government and social action when there are supra-competitive profits in firms. These rents may also strengthen social democracy by increasing envy and perceived unfairness. And they provide more to fight over. Rent-seeking employees may win more often in small economies, especially those whose oligopolistic firms are not fully exposed to world markets.[3]

When product market competition is fierce, rents are reduced and excess profits competed away. One reason for American exceptionalism is that the American economy has been more competitive, making rents in American firms smaller and more fragile (i.e. more easily lost as they will be competed away and therefore less worth seeking).[4] Many of the stronger social democracies have been smaller nations and, in the smaller national economies, rent-seeking below the surface and social democratic ideologies above it could have produced concentrated economies unable to strongly support diffuse stockholders.

---

[2] I expand on this in Ch. 16 and in Mark J. Roe, 'Backlash', 98 *Colum. L. Rev.* 217 (1998).

[3] I expand on this in Ch. 18, in Mark J. Roe, 'Rents and their Corporate Consequences', 53 *Stan. L. Rev.* 1463 (2001), and in Mark J. Roe, 'The Shareholder Wealth Maximization Norm and Industrial Organization', 149 *U. Pa. L. Rev.* 2063 (2001).

[4] Monopoly rents create indeterminacy in corporate ownership and governance. Rents allow different players to get value out of the firm, and different players may win by chance in some political environments and lose in others. Rents might induce concentrated ownership (so stockholders can better ensure that they get a big share of those rents). But if large size of the firm is the predicate to the rents, and concentrated ownership impossible at that large size, then managerial slack might be the price shareholders pay to get a slice of those rents remaining after managerial dissipation. When competition in the American economy was weaker, and oligopoly stronger, mild pressures to soften the work place and to make managers socially responsible to employee constituencies may have been more effective than they would be today. See Mark J. Roe, 'From Antitrust to Corporate Governance? The Corporation and the Law: 1959–1994', in *The American Corporation Today* 102 (ed. by Carl Kaysen, 1996).

These corporate-political results parallel James Madison's famous analysis in the Federalist No. 10: the smaller the nation, the greater the chance that a faction can dominate.[5]

* * *

As the small economies integrate into free-trade zones, the potential for local rent-seeking is diminishing, enhanced product market competition is making traditional social democratic corporate governance harder to maintain, and the demand for securities institutions has been rising.[6] Governments whose firms face intense competition that renders those governments unable to implement a social democratic program through firms or labor markets may either abandon their goals or implement them via social insurance that leaves firms out of the picture.

15.6. CRAVING STABILITY

Social democracy may not fully capture the ideological metric here. Some nations may crave stability more than do others. Markets' fluidity may induce a populace to crave stability. National histories of war, devastation, social instability, market collapse, or starvation can deepen and enlarge this craving. If post-war voters craved stability, they may have insisted on rules and a business atmosphere that made change harder than it would otherwise have been. The core cause though may then not be social democratic ideology, or employee rent-seeking, but a society seeking stability.[7]

Indeed, before the First World War, in an era before Europe's self-destruction and economic instability, securities markets were *stronger on the continent than they were at the end of the twentieth century,* and not that much weaker than they were in the United States at that time.[8] European politics was more conservative then, and social democratic movements were on the political fringe.[9]

---

[5] *The Federalist* No. 10 (James Madison): '[A more populous nation] ... renders factious combinations less to be dreaded. ... The smaller the society, ... the fewer the distinct parties and interests, the more frequently will a majority be found of the same party [and] ... the more easily will they concert and execute their plans of oppression.'

[6] Whether path dependence diminishes the demand for corporate change is analyzed in Lucian A. Bebchuk and Mark J. Roe, 'A Theory of Path Dependence in Corporate Ownership and Governance', 52 *Stan. L. Rev.* 127 (1999).

[7] Cf. Karl Polanyi, *The Great Transformation* (1944) (markets destabilize society, inducing a reactive craving for stability).

[8] See Raghuram G. Rajan and Luigi Zingales, 'The Great Reversals: The Politics of Financial Development in the 20th Century' 61, tbl. 3 (Univ. of Chicago Working Paper, 2001) (arraying data showing that in 1913, total stock market capitalization as a percentage of GNP was higher in France than in the United States and about the same in Germany and the United States). See Table 7.1.

[9] For example: 'The share of [government-mandated] transfer over GDP was less than 1 per cent in Europe *and* in the United States at the end of the nineteenth century, [but in 1996 was 44 per cent in Europe and 14 per cent in the United States].' Alberto Alesina, Rafael Di Tella, and Robert MacCulloch, 'Inequality and Happiness: Are Europeans and Americans Different?' (National Bureau of Economic Research Working Paper No. 8198, 2001) (emphasis supplied).

15.7. MANAGERS' UTILITY FUNCTIONS

Consider managers' utility functions. Human nature does not demand that managers maximize firm size or profitability. In cultures that emphasize other values, and inculcate them through schooling and other means, managers may maximize something else, and that something else may make them less able, or less willing, to do shareholders' bidding. To the extent political and social conditions affect managers' utility functions, they affect to whom managers are loyal, what controlling shareholders want, and hence the type of firm best suited for a society.

15.8. THE ALTERNATIVE FORMULATIONS

I have in this book primarily viewed politics as given, as the starting-point, and from there derived what type of firm is best adapted to the differing political environments.

Politics of course is not everything, and underlying economic and technological conditions surely affect what firms are best suited for any given task. I emphasize politics not because it determines everything in the firm and its ownership structure, but because its effects are grossly under-represented in the financial and legal literature.

And in this chapter we have seen alternative ways of viewing the political phenomena. One could view politics yet more crudely, viewing the corporate contestants as seeking rents inside the firm and then seeking to trump the intra-firm results with political rent-seeking. Or one could see some political environments' hostility to capital as leading them to demolish the institutions that distant shareholders need, so those organizational forms that require little in the way of institutional infrastructure survive better.

One could look at the causal direction as moving from ownership to politics, and not as I have set it out as moving from politics outward. Or one could look at the same political phenomenon but attribute it to a national craving for stability, a preference resulting from a century of war, turmoil, and economic havoc.

16

....

Backlash

Economic systems produce wealth. For some polities, productive arrangements gen-erate a political backlash that can destroy that wealth. Some, perhaps many, economic arrangements may be unstable politically, and this potential for backlash compli-cates economic analysis. Economic analyses of American institutions seldom take backlash into account. This is in general justified because the chances of strong, wealth-destroying backlash here are small. But in other nations it is not small. Property rights in general—and their corporate governance equivalent of secure intra-shareholder arrangements—might be, and usually are, analyzed as preceding the rise of large firms. But productive arrangements and property rights are con-tinually determined. Property rights are not determined once and for all, before business begins. Instead the polity continually, or at least repeatedly, decides which property arrangements to erode and which to protect. While this difficulty of con-tinuous and simultaneous resolution is stronger in other countries than in the United States, it is even relevant although weaker in the U.S. Some secondary American insti-tutions that are hard to justify on normal efficiency grounds become understandable as institutions that either mitigated or resulted from backlash. Glass-Steagall, Robinson-Patman, anti-takeover laws, and chapter 11 of the Bankruptcy Code can be seen as examples of backlash or as means to avoid more serious backlash.

16.1. Instability
16.2. The Efficiency of Stability
16.3. Political Transformations?
16.4. Is Turmoil Un-American? How about Small Changes?
16.5. Conclusion

16.1. INSTABILITY

Politics can disrupt markets. Voters may see market arrangements as unfair, leading them to lash back and disrupt otherwise efficient arrangements. Concentrated ownership, for one example, or powerful financial institutions for another, may for some firms be efficient but unpopular. Pro-shareholder laws and institutions could generate more total wealth, and conceivably be fairly distributed as well, but also be unpopular.

To quell a backlash, differing structures may arise and survive, even if they could not withstand a normal efficiency critique. The prospect of backlash—or of strategically tempering otherwise efficient rules and institutions to finesse it away—complicates an economics inquiry. Some institutions may arise and survive not primarily because they accomplish an economic task well, but because they resist backlash better than other institutions.

Take the following example, admittedly extreme: a rule of free contracting leads a nation to construct large organizations—call them latifundia—in which the senior controllers earn millions of dollars annually, the middle-ranking overseers earn hundreds of thousands of dollars annually, and the lowest paid workers earn tens of thousands of dollars annually. In no alternative organizational configuration could any of the three 'levels' earn more.[1]

The 'twist' in the latifundia system here is that the lowest-ranking workers could fare no better in any known alternative system, the most obvious being a system of small-scale firms. Employees at all levels in the alternative society would earn less. Senior controllers would not be needed there, their talents would not be tapped, and their pay would be reduced, because they would run smaller, less-profitable enterprises. The alternative society's per capita GNP is less than the latifundia's. Not only is the latifundia nation's GNP at its highest possible level but its poorest citizens also live better than they would in any other system.[2]

Suppose that after a few prosperous years, this nation of latifundia becomes politically unstable. Instability was not foreordained, but it arises. Although the lowest-ranking employees have a higher income in the latifundia than in any alternative business structure, after the first few placid years they change their minds. Initially they were happy, but they come to hate the system, the government, and the controllers. They start to envy the controllers, whose power and wealth they resent. They grouse on the job, complain to one another, and finally, many revolt. The controllers resist, and in the years of turmoil that ensue the nation fritters away its early economic advantages. Its GNP declines.

At the same time when the nation of latifundia enjoyed its early happy success, a nearby nation developed different institutions. It outlawed latifundia, taxed senior controllers' income at 90 per cent marginal tax rates, and subsidized small businesses and family farmers. Although its people were initially poorer—less food, smaller homes, fewer clothes, no luxuries—the nation was never afflicted with the latifundia nation's later turmoil. Backlash, voters' eventually destructive resentment of the organization of production, never emerged. Employees at the lowest level—whose income initially was *less* than the income of the lowest ranking latifundia employees—identify with their small firms' owners. They never revolt. They are satisfied. And, because industry and farming are scattered, they neither

---

[1] To describe this society I use the word latifundia, a word that implies a bottom rung living in peonage, as might the more common English word, plantation. Here, though, the lower rungs do not live in misery, and for this reason I use the less common English word, latifundia, to define the economic setting. Obviously, many of history's real 'latifundia' have been both inefficient and oppressive, unlike, at least initially, the one we hypothesize here.

[2] To get a true measure of fairness and wealth, we must adjust each system's value by its nonmonetary costs and benefits. That adjustment contorts but does not cut the main line of thought here.

develop the revolutionary ideology that led the nation of latifundia to turmoil nor—because workers and managers are scattered in many small enterprises—do they find themselves working in a setting conducive to revolutionary organization.

Consider again the *ex-ante* setting. One nation, that of latifundia, has a high GNP and its lowest paid workers do better than their counterparts in the nation of small enterprises. Yet the GNP of the nation of latifundia is about to decline sharply. Suppose we seek to analyze the efficiency of each nation's institutions. In the family farm society, we look at the high marginal tax rate, the distortive regulatory and tax subsidies to small business, the rules that stymie latifundia, and so on, and pronounce each institution inefficient.[3]

Yet which nation is in overall terms more efficient over time? Can we analyze the efficiency of any one of the institutions in the subsidized, regulated, overtaxed nation, most of which would be suboptimal in strict efficiency terms, without considering backlash and the (possibly) politically stabilizing effects of these otherwise inefficient institutions?

16.2. THE EFFICIENCY OF STABILITY

Obviously, the nation that buys immediate prosperity at the price of serious political instability later cannot be said to be more efficient over time than its less productive but more stable neighbor. Accounting for backlash could disable our ability to analyze the efficiency of any single institution or law. What if this law, or this institution, is the one that will tip the nation toward turmoil? Can the law or institution, even if at present productively efficient compared to the next best institution or law, be said to be overall efficient if economic turmoil might result from using it? And if backlash is potentially in play, is accounting for it so amorphous that nothing useful could be said about the law's or institution's efficiency?

We could avoid the problem here by assuming that the odds that any one specific law or its alternative would contribute to turmoil or its avoidance are too slim to consider.

Politics, according to this reasoning, is merely secondary to efficiency, and turmoil, one could assume, is unlikely. To an American, this scenario is plausible. After all, the United States, unlike Argentina, for example, has never gone through deep and upsetting economically-based turmoil. Our social divisions that led to civil war and serious turmoil were based on race. So American analysts can, in a first cut at the

---

[3] 'Efficiency' is surprisingly imprecise, sometimes referring to efficiency in exchange, sometimes to efficiency in production, and usually in economic analysis of law to Kaldor-Hicks style wealth maximization. It usually is a snapshot, a static economic look, with more-efficient arrangements producing more value than less-efficient ones. In this chapter I mean something further: that the productive system is also 'efficient' in maximizing wealth over time. If political backlash did not arise, the initially efficient arrangements would have continued to produce more wealth than would alternative arrangements. The system is not only immediately efficient but would have been dynamically efficient in the absence of backlash. I will not use the term 'dynamic' in the text every time I use the word efficient, but that is what I mean.

problem, ignore politics and turmoil; others living in less politically stable nations may lack that luxury, but we Americans have it. Perhaps for these historical reasons, non-American academics often are puzzled by the American emphasis on productive efficiency. And perhaps for these reasons, American analysts might especially be initially unsympathetic to a political explanation based on, say, social democracy for many important corporate structures: settling and containing economic-based social conflict just has not been a key issue for American business.

Outside the United States, though, in nations where the risk of turmoil has been greater, politics could not be ignored, and efficiency-based analysis has been secondary to ensuring stability. In the United States, because such a risk of turmoil is minimal, the analyst can ignore these risks.

A second exit from the dilemma is also probabilistic, but does not depend on any peculiarly American economic stability. Yes, institutions and laws *can* create turmoil, but we do not know in advance which ones *will*. Perhaps the more productive arrangement will tip the scales toward instability, perhaps the less productive arrangement will. Because, all other things being equal, the more productive arrangement should prove more stable politically since the society is made richer, we can, in the absence of strong showings of turmoil, ignore it and assume that generally higher productivity leads to greater political stability.

16.3. POLITICAL TRANSFORMATIONS?

Societies can transform themselves away from revolutionary collapse. Political institutions can mediate the unrest, and better institutions may reduce costly turmoil. Today, worldwide media can help a latifundia nation succeed in transforming itself peacefully because people can more vividly imagine alternatives: they see them on television.

And maybe the United States is not fully free from these influences. Historically, one could see some American laws, perhaps even some American corporate and financial laws, as fitting with a soft transformation to avoid backlash. One could view American family farm subsidies via the Homestead Act, banking law's fragmentation of finance (via the National Bank Act, the Glass-Steagall Act, and related laws), and, say, America's one-time Robinson-Patman-style antitrust policy as politically 'efficient': each absorbed political backlash with economically inefficient (but degradable) structures that, although imperfect, did not destroy too much economic value directly and still preserved a core of competition and incentives.[4] As later generations adjusted to large-scale enterprise—family farms were absorbed into large-scale agribusiness and for the most part disappeared (except in wistful nostalgic films)—Glass-Steagall faded through regulatory reinterpretation, Von's Grocery-style restrictive merger standards led to more expansive Justice Department Merger Guidelines, and the Robinson-Patman Act

---

[4] Cf. Harlan Blake and William Jones, 'In Defense of Antitrust', 65 *Colum. L. Rev.* 377, 382–4 (1965).

pricing strictures came to be understood as inefficient (and ineffective), leading to its interpretive and enforcement demise.

Economic turmoil can be mediated through political institutions, and the quality of those institutions can determine adaptive success. Moreover, some nations have stronger backlash than others, or the backlash expresses itself in differing ways. Some of the corporate governance pro-shareholder limits seen around the world are due to backlash, or to wise political decisions to suppress some severe institutions or laws.

To see the problem abstractly: the property rights literature tends to see property rights as coming prior to production. A society protects property rights, and then it produces. Constitutionally entrenching strong property rights is seen by some as the best way to protect property, but this approach has its weaknesses.

For some societies this puts the cart before the horse. Constitutions and their enforcement are malleable; having a rule constitutionally enshrined does not tell us whether property truly will be secure. And, providing property rights is a public good. But public goods depend on politics and social support to arise and persist. If property rights of one sort or another are unpopular, the public may not support them.

Property rights thus in turn depend in part on production, because the populace does not see each way of organizing production as equally legitimate; some ways of producing (or of distributing) wealth induce more turmoil and weaker property rights than others. Moreover, some forms of organization are less stable than others, and which ones succeed over time can depend on social and cultural settings. Beliefs about the proper scope of government (such as Jeffersonian limits versus centralization), socialization in schools (respecting property, inculcating a belief in opportunity and in the justice of unequal outcomes), and religion (both in producing beliefs and in providing dimensions other than the economic over which politics can divide a polity) all can affect whether a system of production will or will not yield political backlash.

Property rights, social preferences, and production are resolved continually, not sequentially.

Corporate structures are similar, with legal rights, social preferences, and productive organization resolved continually, not sequentially, with some packages more stable than others.

One might posit that corporate law and supporting structures must be in place for this or that type of modern corporation to arise. But some corporate rules and supporting institutions cannot succeed and prosper because they would induce strong backlash. There is reason to think that strong shareholder-based institutions in many nations would often have induced that kind of backlash.

16.4. IS TURMOIL UN-AMERICAN? HOW ABOUT SMALL CHANGES?

I have analyzed the political problem in a way alien to the American setting. Either I have used abstract illustrations—latifundia run by senior controllers—or alluded to foreign ones. The cost of politics in these illustrations is the risk of revolution, either of the Peronist kind that took over Argentina or of the Bismarckian kind that suppressed and co-opted the socialists, or of the communist kind. These abstract, foreign, and revolutionary settings are so far removed from the American experience that one could dismiss their import for us, as I did earlier in this chapter. By dismissing them as foreign or abstract, we justify the implicit foundational assumption in law and economics analysis, that political effects can be ignored. We also can understand why, as I noted earlier, law and economics scholarship is most deeply rooted in the United States, where such revolutionary potential is low.[5]

But one can believe in the stand-alone efficiency of this or that corporate institution (such as free-wheeling hostile takeovers or putting public companies on the auction block in chapter 11) and still doubt whether its persistence maximizes political efficiency. The dampening rules (that reduce takeovers and bankruptcy auctions) may enhance a system's political stability, preserving the *core* efficiency tendencies of capitalism, private property, and competitive markets, by *conceding* a few economically dubious but politically astute regulations here and there. One could believe a set of legal institutions to be inefficient one by one—anti-takeover rules, slow chapter 11 reorganizations, Glass-Steagall, old-style antitrust, and a list to which we could all add—and still one cannot conclude that the whole set is inefficient, because the inefficient *fringe* may preserve that efficient *core* of private property, mobility, and competition.

Hence we can see the relevance of backlash, albeit diluted, even today in the United States, and even without the alien and improbable risk of fundamental revolutionary political turmoil.

16.5. CONCLUSION

When economic-based political turmoil is unlikely, the American law and economics implicit perspective of analyzing the productive efficiency of an institution or rule need not be modified. The fact that for most of American history, and certainly for the American present, the turmoil risks of this or that rule have been trivial helps to explain the American-centered nature of law and economics. But in some nations turmoil had to be avoided, *and their choice of corporate structure was one way of reaching social peace.*

The hard part about accounting for backlash is that while it is real, it is amorphous: one cannot readily measure it, precisely determine gains and losses to GNP, and thereby calibrate for each law or institution the exact dose of needed

---

[5] This view resonates with the 'consensus' view of American history. See Daniel J. Boorstin, *The Genius of American Politics* 158 (1953); Louis Hartz, *The Liberal Tradition in America: An Interpretation of American Political Thought Since the Revolution* 5–32 (1955); Richard Hofstadter, *The American Political Tradition* ix–x (1948). The consensus view has since been challenged by those seeing conflict simmering beneath the placid surface. See, e.g., Samuel P. Huntington, *American Politics: The Promise of Disharmony* 85–149 (1981).

political accommodation or the exact amount of backlash that explains this or that rule or institution. It cannot be easily modeled with supply and demand curves that would tell us much. It is a matter for judgment calls. And, when backlash is in play, one might simultaneously see the law as a result of backlash (and hence analytically unwise) and as a means to avoid more serious backlash (and hence politically astute).

Fully understanding the origins, persistence, and disappearance of economically inefficient statutes could lead to them being seen not just as policy mistakes or interest group rent-seeking, but also as efficiency interacting with backlash. Statutes that seem inefficient—small farm subsidies, Robinson-Patman-style anti-trust, Glass-Steagall, etc.—could be seen as not just policy errors or interest-group power plays but as ways to avoid destructive backlash (or as the products of mild backlash). They dampen crises and then over time they degrade and disappear.

17

Contract as Metaphor

The political problem of backlash is analogous to the economic problem of producing from a common pool. When society has an asset that it uses in common, over-using it can destroy its value, and private economic incentives militate toward over-using a commonly-owned asset. To make that common asset productive, society must deter extreme over-use. The means that lead to assent and acquiescence do not always yield the most efficient results, but rather could be the politically possible results. Political stability, like a common pasture or a public fishery, is a common asset. To keep claims on the polity from overly destabilizing production, political deals that work, like the economic common pool deals that work, may not be pretty and may not be efficient when compared to the ideal.

The problem of politics, economics, and backlash is analogous to a contracting problem with pernicious externalities, one best illustrated by the destructive drilling in the East Texas oil fields in the 1930s. The basic story is familiar to law and economics analysts: the East Texas oil fields were upon discovery the world's richest. Many landowners sank wells and pumped up oil. If the well operators pumped too quickly, the ultimate total recovery from an entire field would fall, as some oil would be trapped and made unrecoverable. But if a single operator reduced the flow from his own well, a neighbor would gain most: the neighbor would recover her own oil and, because the underground pressure increased whenever the single operator slowed down his own pumping, would also recover some oil that seeped out from the slow operator's land. The single operator, recognizing this potential loss, accordingly refused to reduce his oil flow and kept drilling and pumping, hoping that someone—an industry organization, a field-wide contract, the Texas Railroad Commission, the National Recovery Administration, or the Texas militia—would resolve the over-drilling and over-pumping problem.

   This common pool problem is familiar. Less familiar is its resolution. Many means to resolve the over-pumping problem were potentially available, but each had one practical difficulty or another. Agreements to cut production were hard to enforce: everyone 'agreed' to cut daily production by, say, 50 per cent, which, if everyone carried through, would have more than doubled the expected life of the field. But many cheated and secretly pumped oil anyway. The Texas Railroad Commission issued orders, but the drillers ignored them. The National Recovery Administration issued similar orders and some big oil companies tried to take illegal 'hot' oil off the market, to their disappointment when antitrust authorities sued them.[1]

At times civil order broke down. The military occupied the oil field and restored civil order but failed to keep oil production at the government-mandated level. At times pro-rationing was used despite its inefficiencies. The regulators issued drilling orders based on the density of wells per square mile of land, but influential small landowners wanted to drill more intensively than larger landowners. Occasionally the spacing of wells was regulated successfully, but even the spacing rules usually allowed too many wells from the engineering and economic perspectives.

Unitization, which would have treated all of a field as a single unit and maximized revenue by positioning wells on engineering rather than political grounds, would have greatly enhanced total recovery. But the regulators instead chose pro-rationing with regulated spacing of the wells, because pro-rationing, despite leading to excess wells, facilitated a political consensus for enforcement, voluntary and otherwise, of sensible but suboptimal production without a free-for-all that would have reduced recovery even further. The consensus reduced the extreme waste from the free-for-all, but still lost half of the recoverable oil. That is, agreements to 'unitize' production—split all the revenues from a field and allot oil production only to maximize output—were technically within reach, but politically unfeasible. Political unfeasibility arose from an inability to agree on a sharing formula, because those with 'rich' oil lands did not wish to share in proportion to the acreage contributed, and no obvious other formula popped up.[2]

The analogy to politics and economics is obvious: to create the public good of political tranquility, a system may sometimes choose technically suboptimal production, just as the oil field regulators eventually chose an imperfect engineering result because it was the one that could most plausibly get collective acquiescence.

---

[1] See United States v. Socony-Vacuum Oil Co., 310 U.S. 150, 166–7 (1940).

[2] See Gary D. Libecap, Contracting for Property Rights 5 n.5, 96, 98, 113 (1989). Sharing based on acreage worked only when the field owners unitized before anyone had done much drilling, and accordingly were behind a 'veil of ignorance' as to the richness of their own deposits. See id. at 109. Cf. Samuel L. Popkin, 'Public Choice and Peasant Organization', in Toward a Political Economy of Development: A Rational Choice Perspective 245, 249 (ed. by Robert H. Bates 1988), who describes land division in a hilly Indian farm village: the land was distributed in inheritances in vertical strips, because the land's quality varied vertically. Vertical distribution was seen as fairer, despite that the land is easier to plow horizontally.

18

Rents

Product markets are weaker in some nations than they are in others. Weaker product markets, and the concomitant monopoly rents, can affect corporate governance. They can do so directly by loosening a constraint on managers, thereby increasing managerial agency costs to shareholders, costs that shareholders would then seek to reduce otherwise. The monopoly profits can also affect corporate governance structures indirectly by setting up a fertile field for conflict inside the firm as the corporate players—shareholders, managers, and employees—seek to grab those monopoly profits for themselves. One would expect corporate governance structures, laws, and practices to differ in nations with monopoly-induced high agency costs from those prevailing in nations with more competition, fewer monopolies, and lower agency costs. And we might speculate that these rents when large and widespread could affect democratic politics and law-making: directly by making monopolists political targets (and political forces); and indirectly by tempting the players inside the firm to seek to capture those monopoly profits through political action, with political parties and ideologies (and, in time, laws and standards) that parallel the players' places inside the firm. Data from the industrial organization, finance economics, and political science literature is consistent.

18.1. The Issue: Industrial Organization's Effect on Agency Costs
18.2. The Monopolist's Rectangle
18.3. But Who Gets That Rectangle?
18.4. Slack for Managers
18.5. Capital Markets Alone Cannot Tighten the Slack
18.6. Agency Costs: Effects from Employees
18.7. Higher Agency Costs and Corporate Governance
18.8. Politics Again?

18.1. THE ISSUE: INDUSTRIAL ORGANIZATION'S EFFECT ON AGENCY COSTS

Some economies are less competitive than others. Weaker competition produces higher rents—profits above those needed to stay in business. These rents can affect firms, as the rents cut managers some slack and attract grabs by players inside the firm. And, we might speculate, these rents where large enough and widespread could affect democratic politics, as they must be divided up, and politics can be the arena to divide them.

When rents are widespread, the players inside the firm have more room than they would otherwise have to contest the size of the corporate pie that each takes home. This kind of contest has been strong in 'smoke-stack' type industries in many nations. (The contest would be less important in, say, new economy technologies where labor-stakeholder pressure is weak, and where technological change is rapid, thereby reducing the potential slack for managers.) In nations where these contests are pervasive, some political organization will be devoted to (1) settling this contest at the lowest possible cost; (2) devising corporate and labor law rules to fit the usually prevailing corporate and labor structures; and (3) representing in the broad polity the specific players inside the firm, each of whom wants to get a slice of those rents.

I begin in this chapter with a model of industrial organization being established first, and I speculate on how differing degrees of competition affect corporate governance, corporate ownership, and labor-oriented politics. Higher rents induce higher managerial agency costs for shareholders; higher agency costs induce shareholders to strengthen the inside-the-firm structures that keep higher agency costs within bounds. And higher rents could provide the fuel for political parties, ideologies, and contests on how to divide up those rents in a national economy.

18.2. THE MONOPOLIST'S RECTANGLE

The rent comes out of the consumer surplus that a competitive market would otherwise generate, and that the monopolist can, but a competitor cannot, appropriate for itself. Some consumers would pay a high price for the good, if they had to. But where producers compete, a competitor lowers its price down to the point where it covers its costs and its normal basic profit.

When a single firm dominates a product market, and when competitive entry is impossible (or costly), the monopoly firm has reason to produce less and raise its price. It produces less so that it can raise its price by selling to the high-valuing consumers who will pay more.

The monopolist produces less, raises its price, and seeks the price-quantity combination that maximizes its monopoly profits. Value moves from the wallets of the remaining consumers who still buy (at the higher price) to the monopolist's bank account. This transfer, sometimes called the monopolist's rectangle, obviously due to its shape, is illustrated in Graph 18.1, a stripped-down version of the Economics 101 monopoly graph.

When many firms in different sectors cut back production and increase price, they can affect the basic issues in politics. More firms have potentially high agency costs; and those 'rectangles', if many, yield a valuable pot for political players to contest, a pot providing a basis for conflict and settlement that,

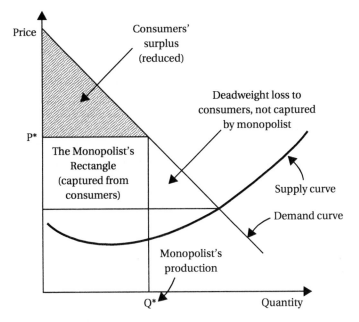

Graph 18.1. The monopolist's 'rectangle'

although possible to accommodate inside the firm, is often divided up nationally by political institutions.

18.3. BUT WHO GETS THAT RECTANGLE?

1. *Merely distributional?* Standard economic analyses downplay the importance of the monopolist's rectangle: the rectangle 'merely' represents a shift in income from the buying consumers (who might be rich, for all we know from examining the graph) to firms (who might be struggling producers banding together in a co-operative, for all we know from examining the graph). The monopolist's core sin is to cut production and raise price, thereby denying the product to consumers who could pay what it would cost the monopolist to make it, but whom the monopolist refuses to serve so that it can raise its price to high-valuing consumers. The diminished consumers' surplus triangle is the loss, and the monopolist's sin in the standard analysis is destroying that triangle, sometimes referred to as the 'deadweight loss', not grabbing the rectangle.

2. *Firms spend to get the monopolist's rectangle.* The classical idea that the monopoly rectangle is 'merely' distributional was badly dented in critiques from Richard Posner and Gordon Tullock. Firms anticipate these excess profits if they can acquire (or keep) a monopoly, and hence they spend to get (or to keep) that monopoly. In the limit case, they dissipate the distributional gain, spending it

ex ante to acquire the monopoly or ex post to keep it.[1] One way of spending to get or keep those monopoly profits is to spend on political organization.

3. *But who is the firm?* Analyses tend to view 'firms' as black boxes, competing to get these rents. The 'firm' is richer. Its owners are richer. The monopolist is richer. That monopolist is usually the 'owner'. Occasionally there are notations that the monopolist-owner can spend some of the monopoly profits on its inputs. So, in some oligopolies, labor, especially unionized labor, can get a piece of the monopoly profits for itself, in the form of wages higher than those of workers with similar jobs elsewhere.[2] For example, wages for members of the UAW (the United Auto Workers union) have typically been higher than those for similar assembly line workers elsewhere in the economy. Autoworkers got a piece of the automobile industry's monopoly rent, especially before international competition among automakers squeezed out much of that rent.

Firms can be decomposed. They are made up of shareholder-owners, managers, employees, and customers. *These* players *also* compete for the rents. Competition for rents and that monopoly rectangle is not just *between* firms but also *inside* firms as the players *inside* the firm—shareholders, managers, employees—compete to grab a piece of that rectangle. (And outside the firm, consumers seek to prevent the monopolist from extracting that rent for the inside-the-firm players.) The way the players compete for those rents is reflected in corporate governance institutions inside the firm and political organizations inside the polity.

18.4. SLACK FOR MANAGERS

Consider a firm with a secure monopoly and consider the monopoly's plausible corporate governance consequences. More monopoly should induce higher potential managerial agency costs in monopoly firms. The monopoly yields a bigger pot of value (bigger, that is, than the pot an equivalent competitive firm would produce) into which managers can stick their fingers. The bigger the 'rectangle', the bigger that pot.

Tightly competitive product markets constrain managers: deliver a defective product and consumers buy a competitor's instead next time. That constraint may not always be tight, if all firms in the market are lax. But, obviously, product markets constraints are lower, or non-existent, for managers of the monopoly

---

[1] Richard A. Posner, *Antitrust Law: An Economic Perspective* 11 (1976); Richard A. Posner, 'The Social Costs of Monopoly and Regulation', 83 *J. Pol. Econ.* 807, 809 (1975); Gordon Tullock, 'The Welfare Costs of Tariffs, Monopolies, and Theft', 5 *W. Econ. J.* 224, 228, 232 (1967).

[2] See W. Kip Viscusi, John M. Vernon, and Joseph E. Harrington, Jr, *Economics of Regulation and Antitrust* 84 (2nd ed. 1995); Thomas Karier, 'Unions and Monopoly Profits', 67 *Rev. Econ & Stat.* 34, 40–41 (1985); Richard B. Freeman and James L. Medoff, *What Do Unions Do?* 52 (1984); John E. Kwoka, 'Monopoly, Plant, and Union Effects on Worker Wages', 36 *Ind. & Lab. Rel. Rev.* 251, 253 (1983) (industrial concentration and high wages correlate); but see Leonard W. Weiss, 'Concentration and Labor Earnings', 56 *Am. Econ. Rev.* 96, 114–5 (1966).

firm.[3] And there is evidence that market concentration reduces productivity and that competition enhances it.[4]

* * *

We have a vocabulary problem to clarify: industrial organization rents—the monopoly profits—could be confused with rents from corporate control—the value that controllers can skim off from the firm with impunity. The two are important and related—a modest *managerial* rent in making mistakes is a kind of controller's 'skim' and it can yield large *monopoly* rent losses to the owners—but the two concepts are neither identical nor even opposite sides of the same coin. A small managerial 'rent' in slack could lose a huge monopoly 'rent' in profits for shareholders.

Enhanced agency costs are important even if monopoly rents do not go, dollar-for-dollar, into managers' pockets. Managers, if insufficiently aggressive, may lose a large slice of the monopoly profits at only modest gain for themselves. Agency *costs* to shareholders could be high even if the manager's *gains* are comparatively modest.

Managers in the standard agency cost analysis tend to expand firms without regard to profitability. Their gain may be less than the shareholders' loss. The shareholders want a mechanism to make managers more profit-oriented than expansion-oriented. When product markets are weak, two of their mechanisms—product market competition and, as next seen, capital market competition—are compromised.

* * *

The point is not that competition *perfectly* constrains managers to operate the firm solely for shareholders nor that a perfect control falls apart as soon as product market competition declines. Even in competitive markets, when the firm has made large fixed investments—in its physical plant, in trademarks, in goodwill—managers can run this sunk capital down without product markets inflicting on them an immediate large penalty.

But product market competition affects managers and less of it loosens the constraints on them. Most managers dislike seeing competitors taking away market share. A weak competitor's profits will decline; and then other corporate governance institutions such as the board of directors or incentive compensation or shareholder action will kick in.

Product market competition does not perfectly constrain managers to work for shareholders, but its absence constrains them less, creating more slack for managers.

---

[3] The converse has been modeled. Oliver Hart, 'The Market Mechanism as an Incentive Scheme', 14 *Bell J. Econ.* 366 (1983).

[4] Stephen J. Nickell, 'Competition and Corporate Performance', 104 *J. Pol. Econ.* 724, 741 (1996); Ravi Jagannathan and Shaker B. Srinivasan, 'Does Product Market Competition Reduce Agency Costs?' 10 *North Am. J. Econ & Fin.* 387 (2000) (managers retain more cash in firms that have weak product market competition).

18.5. CAPITAL MARKETS ALONE CANNOT TIGHTEN THE SLACK

Capital markets constrain managers weakly when product market competition is weak.

Consider how capital market competition constrains managers: managers must go to capital markets for funds. When they do, stock buyers penalize poorly-performing managers by demanding a higher rate of return and a lower stock price, creditors penalize those managers by demanding a higher interest rate, and in the limit case capital providers refuse to give poor managers any new capital. The firm withers. More effective firms with more effective managers eventually grab market-share from the ineffective managers. (True, capital markets do not tightly constrain every competitor: a firm not needing new capital is not immediately constrained. It can run down capital in place and use up retained earnings. In time it should wither, and avoiding that withering can motivate some players. But some corporate players could accept that withering, especially if others pay for it.)

Capital markets constrain the *monopolist's* managers much more weakly than they constrain the competitor's managers. The monopolist's managers can more readily generate sufficient profits internally to pay for needed capital improvements. And as long as they leave *some* of the monopolist's 'rectangle' on the table for the original capital providers, the monopolist's return on invested capital is *still higher* than a competitive firm's.[5] Capital markets constrain the monopolist's managers strongly *not* when the managers dissipate monopoly profits, but when they dissipate *so much* that they need new capital and their return dips below the *competitive* return for capital.[6]

So, if the monopoly rate of return is, say, 25 per cent, when world-wide capital markets demand a 10 per cent rate of return (for this type of company, this class of risk, etc.), then capital markets constraints will starve the capital-needy firm if managers throw away enough that the expected return declines below 10 per cent. But capital markets will *not directly* constrain the managers as they take, share, or squander the *first* 15 per cent of the monopoly's return. That 15 per cent cushion is the monopolist's rectangle, the potential excess profits that create the potential for slack.

---

[5] A refinement that does not change the story: capital markets will bid up the stock price until the return equals the risk-adjusted competitive return. Posit that the competitive, risk-adjusted rate of return is 10% annually. In competitive industries, $100 of investment will return $10 each year. A monopolist builds, with a $40 investment, a monopoly that yields $10 annually. When the monopolist sells the firm to buyers who expect the monopoly to be retained, the buyers will pay $100. The *original* monopolist captures the $60 'rectangle'. If agency costs would diminish the firm's profitability to $7.50 (i.e. losing $2.50 of monopoly profits for capital-providers), then outsiders will pay $75 for the firm.

[6] The capital markets mechanism would, in textbook fashion, be this: when the firm goes fully public, investors capitalize the firm's expected cash flows. These cash flows will be the competitive return, plus the additional monopoly profits before agency costs, minus profits lost to agency costs. The original owner reaps the expected gains from the monopoly and suffers the expected managerial agency cost losses. The future shareholder will capture unexpected reductions in agency costs. The non-classical point to be made here is that if the potential agency costs are high for a monopoly firm, then the original owner would avoid that expected loss by declining to allow the firm to go public.

18.6. AGENCY COSTS: EFFECTS FROM EMPLOYEES

There is more. Employees can claim a share of the monopolist's 'rectangle'. Wages should be higher, hours shorter, the workplace potentially less friendly toward shareholder profitability. Their claims may be straightforward grabs, or may be justified by claims of fairness and just entitlements. (On whose backs and with whose sweat was that monopoly built anyway?)

Employees seeking a piece of the rectangle raise managerial agency costs. They would seek their share of that rectangle in higher wages, in better working conditions, and, sometimes, in corporate governance authority. They thereby would press managers to compromise managerial loyalty, pushing it away from shareholders. German codetermination, for example, fits better with a weakly competitive market (where shareholders can split rents with incumbent employees) than with a fiercely competitive one (one lacking rents for employees). Managers in the first instance have the task of refusing or modulating employees' demands, and for most managers their easiest action is to give employees a piece of the 'rectangle', especially if it is a piece that would otherwise go to shareholders, not to managers.

Conflict is costly, psychologically and otherwise, and settlement and persuasion can be hard. Managers are pressed by the people they work with for better conditions, for more pay, and for continued employment. Why should they favor distant abstract financial interests over the people they see every day? Especially if others (i.e. stockholders) are paying, managers may well use what would otherwise be part of the stockholders' share to end the conflict and buy labor peace.[7]

Labor's goals are frequently not at managers' expense but are goals that many managers would want, such as over-investing in a comfortable work place, shorter hours, etc. Hence, managers and employees should often be on the same side in taking a slice of that rectangle for themselves. (Some monopolies are more susceptible to raising agency costs than others. Smoke-stack industries with large long-lived physical capital and with heavy labor inputs have a higher potential for high agency costs than, say, high technology monopolies with short-lived capital, a short expected life for each monopoly, and different labor inputs.)

18.7. HIGHER AGENCY COSTS AND CORPORATE GOVERNANCE

Thus, more monopoly begets higher managerial agency costs because there is more to 'grab' (by employees and, to some extent, by managers). And managerial slack is higher and less easily controlled (yielding a pot that is more easily 'lost' by managers even when they cannot, or do not, 'grab' it for themselves), and the

---

[7] Michael A. Salinger, 'Tobin's q, Unionization, and the Concentration-Profits Relationship', 15 *Rand J. Econ.* 159, 166 (1984) (data that unions capture whatever long-run monopoly power exists in the U.S. economy); cf. Richard S. Ruback and Martin B. Zimmerman, 'Unionization and Profitability: Evidence from the Capital Market', 92 *J. Pol. Econ.* 1134 (1984) (unexpected collective bargaining agreements lower equity value in the United States).

market's other means to reduce agency costs, such as capital and product markets competition, are weaker.[8]

One powerful means to reduce managerial agency costs is for the stock-owners to act cohesively in a block. The blockholder can monitor managers directly, has greater incentives to do so (because it owns so much stock), has greater means to do so (because managers pay more attention to a large stockholder than to a small one), and can get better information than scattered shareholders can (thereby making the monitoring potentially more effective). All else equal, blockholding should be higher where monopoly (or oligopoly) is higher; some American evidence corroborates.[9]

That is, the original owner has incentives to optimize corporate governance for shareholders, because, when considering whether and how to go public, he or she internalizes what managers would lose in agency costs thereafter. Rational markets do not pay the owner for monopoly profits that will be lost to shareholders. If the original owner cannot build a structure that would maintain these profits, he or she will lose them when taking the firm public. Often he cannot build such a structure and, hence, often he has reason not to let go of control. This potential loss gives the original owner an incentive to maintain block ownership, as that is oftentimes the best, or only, way to retain those monopoly profits.[10] Either the original owner retains the block herself, or sells it intact to a new blockholder. Ownership does not separate from control.

---

[8] American firms in weak competitive markets display higher agency costs than those in more competitive markets: Franklin R. Edwards, 'Managerial Objectives in Regulated Industries: Expense-Preference Behavior in Banking', 85 *J. Pol. Econ.* 147 (1977); Timothy H. Hannan and Ferdinand Mavinga, 'Expense Preference and Managerial Control: The Case of the Banking Firm', 11 *Bell J. Econ.* 671 (1980) (office expenses and employment levels rise in banks in concentrated markets); Gary S. Becker, *The Economics of Discrimination* 31–42 (1957) (managers in monopoly industries indulged a preference to discriminate more readily than managers in competitive industries).

[9] Management-controlled high-market-power firms in the United States historically showed the ordinary profitability of *non*-monopoly firms. But firms controlled by strong owners showed higher-than-normal profits when the firms had market power, but ordinary profits if the firms lacked market power. See John Palmer, 'The Profit-Performance Effects of the Separation of Ownership from Control in Large U.S. Industrial Corporations', 4 *Bell J. Econ. & Mgmt. Sci.* 293, 298 (1973). Product markets and strong owners each constrain managers, albeit imperfectly. When monopoly power is high and ownership concentration low, these imperfect constraints are even more imperfect. Id. at 299. And 'manager-controlled banks operating in noncompetitive markets . . . spend more on items likely to be preferred by managers than do owner-controlled banks in the same situation.' Hannan and Mavinga, supra, note 8, at 671.

[10] Unless the only way to achieve monopoly is via a scale of operations that a single owner cannot handle: the relationship between monopoly and concentrated ownership may be the economist's frequent 'inverted-U' curve. Ownership concentration increases at first as monopoly power increases, because the monopoly can be retained by a small group, who get the best of both worlds for themselves: monopoly profits and low managerial agency costs. As firm size overwhelms a single owner's capacity to provide or hold capital, the big monopoly requires more diffuse ownership. Agency costs rise, but so do monopoly profits, which make up for the inefficiencies for shareholders. I focus in this chapter on the first part of the curve, the rise in ownership concentration, a result that probably was more common historically in smaller, less-competitive economies than in larger ones.

18.8. POLITICS AGAIN?

Monopoly is not inevitable. It partly depends on technology, partly on the size of the market. Small economies closed to trade are more susceptible than large economies, or than economies open to trade.

But these results are not independent of political forces. Internal political forces can open up a national economy to international trade, thereby diminishing monopoly rents. Or political coalitions can propel antitrust policy, make it effective, and thereby reduce pernicious monopolies (and perhaps even natural ones or even those acquired by skill, foresight, and industry); this was the American result but until recently not a common one around the world. Conceivably one could tie competitive markets and weak social democracy to some similar underlying characteristic, such as a strong individualist culture. Or perhaps concentrated owners come first, capture enough of the democratic polity to impose monopoly, and then the owners coalesce with their employees to retain the monopolies in the face of consumer interests. Suffice it to say that real world causal directions are complex, but that the association is there, with monopoly tying in to both ownership concentration and labor laws that are protective of employees with jobs-in-place. Why consumers win in some nations (with an effective antitrust policy or via borders open to trade) but lose in others is a question worthy of study. Here I simply analyze the consequences of the result: if consumers do not win in the antitrust arena and if monopoly profits in smoke-stack type industries are high, what, I ask, are the plausible consequential pressures on corporate ownership, labor laws, and basic democratic politics?

19

Rents and Politics

If a nation has many firms capturing monopoly rents, then we should expect two major corporate governance consequences: first, potential managerial agency costs to shareholders will be higher than elsewhere, making owners try to tighten up to avoid those potentially heavier costs. Second, with more rents for the players to split, we could speculate that the corporate governance splits could have political correlates, as the players would seek to use politics to grab, or block, rent acquisition.

19.1. PRIMARY CONSEQUENCES

1. *Of higher agency costs.* If agency costs are potentially higher inside the firm, shareholders should demand more public provision of institutions that would reduce agency costs. These might include statements of corporate fiduciary duties, related causes of action, incentive compensation (with facilitating tax laws), pro-shareholder norms, and so on.

But while the demand for these institutions *from shareholders* would be high, the resistance from, or indifference of, the *other* players, who have more votes, could block them.[1] And public-regarding political players might see that enhancing shareholder institutions could demean national wealth. Certainly, it would be easy for them to see that enhancing shareholder wealth would initially shift wealth from consumers to the firm's owners. (Imagine the founders seeking to sell their firms into a diffuse market. With agency costs expected to be high because of the monopoly profits, and hence the price buyers would pay lower than the full monopoly

---

[1] This tension can be seen vis-à-vis incentive compensation in France: business interests call for favorable taxation of stock options to align managers with shareholders; socialist politicians block such changes.

price, they ask the Finance Ministry for good, pro-shareholder takeover law. When public-spirited officials understand that the founders want good takeover law to protect monopoly profits, they balk at helping the owners out.) And political players would often see that they could get more votes by pleasing the monopoly firm's employees than by pleasing its shareholders. Political parties might be organized around this concept, we might speculate. Supporting ideologies of fairness and justice could develop.[2]

Then, if public provision of shareholder-enhancing institutions is weak, the firm will seek to enhance them privately. Enhancements would include more concentrated stock ownership, more continued family control of firms through several generations, and more tailoring of capital structure to reduce agency costs.

2. *Of higher rents for the players to split.* Politics when successful settles conflict. The monopolist's 'rectangle' is a fertile field for conflict, as the corporate players—owners, managers, and employees—stake their claims to part of that field. This enhanced potential for conflict inside the firm should, if such firms dominate an economy, raise the demand for political institutions that can settle this conflict. How politics settles conflict is probably not fully determinate, but depends on interactions with other institutions in that nation: the settlement could favor shareholders, employees, or consumers. Alliances could shift; coalitions could form.

Social democracy settles this conflict in one important way, by creating a collective sense of belonging and by regulating the firm to produce more equality and more employee voice in the firm's decisions. Workers feel they have more collective control over their destinies in the work place, because they do. Corporatism is another way to reduce this conflict; centralized associations of employers, employees, and the government meet to hammer out bargains on wages, employment levels, and monetary policy. The corporatist associations thereby divide up those monopoly and oligopoly rectangles.[3] Social democratic parties represent incumbent labor as the political arm for employees to garner a 'fair' share of the monopoly firm's rents. Indeed, monopoly power correlates, albeit weakly, with employment protection law.[4]

Owners have reason to 'invest' in politics to keep those monopoly profits for themselves. In democracies they often lose, as other players (their employees, the unions, sympathetic bystanders) have more votes, inducing democratic politicians to go where the votes are, disfavoring the owners. (Perhaps the American result is unusual; one might see consumers as the principal winners, with a satisfactory antitrust policy keeping the rents down over the long haul.)

Because owners in a weak democracy could more often win (than owners in a strong democracy), they have reason to resist strong democracy.

---

[2] Consumers, presumably poorly organized politically or unsympathetic with owners' pleas, may end up losing more. But even consumers might be rationally indifferent if (1) monopoly is unavoidable (because, say, the economy is too small to be competitive); and (2) the primary political issue is whether the firms' owners or their employees get the lion's share of the monopoly profits.

[3] E.g. Charles S. Maier, 'Preconditions for Corporatism', in *Order and Conflict in Contemporary Capitalism* (ed. by John H. Goldthorpe, 1984).

[4] I compared the OECD's job protection index, displayed in Table 19.1, with the mark-up index from Table 20.1. The two correlated, although not powerfully.

Democratic consumers might take those rents away from owners one way; democratic and organized workers might take them away another way. Whether this factor—protecting rents—describes why some owners resisted democratization in historically conservative dictatorial regimes in Latin America and Asia could be investigated.

19.2. CONVERSE: CONSEQUENCES WHEN PRODUCT COMPETITION IS STRONG

Reflect the monopolistic scenario in a mirror. Imagine another nation, B, similar in all other respects to the nations just discussed in section 19.1 except that B's major firms are *not* organized monopolistically. Imagine how the competitive consequences play out inside the firms and how the demand for social democratic and corporatist politics will be lower in B than in the nations in section 19.1.

Competition in nation B makes rents inside B's firms lower than those in nation A, the firms from Section 19.1. There are no monopoly 'rectangles' (or they are smaller). With the rectangles gone (or reduced), managerial agency costs inside the firm are lower in nation B than in A. Shareholders can relax their most costly agency-cost control institutions, which might be concentrated ownership and tight shareholder control over managers. They can cut managers *a little* slack (because there are no monopoly rectangles that already cut the managers *a lot* of slack, making it worthwhile to use even expensive agency-cost-reducing tools because the gains would be so high), by reducing the size of their large blocks so that they can benefit from more liquidity and more diversification.

The monopoly rents for shareholders, employees, managers, and customers/ consumers to fight over in the political sphere are smaller in this competitive nation B. The private manifestations of that struggle—unions and concentrated ownership in a small, monopolistically-organized nation—should diminish. The corporate law manifestations—opposition to shareholder wealth institutions from the non-shareholders—should diminish because there is less (or nothing) for the other non-shareholder players to capture out of those shrunken (or non-existent) monopoly rectangles. And the political manifestations of that struggle should also be weaker for similar reasons. Hence, social democratic parties (as the political arm of employees' fight for a share of the rents) should, all other things equal, be weaker in nation B than in A.

19.3. CONSEQUENCES FOR LABOR LAWS AND OWNERSHIP CONCENTRATION

Strong ownership concentration should result in a democratic nation if its laws and politics are strongly pro-labor (actually if they are more pro-employees-with-

Table 19.1. *Labor Laws, Strong and Weak, and Ownership Concentration*

Country	Employment protection (1 = lowest)	Portion of mid-sized public firms without a 20 per cent stockholder
United States	1	0.9
Canada	3	0.6
Australia	4	0.3
Denmark	5	0.3
Switzerland	6	0.5
United Kingdom	7	0.6
Japan	8	0.3
Netherlands	9	0.1
Finland	10	0.2
Norway	11	0.2
Sweden	13	0.1
France	14	0
Germany	15	0.1
Austria	16	0
Belgium	17	0.2
Italy	21	0

jobs-in-place, because law-induced labor power does not always favor unemployed people looking for jobs). In Table 19.1, I array an OECD index of employment protection and a standard measure of ownership concentration in the world's richest nations.[5] They correlate strongly. Graph 19.1 depicts the result.

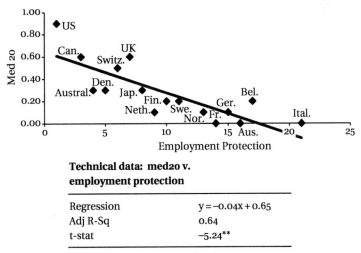

Technical data: med20 v. employment protection

Regression	$y = -0.04x + 0.65$
Adj R-Sq	0.64
t-stat	-5.24**

** Significant at the 0.0005 level.

Graph 19.1. Employment protection as predicting ownership concentration

[5] The index of employment protection is for the years 1985–93 and comes from Organization for Economic Co-operation and Development, *The OECD Jobs Study: Evidence and Explanations*, Pt II:

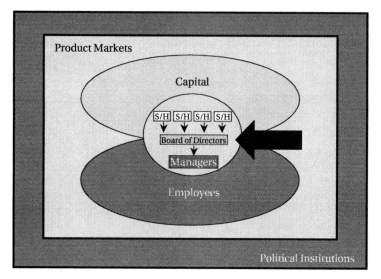

Fig. 19.1. Product markets and the corporate governance environment

Although the strong American correlation—very weak labor protection and strong ownership diffusion—might make one think that it alone 'drives' the strong statistical results, it does not. One could drop the United States from the list and strong employment protection would still significantly correlate with ownership concentration. In fact, one could drop the next strongest—Canada and the United Kingdom—and the correlation would remain strong.

19.4. CAUSATION'S DIRECTION

I have presented product markets as coming first, with uncompetitive product markets raising managerial agency costs, thereby both calling forth concentrated ownership and, I speculate, fueling labor-based politics in the democratic West. I illustrate this direction, and these effects on the corporate governance environment in Figure 19.1.

Product markets could affect politics, as I have posited, but causation might run in the opposite direction. Politics could come first. If social democratic politics heavily favored employees with jobs in place, then entrepreneurs might not have entered industries to the point where profits would have been fully competitive, if they knew that one key input, labor, had to be paid accordingly. Politics could come

The Adjustment Potential of the Labour Market 74 (1994); the index of ownership concentration comes from Rafael La Porta, Florencio Lopez-de-Silanes and Andrei Shleifer, 'Corporate Ownership Around the World', 54 *J. Fin.* 471, 474–80 (1999).

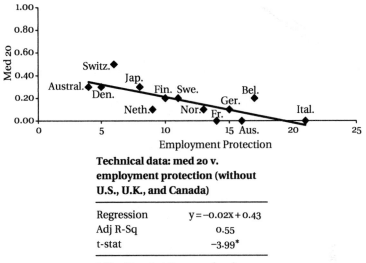

Graph 19.2. Employment protection as predicting concentration, without U.S., U.K., and Canada

first in another way: well-placed players could have seized government levers to get themselves a monopoly, and from that monopoly could flow social democratic, pro-labor politics and concentrated ownership. Or social democratic governments may facilitate, or at least tolerate, monopolies, not breaking them up as long as some of their largesse—i.e. a piece of that rectangle—goes to the social democrats' constituencies.[6]

Other causal chains are possible. Controlling shareholders may induce governments to support their monopolies. Then, with the monopolies in place in a democracy, the benefited owners have to get other players' political support. Union and employee benefits, instead of being 'grabs', could be 'pay-offs' from owners, to keep political and internal support strong for hampering competitors.

Or, slightly differently, employees and owners can coalesce politically, aiming to weaken competitors, both domestic and foreign, via blocking rules, subsidies, and trade barriers. Once they secure the monopoly profits for their firm or their industry, then owners would be motivated to protect their share of the split of the monopoly profits, by maintaining close ownership of the firm and a tight hand on managers' actions.

---

[6] Japan's Ministry of International Trade and Industry limited entry into key industries, facilitating oligopolies with lifetime employment for core workers. Nobuhiro Hiwatari, 'Employment Practices and Enterprise Unionism in Japan', in *Employees and Corporate Governance* 275, 290 (ed. by Margaret M. Blair and Mark J. Roe, 1999).

[7] Marco Pagano and Paolo Volpin, 'The Political Economy of Corporate Governance' (Universita Degli Studi di Salerno Working Paper No. 29, 1999).

This alliance could be seen as a means for the controlling shareholder and the employees to jointly extract private benefits of control out of the *minority* stockholders' pockets.[7] But, while logically possible and intellectually intricate to outline, such an alliance would demand that employees and unions (or their leaders) get involved in the nitty-gritty of corporate law rules' formation, and that seems both implausible and too attenuated as a way for employee or union gains. More plausible is that the two—owners and employees—easily understand their direct interests in garnering monopoly profits for the firm, in shutting down competitors, and in blocking international competitive entry. This is a more usual and a simpler story.

* * *

Thus, while for some nations at key times the product market is settled first, it is not that way for all nations at all times. A modest restatement of this Part's thesis here would be that the world's wealthy democracies have two broad packages: (1) competitive product markets, dispersed ownership, and conservative results for labor; and (2) concentrated product markets, concentrated ownership, and pro-labor results. The three elements in each package mutually reinforce one another.

19.5. POLITICAL CONSEQUENCES WHEN GLOBALIZATION AND INTERNATIONAL COMPETITION INCREASE

Owners may get product market rents in the first instance, but they might be unable to keep them. The other players, such as the employees, want representation when the political decisions are made to divide up these rents. Social democratic ideology is a statement that the rents belong primarily to the employees.

You would expect *less* social democracy in *big*, democratic, technologically advanced countries with strong product market competition. *And* globalization, by squeezing rents, changes what is up for grabs inside the firm, even in smaller nations. *Then*, by reducing what is up for grabs inside the firm, globalization weakens the social democratic parties and the polity's demand for the related corporate and labor laws.[8] So it is no accident that as global competition heats up, French corporate law, which tells managers to manage their firms in the 'social interest', gets challenged by official commissions not unlike the American Law Institute via reports that extol a more shareholder-oriented approach to the French firm.[9] Something similar happened in

---

[7] Marco Pagano and Paolo Volpin, 'The Political Economy of Corporate Governance' (Universita Degli Studi di Salerno Working Paper No. 29, 1999).

[8] And it weakens shareholders' preference for concentrated ownership. Enhanced product market competition shrinks the rectangle that managers can grab from (or lose for) shareholders. And enhanced product market competition constrains managers more than monopoly. Hence, globalization should diminish ownership concentration and promote separation. The Canadian experience is consistent: '[D]iffuse ownership is more commonplace in Canada subsequent to that country's free trade agreement with the United States.' Randall K. Morck, 'Introduction', in *Concentrated Corporate Ownership* 1, 6 (ed. by Randall K. Morck, 2000).

[9] Association Française des Entreprises Privées, *Recommendations of the Committee on Corporate Governance* (1999) (Viénot Report II); Philippe Marini, *La modernisation du droit des sociétés: rapport au premier ministre* 12 (1996) (legislative report to Prime Minister says that the French corporate code's social interest duty mistakenly masks an allocation of power).

the U.S.: regulation of some industries, like trucking, led to union employees capturing some of the monopoly rent. Deregulation wiped out the rents and the union's ability to grab a share of those rents for its members. As deregulation took off, union membership and power declined.[10]

We have now just traced out a linked explanation for the observation that globalization and increased competition are pressing social democratic ideologies in Europe. A socialist party in France in the 1990s did not nationalize further, but privatized. A former communist became the prime minister in Italy and maintained private markets. A German prime minister fulminated against a huge hostile takeover, but let it proceed, although his predecessors had blocked similar hostile takeovers. As even local firms in previously-monopolistic markets face increasingly *international* competition, some via the European Union and the Common Market, those rectangles shrink, and there is less for the players inside the firm—managers and employees—to grab. Then the players' (that is, the employees' and the owners') demand for their political correlates declines, because there is less to grab (or protect), making political action less valuable. And hence social democratic parties should, all else equal, move to the right, as they have been.[11]

For now, integrating Europe economically increases competition, reduces the monopoly rectangles, and diminishes the fuel for social democratic politics. But possibly Europe is in transition, and the end point might not be less monopoly. As Europe integrates, firms formerly confined to national boundaries may merge and, in time, yield a new weakly competitive continent to replace yesterday's weakly competitive nations. If so, then the fit outlined in this book—social democracy, monopoly, and ownership concentration—could replace the now emerging fit of middle-of-the-road politics, competition, and growing securities markets. Politics could cause the shift. Some European politicians want more political integration to better implement a social democratic labor policy, a labor policy that fragmented nations in competitive markets cannot implement.[12] Or, incumbent groups could react against increasing economic integration when they see integration eroding their rents.

---

[10] Nancy Rose, 'Labor Rent Sharing and Regulation: Evidence from the Trucking Industry', 95 *J. Pol. Econ.* 1146, 1163 (1987).

[11] Cf. *The Federalist* No. 10 (James Madison). Madison said the Constitution would diffuse the political power of factions and leave less room for political rent-seeking, which is analogous to the claim here that increased global competition widens the economic space and thereby shrinks the rents that political factions would fight over.

[12] See 'Workers' Rights in the EU—Inform, Consult, Impose', *Economist*, 16 June 2001, at 79 (a 'new [European Union] directive [requiring owners to consult with workers on managerial strategy] has unions cheering and company bosses fuming' as socialists praise an emerging 'social Europe'); 'Europe—A French Lesson', *Economist*, 1 July 2000, at 47.

20

Rents and Ownership Concentration

Where product market rents are higher, two key constraints on managers—product and capital market competition—weaken. When these constraints on managers weaken, managerial agency costs in the fully public firm and the demand for alternative means to reduce those costs would both rise. One would thus predict that where product market rents are higher, then, all else equal, ownership concentration would also be higher.

20.1. Implications for Ownership Concentration
20.2. Implications for Private Benefits of Control Theories
20.3. Twilight of the National Monopolies
20.4. Implications for Going Public and Growing When
  Monopoly Trade-off are Large: A Proviso
20.5. Rents and their Corporate Effects: Summary

Chapter 18's analysis of high product market rents as inducing higher managerial agency costs and stronger stakeholder demands on the firm has implications for current theories of corporate ownership structure.

20.1. IMPLICATIONS FOR OWNERSHIP CONCENTRATION

A currently popular academic theory is that the quality of corporate law largely determines whether ownership will separate from control. While this theory is quite strong for understanding why ownership separation is difficult to maintain in, say, Russia, the transition economies, and many developing nations, it does less well in explaining weak separation in richer, democratic nations, some of which have good corporate law and several of which would not have had much trouble getting good corporate law if the polity had sought to promote a stock market.[1]

The agency cost theory I have offered here poses an additional explanation. Law might be fine, but if agency costs would be much higher after separation because weak product market competition constrains managers only mildly, the founding owners would be reluctant to push separation. In statistics-talk, competitive

[1] See Part VI.

conditions could be an 'omitted variable' in the quality-of-corporate-law literature for the world's richer nations.

To see whether widespread monopoly correlated with ownership concentration (thus posing an alternative explanation for ownership concentration), I compared monopoly power in heavy industries in the world's richest nations with ownership concentration in the same nations.

This comparison examines the world through a very crude lens, one that gives us a 'reality check', not a conclusive demonstration. The heavy industries were the 'usual suspects' for large factories, large firms, and the potential for both high labor-owner conflict and large packets of market power: iron and steel, machinery and equipment, metal products, motor vehicles, and petroleum refineries. I did not refine the crude index: that is, these were the first five industries I chose; none was added, deleted, or adjusted.[2] Monopoly power was measured by the size of an industry's mark-up: if an industry could charge much more for its output than it paid for its input, then it had more monopoly power than a similar industry in another country that could not mark-up its prices as much over its costs. I compared this mark-up ratio to a standard measure of ownership concentration from the finance literature and measured concentration by counting the portion of the twenty firms just over $500 million in stock market capitalization that do not have a 20 per cent blockholder.[3] The raw data is in Table 20.1 in this chapter's appendix, and the statistical measures (which are significant) follow Graph 20.1. The data, although quite unrefined, suggests that nations whose firms have more market power have higher ownership concentration.

I also arrayed a standard measure of political position from the political science literature, one measuring a nation's governing party's 'leftness' versus its 'rightness'. High product market monopoly (or oligopoly) power also strongly correlates with a nation being more to the political left. The theory here is that widespread monopoly profits fuel distributional politics; voters dislike the profits and power that the monopoly accords, especially when owners are visible (not, say, quasi-public entities like CalPERS, but well-to-do families). And the widespread monopoly rectangles provide a pot of value that political players can allocate to the mass of voters and the firms' own workers.

This data is also suggestive but crude. In a complex world, there are many causes and effects of institutions, histories, and cultures, and many economic features vie to influence corporate governance structure and political policy. I hardly mean that we have here captured *the* fundamental relationship among corporate governance structure, competition, and political orientation, but we have captured *an* important one, maybe a very important one, and one absent from the literature.[4]

---

[2] I did not refine the index to weight it by the size of the industry in the economy. (An industry might not be a big part of the economy.)

[3] The mark-up data is from Joaquim Oliveira Martins, Stefano Scarpetta, and Dirk Pilat, *Mark-up Pricing Ratios in Manufacturing Industries: Estimates for 14 OECD Countries* 18–19 (Org. for Econ. Cooperation and Dev., Econ. Dept Working Paper No. 162) (arraying mark-ups for 1970–92).

[4] With 14 nations in the test, a few nations might drive the results. Thus, the United States and Britain both have strong competition and diffuse ownership. One could drop them from the sample, though, and still get some support for the relationship: the t-statistic loses significance, but the sign remains as predicted.

20.2. IMPLICATIONS FOR PRIVATE BENEFITS OF CONTROL THEORIES

As I noted, other features could explain the correlation. The less-competitive nations tend to be civil law countries, the more competitive ones common law countries. Perhaps the legal system induces high (or low) quality securities markets and low (or high) ownership concentration. This possibility has been suggested.[5]

The competitiveness of the economies provides an alternative explanation (i.e. competitive, not legal, differences may drive the result).

Globalization and weakening national monopolies help to explain why the law-driven theory has become prominent in recent years. As globalization reduced oligopoly's rents, managerial agency costs should also have declined, making the public firm and separation more stable.

Thus an alternative explanation for Western Europe's historically concentrated ownership and smaller stock markets arises from product market rents. When the monopolist's rectangle was large, the total value that the firm could *potentially* yield to stockholders was also large. True, the value that the controlling shareholder could shift to itself away from minority stockholders could have been in play. Two important potential shifts in value were in play, each of which could determine ownership structure: one a potential shift from minority stockholders to the majority; and the other a loss from all stockholders if managers did not maximize shareholder profits.

Stockholders had reason to be more concerned with keeping the firm's total value for stockholders as large as possible (and keeping it for stockholders as a group), and less concerned than they would be today about whether the controller could grab some of it away from minority stockholders. The potential loss to stockholders as a group was historically plausibly more important than the problem of diversion to controlling stockholders.

That is, when the 'rectangle' is large, who gets it—the political and distributional contest between shareholders, managers, and employees—swamps the importance to shareholders of the intra-shareholder contest for the private benefits of control. In such settings, private-benefits-of-control theories explain less than they do elsewhere. Controlling shareholders' private benefits and corporate law's capacity to reduce them can account for ownership concentration in important settings, but not when managerial agency costs in diffusely-held public firms are very high and reducible by a concentrated owner.

20.3. TWILIGHT OF THE NATIONAL MONOPOLIES

It is thus sensible that the law-driven, private-benefits-of-control literature is now reaching its zenith theoretically and empirically for Europe. In prior decades, the

[5] Rafael La Porta *et al.*, 'Legal Determinants of External Finance', 52 *J. Fin.* 1131, 1138 (1997).

monopoly 'rectangles' made more of the value of the firm up for grabs among European shareholders, managers, and employees. Managers could easily lose a good fraction of it for shareholders, because (1) it was there, and (2) they faced weaker product market and capital market constraints but stronger stakeholder claims.

As markets have become more competitive, the amount of what is up for grabs among all the players has diminished, while the amount that is up for grabs only between controllers and minority stockholders has become relatively more important now than it was before. And, as the latter became relatively more important, theory and empirical work should have followed, as they have.

Now that there is less bargaining among owners, managers, and employees to grab value because strengthening competition makes less value available for grabbing as those monopoly rectangles shrink across Europe, we can finally focus more on what historically was the smaller problem of the two, the potential diversion among shareholders.[6] As the monopolies shrink, the social democratic politics that they supported recede, and technical issues such as the private benefits of control for shareholders can be more determinative than previously. And as trade liberalizes and monopolies shrink, pro-shareholder institutions become more functional and pressures increase to improve them.

20.4. IMPLICATIONS FOR GOING PUBLIC AND GROWING WHEN MONOPOLY TRADE-OFFS ARE LARGE: A PROVISO

But monopoly cannot always coexist with concentrated ownership: the monopolist must acquire size, and to acquire size it oftentimes needs to get access to capital beyond that which a single person, or a single family, can provide. Thus the locally maximizing decision for shareholders might be to *allow* agency costs to increase, by diffusing ownership, if growth (obtained by diffuse ownership) is the only road to increased monopoly profits. This trade-off in very large economies may induce more diffuse ownership than otherwise: to get the monopoly, the firm must grow, but to grow it must raise capital from outsiders. Thus the monopoly-driven ownership story is more complex than a simple linear relation (of more monopoly, more ownership concentration). Perhaps its analytic complexity has obscured its importance.

---

[6] An analogous result occurred in the U.S.: shareholder wealth maximization institutions, such as the hostile takeover and incentive compensation, came to the fore starting around the early 1980s. It was then that competition in the U.S. economy, already moderately good and stronger than that in most other national economies, strengthened as foreign manufacturers 'caught up' with the big U.S. firms and delivered competitive, often better, products into the U.S. heartland. Enhanced competition reduced the wiggle-room inside those already small rectangles, as the small rectangles shrank further. Corporate governance became more important, or at least more visible, than it had been, often in managing the transition from a moderately competitive to an intensely competitive environment.

Monopoly's effect on corporate structure in the large nation thus would seem to differ from that in the small nation: the monopolist *must pay* in increased agency costs in order to get (or keep) the monopoly, because it must raise capital through diffuse ownership to maintain the size needed (or to get the size needed) for supra-competitive profits. This trade-off in favor of size and more diffuse ownership was easier for shareholders in a nation like the U.S., where employee pressures were relatively weak.

Thus monopoly's effect here looks like a 'U' curve, a shape familiar to economists. When monopoly is weak and competition strong, then all else equal, separation is easy and ownership should in time diffuse. If competition is weak *but control is within the grasp of a family or small group,* the ownership concentration should persist. This would seem to be the plausible relationship in smaller national economies. But if the size of the economy and of the most profitable scale for the firm are much larger, then owners face a trade-off. If there would be more monopoly profits from increasing the firm's size, the potential for increased managerial agency costs pushes owners to hold on to control; but if owners cannot get those profits without 'paying' for them in increased agency costs, then they would, within limits, pay those managerial agency costs, as a price of acquiring those monopoly profits.

This last proviso may be a big one, helping to explain the evolution of the American corporation. That is, it's arguable that American corporate law was not all that conducive to building big firms in the nineteenth century: minority stockholders were not extremely well-protected, information disclosure was haphazard, common law protections were precarious, and securities regulation was something for the future, for 1933 and 1934 or certainly no earlier than the early twentieth century New York Stock Exchange reforms. The scenario we could have is this: despite mediocre law, ownership could diffuse because the only way owners could get the excess profits from large size (either because of monopoly or efficiency) was via growth and ownership diffusion. Diffusion cost shareholders something, maybe a lot, but their increased monopoly (or efficiency) profits paid for it. Then, once the large firms were built, the corporate and other protections could be put in place. There was a constituency of new owners who were happy to see better corporate protections.

(A more difficult question then arises: why did the American monopolies not induce the same *political* effect as Europe's? One possibility is that *independent* political differences between the two, such as a traditionally weak central government in the U.S. and a strong central government in European nation-states, were important.[7] Another is that Europe's *concentrated* owners of monopolies induced a more intense political reaction than did America's *diffuse* owners. A last one is that there *was* an important American reaction: to enhance product competition via government action, to limit financial holdings in industrial firms because they were

---

[7] Mark J. Roe, *Strong Managers, Weak Owners: The Political Roots of American Corporate Finance* (1994).

seen to promote monopoly, and to break up perceived monopoly-promoting financial power centers via Glass-Steagall type rules.)

* * *

To illustrate: the pressure to grow and diffuse *even if* agency costs increased may have once been more important in the United States than in, say, Sweden. The American economy was much larger than that of Sweden, where the controller *could* keep control and *still* have the scale needed for market monopolization. But even in the United States, that period of weaker competition may have been the closest the U.S. came to being somewhat 'social democratic'. Statements of managerial goals cited stockholders as a primary constituency, along with employees and consumers.[8] And one saw controllers in oligopolistic industries hanging on to control for quite some time. The Ford Motor Company and the Ford family, and General Motors and the duPont family (and maybe IBM and the Watson family), come to mind.

In any case, this demand-for-size effect on ownership structure just means that we have more than one dimension in a full analysis. But the undertow of mid-sized monopolies with concentrated ownership as fitting with social democratic politics and corporate governance structures that control agency costs is there.

* * *

The product market focus I offer here could inform the American 'race-to-the-bottom' versus 'race-to-the-top' theory. State corporate law has been seen as a 'race-to-the-bottom', one that provides the weakest possible corporate law that leads managers to incorporate in the racing states. This view was once dominant, and still has important support. Alternatively, the race could be to the top, as the prevailing wisdom now has it: states provide shareholder-oriented efficient corporate laws, so as to attract managers to incorporate in the racing states. If the corporate laws were grossly inefficient, then capital markets would punish the firm's managers via a weak stock price.

Consider two time periods, period one and period two. If product market competition is relatively weaker in period one than in period two, then *identical* corporate law rules and structures in the two periods could have differing 'race'

---

[8] Francis X. Sutton, Seymour E. Harris, Carl Kaysen, and James Tobin, *The American Business Creed* 64–65 (1956), in which leading economists state a managerialist philosophy for the time, and, I would argue, a justification for oligopoly: '[C]orporation managers... [are] responsib[le] to consumers, to employees, to stockholders, and to the general public..., each... equal[ly]; the function of management is to secure justice for all and unconditional maxima for none. Stockholders... are entitled to a fair return on their investment, but profits above a "fair" level are an economic sin.' Although even back then the interests of stockholders were not submerged to those of the other players (as they have been in other nations), 'fair' profits fit with an economist's prescription for an oligopolistically-organized industry. An 'oligopoly-conscious' managerial creed would give managers discretion to invest and expand, encouraging them to 'plow' earnings back into the firm. And indeed the 'creed' so recommends. Sutton *et al.*, supra at 85, 87. Cf. Sanford M. Jacoby, 'Employee Representation and Corporate Governance: A Missing Link', 3 *U. Pa. J. Lab. & Emp. L.* 449 (2001).

implications. The weaker product competition in the earlier period made for more managerial slack that neither product nor capital markets could fully control. This slack could then have induced reformers to call for tighter corporate law regulation and have induced analysts to see the race as one to the bottom. But when product markets become more competitive by period two, the same loose rules could be a race to the top (or at least not as steep a race to the bottom) because flexibility would have become relatively more important and managerial agency costs would have declined by period two. Intense product market competition would have pressed firms to improve corporate governance even if corporate law did not.

20.5. RENTS AND THEIR CORPORATE EFFECTS: SUMMARY

When product market rents are high, managerial agency costs to shareholders are high. They are high for two reasons: managers have more slack; and employees expect a piece of the monopoly rent, which managers may be ready to yield to them.

Sometimes this increased managerial agency cost is the 'price' that shareholder-owners have to pay to get and keep their monopoly profits. But when they can, the owners would like to reduce those agency costs. They have more reason to try to rein in managers and reduce the agency costs when managers have more value in their hands to allocate. To rein them in, and to divide the pie more in their favor, owners would tend to keep their ownership concentrated, as concentrated owner-ship is often their best means to control managerial agency costs. And owners would want direct representation at the national political level, where some of the spoils have been divided. In the political arena, social democratic ideologies should be more viable, because their implementation can be paid for out of the mono-polist's excess profits, not extracted out of the more-difficult-to-divert competitive profits. Moreover, owners found concentrated ownership more valuable than otherwise, and this concentrated ownership induced counter-ideologies and organizations that sought to constrain the rich owners.

As product competition increases, managerial agency costs inside the firm decrease. The rectangle that managers can grab—or give away—diminishes. Political conflict over dividing that rectangle also changes as the pot to divvy up shrinks. As managerial agency costs inside the firm diminish, the owners' demand for con-centrated ownership (as their next best means to rein in agency costs) decreases and their willingness to allow ownership separation increases.

APPENDIX

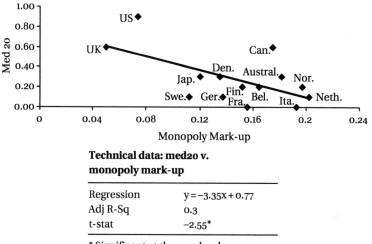

Technical data: med20 v. monopoly mark-up

Technical data: med20 v. monopoly mark-up

Regression	$y = -3.35x + 0.77$
Adj R-Sq	0.3
t-stat	-2.55^{*}

* Significant at the 0.05 level

Graph 20.1. Monopoly mark-up as predicting ownership concentration

Table 20.1. *Mark-up Measure of Monopoly in Heavy Industry* (1970–1992)

Country	Metal products	Machinery and equipment*	Iron and steel	Petroleum refineries	Motor vehicles	Unweighted average minus 1	Widely-held at 20% cutoff for mid-sized public firms
United Kingdom	1.03			1.07		0.050	0.60
United States	1.09	1.06	1.10	1.03	1.09	0.074	0.90
Sweden	1.13	1.07	1.10		1.15	0.113	0.10
Japan	1.11	1.09	1.19	1.04	1.17	0.120	0.30
Denmark	1.15	1.12				0.135	0.30
Germany	1.20	1.06	1.14		1.15	0.138	0.10
Finland	1.19	1.14	1.18	1.11	1.14	0.152	0.20
France	1.18	1.12	1.16	1.19	1.13	0.156	0.00
Belgium	1.08		1.25			0.165	0.20
Canada	1.16	1.15	1.25		1.14	0.175	0.60
Australia	1.17	1.17	1.14	1.35	1.08	0.182	0.30
Italy	1.39	1.19	1.17		1.02	0.193	0.00
Norway	1.15	1.10	1.33		1.21	0.198	0.20
Netherlands	1.13	1.16	1.40		1.12	0.203	0.10

* The OECD data are incomplete, lacking data for some industries such as U.K. machinery and equipment. Some cells are blank because of insufficient reliable data.

Note that the relationship becomes less compelling if one drops the U.S. and the U.K. from the regression. (It was also weaker with later mark-up data.) But still, this relationship might prove important: the mechanism by which the U.S. and the U.K. facilitate ownership separation might be their more intensely competitive product markets as much as any of their other institutions.

21

Political Change in Continental Europe

A plausible test of the political theory would examine sharp political movements to see if corporate structures moved in parallel. Although that kind of precise data on changes in corporate ownership around the world is unavailable, the recent demand for more pro-shareholder corporate governance in continental Europe and for legal structures that would facilitate ownership separation follows European politics' move rightward, away from its late twentieth-century history of strong social democratic politics.

21.1. Political Change and Time Series Data
21.2. Political Change and Path Dependence
21.3. Simultaneity

21.1. POLITICAL CHANGE AND TIME SERIES DATA

As politics changes, the pressure on ownership structure would also change. Thus, one could try to measure political change to see if ownership changes with it, perhaps with a lag. But this kind of longitudinal study is not technically possible right now because the multi-nation historical ownership data are unavailable or unreliable.[1] Moreover, there are surely lags of uncertain length in economic reaction to political change. And, most importantly, one would need to hold the *other* conditions constant. Economic, technological, and institutional conditions have changed greatly during the past decades. It will be hard, or impossible, to do a time-series test that holds these other conditions constant, and measures only politics' effects on ownership structure.

But in gross, recent shifts in Europe are consistent with the social democracy thesis. Economic policy has moved rightward in recent decades in Europe, and

[1] In a major undertaking, the European Corporate Governance Network has pulled together Europe-wide ownership data for the mid-1990s. Marco Becht and Ailsa Röell, 'Blockholdings in Europe: An International Comparison', 43 *Eur. Econ. Rev.* 1049, 1053 (1999). The data are hard to assemble because many nations lack transparent ownership data (i.e. no immediately ready historical databases from SEC filings). Coming up with nation-by-nation data that stretch back for decades (and onto which one could regress political change) is a task for the future, perhaps an impossible one.

Table 21.1. *Europe's Social Democratic Parties Move to the Right*

Country	1984	1995
Austria	3.00	4.80
Belgium	2.50	4.20
Denmark	3.80	4.20
Finland	3.00	4.40
France	2.60	4.10
Germany	3.30	3.80
Italy	3.10	3.50
Netherlands	2.60	4.20
Sweden	2.90	4.10
United Kingdom	2.30	4.40

Source: Seymour Martin Lipset and Gary Marks, *It Didn't Happen Here—Why Socialism Failed in the United States* 275 (2000). (The authors calculate their index of political orientation from data similar to that used in the regressions in Chapter 6; lower numbers are more left, higher ones more right.)

social democratic parties have abandoned many of their first principles, as Table 21.1 indicates. One cannot simply measure 'social democracy' by the name of the political parties in power because their programs have changed, with social democratic parties becoming less hostile to shareholders. Or, descriptively:

A decade ago [in the early 1990s], Europeans (except perhaps the British) overwhelmingly favoured a stakeholder model of society and business. The model took different forms: state centrism in France, paternalism in Germany, social democracy in Scandinavia. But all were distinct from the financial market-driven system of the U.S.

Financial markets were viewed as the enemy...[2]

This European movement to the right could lead to other predictions: as economic politics has moved rightward, diffuse ownership has become more feasible in Europe. As it becomes more feasible, the demand from policymakers and investors could increase (as it has) for institutions that better support diffuse ownership. The recent rise in stock-market institutions was preceded in Europe by a (necessary) precondition: a *political* shift to the right.

21.2. POLITICAL CHANGE AND PATH DEPENDENCE

The historical explanation for the emergence of an institution need not explain its current persistence. Political or economic condition A may induce institution X.

---

[2] Wolfgang Münchau, 'Pondering the Power of the Market in Europe's New Capitalism', Pt 4, *Fin. Times*, 8 Feb. 2001, at 2.

Institution X then could become embedded in the society. Condition A may disappear, but the embedded institution may then persist.

1. *Technological and economic preconditions.* The United States in the late nineteenth and early twentieth centuries had a key political precondition for public firms—the absence of a strong social democracy—but may have needed other forces too. American technological progress and business conditions at the end of the nineteenth century made firms demand capital beyond that easily provided via family ownership: huge enterprises became technologically possible, and a massive merger movement needed massive financing. Not every nation, even today, meets the technological and economic preconditions for large diffusely-owned public firms.

2. *Suppressing financial institutions inside the large firm versus suppressing the public firm's political support.* Capital movement is fluid and can be channeled. Capital, corporate structure, and financial flows attract political attention, and the political result deeply affects the organization of the large firm. In the United States, populist politics historically suppressed powerful financial institutions and their voice inside the large firm.[3] This suppression especially affected the structure of the very largest firms, because the largest American firms were (and are) too large for even the richest American families to take and retain long-term big blocks; for many of the biggest firms, only financial institutions could. Complementary pro-shareholder institutions developed to support distant shareholding in public firms, both in those public firms that were very large and in those that were merely large, and hence the public firm dominates in the United States.[4] In contrast, modern European social democratic politics has pressed on invested capital, and weakened or barred those complementary institutions that support the public firm. Hence close ownership, both family and institutional, thus far persists in Europe.

I offer this path-dependent account—with the original reasons differing from the reasons that explain persistence—for completeness, not as necessary for the political preconditions thesis. Whatever explains the rise of the public firm in the United States and the persistence of concentrated ownership in Europe until now, there are political preconditions to the rise and persistence of the public firm. In the United States these conditions were met early; in contrast, modern mid-twentieth-century continental social democracies until recently mixed badly with the American-style public firm.

21.3. SIMULTANEITY

Europe's recent increasing demand for securities markets might give comfort to supporters of one determinant or another as primarily determining whether ownership diffuses or not. Proponents of a legal theory might look to recent European efforts to build stronger stock exchanges, or to reform corporate and securities

---

[3] Mark J. Roe, *Strong Managers, Weak Owners: The Political Roots of American Corporate Finance* 51–101 (1994). [4] Id., at 7–8.

laws, as supporting their theory.[5] Proponents of a political theory based on the relative strength of stakeholder pressures could point to the sharp rightward movement of Europe's social democratic parties. And proponents of a competition-based theory could point to European economic integration as squeezing out rents and, if not reversed by a political reaction, as increasing the demand for public firms and better means of capital-gathering.

All could do so, but the basic analytical problem is that all four institutions— politics, product markets, efforts to improve corporate law's institutions, and new capital-raising methods—*are moving simultaneously*. Anyone pointing to recent simultaneous movement as ending debate on which determinant is key is over-interpreting the evidence. All we can say is that each is usually moving at roughly the same time in the expected direction, and one just cannot yet tell whether any one is the underlying, primary cause that induces the others to move. Perhaps reality is too complex for such a reductive theory, and each reinforces the other, as small steps in one institution pull along the other three, and then momentum in one of the other three pulls along the institution that first moved.

[5] See John C. Coffee, 'The Rise of Dispersed Ownership: The Roles of Law and the State in the Separation of Ownership and Control', 111 *Yale L.J.* 1 (2001).

22

....

Alternative Formulations: Data

We now have several overlapping explanations for differing levels of ownership separation: the relative strength of social democratic politics; the degree of product market competition; the quality of legal institutions; and standard ones such as the wealth and technological level of the nation and the size of its economy. Here we provide some data comparing the explanations. Even when we add the standard explanations and the newly-popular legal explanation, the political variables retain considerable strength. Politics' strength suggests either that it is a strong independent cause, or that it may even underlie some of the other causes. When politics is conducive to ownership separation, the supporting technical institutions may prosper. And when it is not, they have little reason to flourish.

22.1. THE THEORIES

The political explanations thus come in several flavors: an interest group version is the clearest. But others are plausible, such as a craving for stability in nations devastated by war and economic turmoil, or a backlash against powerful financial interests and business owners.

The political explanation could interact with product market competition as well: product market competition, when weak, could directly raise managerial agency costs by eliminating one constraint on managers, thereby calling forth other means from shareholders to tie managers to them more tightly. And the relative strength of product market competition in a nation could also affect what kind of politics is easy to practice: if monopoly rents are high, politicians have more leverage in dividing out these rents than when they are low.

And we have a potentially overlapping, potentially alternative theory, that of the quality of a nation's corporate law institutions. In its strongest form (which even its proponents would not adopt, but we state it here to make the distinctions among the theories sharp), the quality of a nation's corporate institutions in

protecting minority stockholders determines whether that nation will have ownership separation or close ownership. If the institutions are good quality, separation
will proceed. If they are poor, ownership does not separate from control.

I state the corporate-law-driven theory in more detail in the next Part, and then I
show its limits, both theoretical and empirical. Here I present data to motivate that
discussion: the quality of corporate law helps to predict the degree of ownership
separation. *But when we add political variables to the corporate-law-driven
'model', we get much stronger predictive power.* Law alone does not do as well as
law and politics.

22.2. THE TESTS

Two tests are suggestive. A correlation matrix can set up each of the relevant
variables, and reveal which of them fit together. In Table 22.1, I array two measures
of ownership separation and securities market development, three political measures (the political scientists' index, the OECD employment protection index, and
the Gini income inequality index), two measures of the quality of corporate law
(a qualitative index and an index of the value of the voting right, both discussed in
the next Part), and, lastly, an index of monopoly power.

For the most part, the correlations are as predicted: law, politics, and competitive
strength all predict ownership separation and stock market strength. Two political
indices—the political scientists' index and employment protection—are particularly strong in predicting ownership separation. And the monopoly index and the
employment protection index are especially strong in predicting the size of a
nation's stock market.

A more sophisticated test measures whether a factor significantly adds power in
explaining the results. Take the legal theory: the qualitative index of corporate law
quality predicts ownership separation plausibly. (Another index of corporate law's
quality does less well; more about that in the next Part.) We see in line 1 of Table 22.2
that the qualitative index predicts much of the degree of ownership separation,
with several of the results statistically significant.

But should we stop there?

When we add political variables, we get greater explanatory power, as the next
two lines of Table 22.2 show. The numbers suggest that even if law is important,
politics is independently quite important too.

We could analyze the relationship by thinking in the opposite causative
direction. Starting with law and adding politics, as we do in Table 22.2, reflects a
bias that the technical legal institutions come first, and politics second. But the
political institutions plausibly come first and the legal institutions second. (And it
is even more plausible that the two interact, but this kind of interaction cannot be
readily measured.) If we view politics as coming first, and law as coming along
second, then we would run the tests differently. We start by measuring the degree
to which politics predicts separation, and then add a measure of corporate law
quality to see what that adds. If it adds little, then we would reject law as a

significant addition. This direction for the test is in Table 22.3. Politics predicts well, but the legal index adds to the predictive power. The two do not run together, but reinforce the other.

Another means to investigate the factors that contribute to ownership separation is to look at those nations that do not correlate nicely. That is, one looks for good corporate law countries that do not have much ownership separation. If they are all strong social democracies, then one could draw conclusions of which explanation is stronger, which came first, etc. This kind of inquiry, a cross-sectional one in statistical terms, might be fruitful: there are several nations that by measurement have good corporate law, but weak ownership separation. All are strong social democracies. But the number of nations that we have to deal with is so small that our discussion must be qualitative, a discussion we have next, in Part VI.

22.3. THE DATA

Table 22.1 correlates a set of political, ownership, legal, and competitive variables. All three of the political variables are significant predictors of ownership separation here and of the depth of a nation's securities market. The two legal variables are generally good predictors of separation and stock market depth, as is the measure of monopoly strength.

Some data in Chapter 6 differs from that here, because there are no data for some entries for four countries (mostly voting premium and, for Japan, no comparable GINI). The data gap reduces the number of nations in the Table 22.1 correlation matrix from 16 to 12 nations.

The correlation matrix shows that politics persistently correlates with dispersion: the more conservative, the more disperse is ownership. Several of these correlations are bold-faced in the matrix. The matrix also shows that good quality corporate law correlates pretty well with dispersion as well: the higher the quality of corporate law, the more dispersed is ownership. Several of these correlations are also bold-faced.

Sorting out which factor is the base-line cause is hard. But statistics can illuminate some of the issues. We might want to know if the two potential causal institutions—corporate law quality and politics—are co-linear: is corporate law good everywhere that politics is conservative, or at least middle-of-the-road? And do left nations uniformly have weak corporate law protections for minority shareholders? As it turns out, adding political measures to the legal explanation increases explanatory power.

Table 22.2 first correlates two measures of corporate law quality with ownership separation, showing that each can explain separation. But when we add political measures, the explanatory power increases dramatically.

Table 22.3 begins from the assumption that politics more often comes before corporate law. The table shows that politics predicts ownership separation nicely via three separate measures. But it also shows that if we add measures of corporate law quality, we usually but not always get better explanatory power.

Table 22.1. Correlation Matrix

	Political place	Employment protection	Gini	La Porta law	Voting premium	Monopoly mark-up	Stock market cap/GDP	Widely-held mid-sized firms
Political place	1.00							
Employment protection	-0.41	1.00						
Gini after-tax	0.49	-0.53	1.00					
La Porta Law	0.39	-0.95	0.65	1.00				
Voting premium	-0.26	0.50	0.28	-0.39	1.00			
Monopoly mark-up	**-0.57***	0.35	-0.42	-0.41	0.39	1.00		
Stock mkt capitalization/GDP	**0.55***	**-0.56***	**0.64***	**0.70***	-0.23	**-0.80****	1.00	
Widely-held mid-sized firms	**0.67***	**0.84****	**0.67***	**0.87****	-0.46	**-0.57***	0.73	1.00

* Significant at 0.10 level.
** Significant at 0.01 level. (Not all significant correlations are highlighted.)

Table 22.2. *Law and Politics as Predicting Separation*

Corporate law alone (via La Porta legal quality index)	0.52 0.14 (3.69***)		Corporate law alone (via measured legal quality from control premium)	0.18 −1.07 (−1.94*)	
La Porta law + Politics (via Gini)	0.71**		Measured legal quality + Politics (via Gini)	0.54**	
	Law 0.10 (2.92***)	Politics 0.03 (2.60**)		Law −0.49 (−0.96)	Politics 0.04 (2.57**)
La Porta law + Politics (via political scientists' rankings)	0.76***		Measured legal quality + Politics (via political scientists' rankings)	0.55**	
	Law 0.11 (3.60***	Politics 0.23 (3.30***)		Law −0.59 (−1.24)	Politics 0.27 (2.76**)
La Porta law + Politics (via employment protection)	0.71**		Measured legal quality + Politics (via employment protection)	0.72***	
	Law −0.03 (0.57	Politics 0.03 (−2.62**)		Law 0.43 (0.87	Politics −0.05 (−4.39****)

* Significant at the 0.10 level.
** Significant at the 0.05 level.
*** Significant at the 0.01 level.
**** Significant at the 0.001 level.

The numbers beneath the R^2 number in the one-variable model are, first, the coefficient and, next, its t-statistic, with the asterisks denoting statistical significance. The numbers underneath the R^2 in the two-independent variable lines are, first, the coefficients for each variable, and, second, in parentheses, the t-statistic for each coefficient. The first is the t-statistic of the corporate law variable, the second that of the political variable. Politics always significantly increases explanatory power. For four of our six cells politics is a stronger determinant than the corporate law measure.

For the two-variable R^2, significance means that adding the political measure significantly increases explanatory power.

Sources: The measured quality of corporate law comes from Alexander Dyck and Luigi Zingales, 'Why are Private Benefits of Control so Large in Certain Countries and What Effect Does this Have on their Financial Development?' (Working Paper, 2001). They measure the premium a blockholder gets on a sale of a block of stock over the trading value of minority shares. (A higher premium indicates weaker protection of minority stockholders than a lower premium.) The other data is described in Chapter 6. Separation is the number of medium-sized firms without a 20% + shareholder; this data is also displayed in Chapter 6. Slight differences with Table 22.1 are due to our having data from a few more nations available for this test.

Table 22.3. *Politics and Law*

Politics alone: Gini as predicting separation	0.48***	Political place as predicting separation	0.49***	Employment protection as predicting separation	0.70****
Gini + La Porta law	0.71***	Political place + La Porta law	0.76***	Employment protection + La Porta law	0.76
Gini + Measured legal quality	0.52	Political place + measured legal quality	0.55	Employment protection + measured legal quality	0.72

Significance and data sources are as from Table 22.2. Co-efficients and t-statistics are omitted for brevity. Politics consistently predicts ownership separation; and, of the six combinations of law and politics, legal quality strongly buttresses the prediction twice, but does not significantly buttress it the other four times.

Overall: If one blindly followed the regressions, one could never here reject politics as significantly determining ownership separation. For four of the twelve cells one could not reject corporate law as a significant determinant; for eight of the cells one could reject it.

VI

CORPORATE LAW'S LIMITS

Other forces affect corporate governance and the degree to which large firms' ownership separates from control. A strong theory has emerged in recent years that the quality of corporate law in protecting distant stockholders determines whether securities markets arise; whether ownership separates; and whether the modern corporation prospers. The theory has been used convincingly to explain why we see weak corporate structures in transition and developing nations, less convincingly to explain why concentrated ownership persists in continental Europe, and probably incorrectly to explain why ownership separated from control in the United States. Surely, when an economically-weak society lacks regularity—a gap that may be manifested by weak or poorly enforced corporate law—that lack of regularity and that lack of economic strength preclude complex institutions like securities markets and diffusely-owned public firms. But in several nations in the wealthy West although legal structures are quite good and, by measurement, distant shareholders are protected, ownership has still not yet separated from control. Something else has impeded separation.

We can hypothesize what that something is by examining the calculus of owners and investors when they decide whether to diffuse ownership. They cannot readily let ownership separate from control when they expect managerial agency costs to be especially high. And we need to add to current theory, empirical work, and discourse the basic concept that even American corporate law—usually seen as high quality nowadays—does not burrow into the firm to root out those managerial agency costs that arise from mediocre business decisions. Judicial doctrine and legal inquiry attack self-dealing, not bad business judgment. The business judgment rule, under which judges do not second-guess managerial mistake, puts the full panoply of agency costs—such as over-expansion, over-investment, and reluctance to take on profitable but uncomfortable risks—beyond any direct legal inquiry. (This limit from the business judgment rule is not a 'defect' in corporate law: aggressive judicial attack on managerial error would replicate the costs of government management of business. Something other than direct legal attack has to control basic managerial agency costs, because judicial action here is far too costly.)

The consequence is that even if corporate law as usually conceived is 'perfect', it eliminates self-dealing, not managerial mistake. But managers can lose for shareholders as much, or more, than they can steal from them, and law directly controls only the second cost not the first. If the risk of managerial error varies widely from nation to nation, or from firm to firm, ownership structure should vary equally widely, even if conventional corporate law tightly protects shareholders. There is also good reason, and some new data, consistent with this analysis: by measurement several nations have fine enough corporate law; distant stockholders seem protected from controlling stockholder and managerial thievery, but uncontrolled agency costs seem to be especially high in those very nations.

A roadmap for this Part: I outline in Chapter 23 the quality of corporate law argument and why it is important. I show in Chapters 24 and 25 why when the potential for dissipatory managerial agency costs is high, but containable by domin-ant stockholders, corporate law quality is irrelevant or tertiary: even if it is good, ownership will not separate from control. (I distinguish two types of agency costs: those that shift value away from stockholders to controllers and those that dissipate shareholder value.) Conventional corporate law can contain managerial agency costs due to the shifting of value by thievery, but does not directly contain manag-erial agency costs due to dissipation by mismanagement. Concentrated ownership persists in firms in high-agency-cost nations, even if conventional corporate law quality is high, as long the strong owner can contain enough of these costs. In Chapter 26 I show why the data indicates that the quality of corporate law argument, although it explains transition economies nicely, is over-stated for several of the world's richest nations: in too many of them, even with good shareholder protec-tions, stock can be and is sold, but ownership does not separate from control. Something else has made concentrated control persist.

In Chapter 27, I conclude the analysis of corporate law quality's effect on separation. High-quality, protective corporate law is a good institution for a society to have. It lowers the costs of building strong, large business enterprises. It can prevent, or minimize, controlling stockholder diversions, a necessary condition for separation. But among the world's wealthier nations, it does not primarily determine whether it is worthwhile to build those enterprises. It is a tool, not the foundation.

Corporate Law as the Foundation for Securities Markets: The Theory

*The critical precondition to developing modern securities markets, and the indus-
trial, technological wealth that goes with deep and vibrant securities markets, most
recent analyses posit, is a foundation of highly developed corporate and securities
laws that protect minority stockholders from the rampages of the dominant majority
stockholders. Without such corporate law protections, securities markets, it is said,
will not arise. And if corporate law is good enough in technologically-advanced
nations, ownership will diffuse away from concentrated ownership into dispersed
stock markets. In this chapter we set forth the theory, so that in the next chapters we
can evaluate its importance and its limits.*

23.1. INTRODUCTION

Today's law-based perspective contributes greatly to our understanding the
fragility of capital markets in transition and third world economies. But there is too
much that is critical to separation that corporate law does not reach in the world's
richest, most advanced, nations.

Too many other conditions that depend on institutions other than corporate law
have to be met before ownership can diffuse. And in nations where those other conditions are absent, there would be little reason for public policymakers to invest
deeply in developing good corporate law institutions, because they just would
not be used.

The conceptual problem is basic: current academic thinking lumps together
costly opportunism due to a controller's self-dealing and costly managerial
decision-making that inflicts losses on the owners. The first, self-dealing, law seeks
to control directly; the second, bad decision-making that damages shareholders, it
does not. Other institutions must control the latter and their strength varies from

nation to nation. Owners tend to stay as blockholders if they expect managerial agency costs from mistake or disloyalty to be very high after full separation.

Corporate law *does not even try* to directly control the cost of managerial mis-management or non-conflicted disloyalty, from managers not working hard enough for shareholders. *Other* institutions do. But for these other institutions (product market competition, incentive compensation, takeovers, shareholder primacy norms, etc.), corporate law (other than for takeovers) is at most a supporting prop, not the central institution. And, even if one thinks that law has an equal role to play in both, that supporting props are as important as core institutions in deterring insider machinations and in motivating managers, the two— machination prevention and managerial motivation—depend on *different* laws and *different* institutions (corporate law for insider machinations, for example, but antitrust law for competition, tax law for compensation, etc.). These vary in strength, because of differing national histories, politics, and economic conditions; some countries can, and do, better deal with one than the other, thereby affecting which organization—close or diffuse ownership—its institutions favor. One could get all of the corporate law institutions 'right', but if other institutions are missing that are needed to keep managerial agency costs low enough (or if *other* institutions *raise* managerial agency costs), then ownership will not sharply separate.

* * *

Among the world's richer nations, several by measurement have *good* minority stockholder protection, which the quality-of-corporate-law theory would predict should have long ago facilitated separating ownership from control. But despite protective results that keep the rampages of the majority stockholders in check, ownership has *not* yet neatly separated from control. Our task is to assess the theoretical implications of why separation did not happen, since these counter-examples tell us that deficient corporate law was not the basic impediment.

The fact that ownership did not separate from control in a nation does not tell us whether it failed to separate because *blockholder* rampages were uncontrolled or because *managerial agency costs* would have been far too high if ownership and control had separated. If underlying economic, social, or political conditions made potential managerial agency costs very high and best contained by a controlling shareholder, *then concentrated ownership would have persisted whatever was the state of corporate law in checking blockholder misdeeds.*

Many business features could keep agency costs higher in one nation than another: a weak product market is one; an especially opaque and hard-to-understand business technology is another; an inability to use incentive compensation effectively because it would, say, disrupt relationships within the firm is a third; a high level of social mistrust that impedes professionalization of management could be a fourth; the social politics pressures outlined in prior Parts of this book is a fifth.

Corporate law, when effective, impedes insider machinations: it stops, or reduces, controlling shareholders from diverting value to themselves, and bars managers from putting the firm into their own pockets. When, for example, controllers obtain very high private benefits from control, because they divert firm value into their own pockets, then distant shareholders mistrust the insiders, and are unwilling to buy. Ownership concentration should, all else equal, persist. Good corporate law (or substitutes like stock exchange rules, contract, media glare, or reputational intermediaries) can, by reducing this potential for thievery, facilitate separating ownership from control.

But there is more to running a firm than controlling insider machinations. Managerial agency costs to distant shareholders come in *two* basic flavors: thievery and mismanagement. Law can reduce the first, but does very little directly to minimize the second. American law *avoids* dealing with the second. The business judgment rule has courts *refusing* to intervene when shareholders attack managerial mistake. Indeed, one might argue in only a modest over-statement that in modern American business history, there has been only one significant successful judicial attack on managers for mistake, that in *Smith* v. *Van Gorkom*, an attack the legislature promptly reversed.

It is business conditions, incentives, professionalism, capital structure, product and managerial labor market competition, and financial alignment with shareholders that directly impedes managerial mistakes, *not* corporate law. Conventional, technical corporate law has little to say here. (True, law can create or destroy anything, so law is not irrelevant, but it is a second-order phenomenon: other institutions primarily control managerial mistake.)

Even if one believed law to be central to the institutions that cut managerial agency costs—such as antitrust law to competition, tax law or corporate committee structure to compensation, and so on—one must recognize that these laws differ from the core corporate law that controls insider machinations, and their efficaciousness could differ: one nation's laws might control machinations well but managerial error poorly. Antitrust might handle competition nicely or badly, and that does not require that corporate law handle insider machinations equally well or equally badly.

Today's corporate theory cannot explain why several wealthy European nations protect minority shareholders well, but nevertheless *still* have concentrated ownership. The most plausible theory is that ownership has not yet separated there not because, or not just because, of poor corporate law but because firstly managerial agency costs from dissipating shareholder value would be very high after full separation; and secondly concentrated ownership reduces those costs to shareholders enough.

This, then, is the first limit to the quality-of-corporate-law argument: a good core of corporate law—that attacks and destroys insider thievery—is not enough to induce separation. Recognizing that it or an effective substitute may well be necessary is an important contribution to our understanding of how and why financial markets do and do not develop. But managerial agency costs of another sort must also be contained—costs that come from dissipating shareholder value—and corporate law as conventionally understood does little directly to contain these managerial agency costs. When managerial agency costs are very high, ownership cannot readily without subsidy separate from control.

* * *

Managerial agency costs come in two 'flavors'. One, machinations that transfer value to the managers—'stealing'—corporate law seeks to control. But the other — 'shirking', or pursuing goals other than shareholder value—corportate law largely leaves alone.

Moreover, by shifting our focus from legally malleable private benefits to managerial agency costs, we can see why substandard corporate law persists in a few of the richer, well-developed nations. Low-quality law might in some nations be a *symptom* of weak separation, not its base-line *cause*. If these kinds of managerial agency costs from dissipating shareholder value would be too high *anyway* for there to be much separation *even if* corporate law were perfect, then the players (public policymakers, investors, owners) have little reason to build good corporate law, because it would not be much used anyway.

* * *

A second theoretical limit afflicts the quality-of-corporate-law argument. High-quality corporate law could propel diffusion. But it can just as easily propel concentration. Its effect is indeterminate.

High-quality corporate law makes distant stockholders comfortable with blockholders, because good law channels blockholders away from stealing from distant stockholders and into productive activity (such as overcoming shareholder free-rider and informational problems or monitoring managers, for example). Channeling blockholders away from anti-stockholder action should mean in theory that improving the quality of corporate law could, all else equal, *increase* blockholding as easily as it could decrease it. Minority stockholders have less reason to fear the big blockholders when corporate law protects them. If the blockholders increase value, then we could see more of them develop, not fewer of them, as corporate law quality improved.

* * *

Good corporate law that stymies a grasping controller, or good substitutes like effective stock exchanges, effective reputational intermediaries, and the like, is good for a nation to have. It reduces the costs of running a large enterprise. But it is insufficient to induce ownership separation. Some reformers may thus be pinning their hopes too heavily on good corporate law institutions to propel development in third world and transition countries.

My logic here is that the current wisdom and theory tell us that when the core of corporate law is atrocious, and substitutes unavailable, complex firms cannot be stabilized. This is true, and the empirical contributions here are considerable. Bad law impedes separation. But the *converse* of the current wisdom is often believed as well, although it is false: where there is no separation, law could *still* be good with *something else besides corporate law* impeding that separation. Since several nations *have* protective corporate law but *little* separation, this aspect of the conventional wisdom—if a rich nation gets good corporate law, separation will begin—is thus contradicted empirically, and we need some new theory to explain why.

23.2. THE ARGUMENT: CORPORATE LAW AS PROPELLING DIFFUSE OWNERSHIP

Today's most popular academic explanation for why continental Europe lacks deep and rich securities markets is the purportedly weak role of corporate and securities law in protecting minority stockholders, a weakness that is said to contrast with America's strong protection of minority stockholders. A major European-wide research network, leading financial economists, and leading legal commentators have stated so.[1] One can imagine the Nobel Prize winning Franco Modigliani shaking his head in disappointment when writing that nations with deficient legal regimes cannot get good stock markets and, hence, 'the provision of funding shifts from dispersed risk capital [via the stock market] ... to debt, and from [stock and bond] markets to institutions, i.e. towards intermediated credit.'[2] In a powerful set of articles, insightful economists showed that deep securities markets correlate with an index of basic shareholder legal protections.[3] These protections are important: '[P]rotection of shareholders ... by the legal system is central to understanding the patterns of corporate finance in different countries. Investor protection [is] crucial because, in many countries, expropriation of minority shareholders ... by the controlling shareholders is extensive.'[4]

23.3. PROTECTING MINORITY STOCKHOLDERS

The basic law-driven story is straightforward: imagine a nation whose law badly protects minority stockholders against a blockholder extracting value from small minority stockholders. A potential buyer fears that the majority stockholder would later shift value to itself, away from the buyer. So fearing, the prospective minority stockholder does not pay pro rata value for the stock. If the discount is deep enough, the majority stockholder decides not to sell, concentrated ownership persists, and stock markets do not develop.[5]

---

[1] Rafael La Porta, Florencio Lopez-de-Silanes, and Andrei Shleifer, 'Corporate Ownership Around the World', 54 *J. Fin.* 471, 492 (1999); Rafael La Porta *et al.*, 'Law and Finance', 106 *J. Pol. Econ.* 1113, 1136–7 (1998); Rafael La Porta *et al.*, 'Legal Determinants of External Finance', 52 *J. Fin.* 1131, 1138 (1997); Lucian A. Bebchuk, 'A Theory of the Choice Between Concentrated and Dispersed Ownership of Corporate Shares and Votes' (Harvard Law & Economics Working Paper, Oct. 1998); Marco Becht and Ailsa Röell, 'Blockholdings in Europe: An International Comparison' 43 *European Econ. Rev.* 1049 (1999); Wendy Carlin and Colin Mayer, 'Finance, Investment and Growth', at 13, 33 (Oxford Working Paper, Oct. 1998); John C. Coffee, 'The Future as History: The Prospects for Global Convergence in Corporate Governance and its Implications', 93 *Northwestern U. L. Rev.* 641 (1999).

[2] Franco Modigliani and Enrico Perotti, 'Security Versus Bank Finance: The Importance of a Proper Enforcement of Legal Rules', at 5 (Working Paper, November 1998); see also Franco Modigliani and Enrico Perotti, 'Protection of Minority Interest and the Development of Security Markets', 18 *Managerial & Dec. Econ.* 519 (1997).

[3] See La Porta *et al.* articles, cited supra, note 1.

[4] Rafael La Porta, Florencio Lopez-de-Silanes, Andrei Shleifer, and Robert Vishny, 'Investor Protection and Corporate Governance', 58 *J. Fin. Econ.* 3, 4 (2000).

[5] If the public stock-buyers are non-naive, the selling blockholders are not without self-help contractual remedies to stymie raiders. Capped voting, mandatory bids, and voidable interested-party transactions can reduce or end the buying stockholders' fears if the nation enforces contract satisfactorily, even if its corporate law is weak. Moreover, whether the common law—as opposed to other non-law-based institutions—did in fact well protect minority stockholders during the early development of the public firm is open to question. See Mark J. Roe, 'The Quality of Corporate Law Argument and its Limits: History's Gaps' (Working Paper, 2000); Mark J. Roe, 'Political Preconditions to Separating Ownership from Corporate Control', 53 *Stan. L. Rev.* 539, 586 n.124, 590–1 (2000). But here we are making the quality-of-corporate-law argument, not yet evaluating it.

Or, approach the problem from the owner's perspective. Posit large private benefits of control. The most obvious that law can affect are benefits that the controller can derive from diverting value from the firm to himself or herself. The owner might own 51 per cent of the firm's stock, but retain 75 per cent of the firm's value if the owner can over-pay himself or herself in salary, pad the company's payroll with no-show relatives, use the firm's funds to pay for private expenses, or divert value by having the 51 per cent-controlled firm over-pay for goods and services obtained from a company 100 per cent-owned by the controller. Strong fiduciary duties, strong doctrines attacking unfair interested-party transactions, effective disclosure laws that unveil these transactions, and a capable judiciary or other enforcement institution can reduce these kinds of private benefits of control. (Private benefits also arise from pride in running and controlling one's own, or one's family's, enterprise. On this, corporate law has little direct impact.)

The owner considers whether to sell to diffuse stockholders. With no controller to divert value, the stock price could reflect the firm's underlying value. But the rational buyers believe, so the theory runs, that the diffuse ownership structure would be unstable, that an outside raider would buy up 51 per cent of the firm and divert value, and that the remaining minority stockholders would be hurt. Hence, they would not pay full pro rata value to the owner wishing to sell; and the owner wishing to sell would find the sales price to be less than the value of the block if retained (or if sold intact).

Hence, the block persists.[6] The controller refuses to leave control 'up for grabs' because if it dips below 51 per cent control, an outsider could grab control and reap the private benefits.[7]

23.4. THE ATTRACTIONS OF A TECHNICAL CORPORATE LAW THEORY

One sees the appeal of the quality-of-corporate-law argument. Technical institutions are to blame, we can conclude, for Russia's and the transition nations'

---

[6] See Bebchuk, supra, note 1; cf. La Porta *et al.*, supra, notes 1–4.

[7] The literature focuses, correctly I believe, on corporate law's capacity to contain controlling stockholder thievery. Other features of corporate law—agency theory in determining who can represent the corporation, corporate transactional flexibility, limited liability—are downplayed. Managerial capacity to mismanage the corporation is also downplayed, but it *is* quite relevant. It tends, improperly, to be ignored in the current literature.

The text fairly states the theory. The theory does have some gaps. When the founder is in the second stage of selling out all of his or her stock, the potential stock buyers discount the purchase, the theory runs, because they anticipate a raider buying up the stock cheap and then diverting value to itself. But when raiders compete, the winning raider will bid the stock up to the value of the private benefits of control. Savvy minority buyers would anticipate this competition and pay approximately full pro rata value for the stock when the founder sells. (The theory needs non-competitive—or secret—raiders.) Similarly, when the seller first goes public, the first minority stockholders might also pay nearly full pro rata value, even if corporate law is weak, if the founder credibly commits not to divert value before giving up control.

economic problems. The fixes, if they are technical, are within our grasp. Human beings can control and influence the results. Progress is possible if we just can get the technical institutions right. If we do not see ownership separation in Germany, France, and Scandinavia, it must be because a technical fix is missing, one we can handle as easily as downloading a computer program across the Atlantic Ocean. If it turns out that deeper features of society—industrial organization and competition, politics, conditions of social regularity, or norms that support shareholder value—are more fundamental, we would feel ill at ease because these institutions are much harder to control. (To be clear here, I am not speaking simply of corporate law as just the 'law-on-the-books' alone, but as 'law on-the-books' plus the quality of the regulators and judges, the efficiency, accuracy, and honesty of the regulators and the judiciary, the capacity of the stock exchanges to manage the most egregious diversions, and so on.[8])

* * *

As a self-contained academic theory, there is little to quarrel with in the quality-of-corporate-law argument. It is sparse and appealing. Good corporate law lowers the costs of operating a large firm; it is good for a nation to have it. But we need *more* to understand why ownership does not separate from control *even where core corporate law is good enough*. Where managerial agency costs due to potential dissipation of value are substantial, concentrated ownership persists *even if conventional corporate law quality that prevents diversion of value is high*.

Given the facts that we shall develop in Chapter 25—there are too many wealthy, high-quality corporate law countries *without* much separation—the quality-of-corporate-law theory needs to be further refined, or replaced. This we do in Chapter 24.

---

[8] The best description of the institutions that complement and substitute for basic corporate law is in Bernard S. Black, 'The Core Institutions that Support Strong Securities Markets', 55 *Bus. Law.* 1565 (2000).

Its Limits: Theory

Even if corporate law tightly controls self-dealing, there is more to running a firm than avoiding self-dealing. Ownership cannot readily separate from control if managerial agency costs are very high for shareholders, and law does not directly affect all managerial agency costs. In fact, elaborate legal doctrine—the American corporate law's business judgment rule—bars judicial inquiry into managers' basic business decisions, treating such inquiries as no wiser than government direction of the economy. Other, primarily non-legal institutions control the size of managerial agency costs, and these vary in efficacy from firm-to-firm and nation-to-nation. Hence, core corporate law can at most only be one-half of the central story in understanding why ownership separates or does not separate.

24.1. Where Law Does Not Reach: How Managerial Agency Costs
     Impede Separation
24.2. Improving Corporate Law *without* Increasing Separation
24.3. Corporate Law's Limited Capacity to Affect Agency Costs
24.4. Law's Indirect Effect on Agency Costs
24.5. Even if Laws Critically Affect Both Types of Agency Costs
24.6. Precision in Defining Agency Costs and Private Benefits
24.7. Ambiguity in Recent Legal Theory: When Does Better Law Reduce Separation?
24.8. Limits to the Purely Legal Theory

24.1. WHERE LAW DOES NOT REACH: HOW MANAGERIAL AGENCY COSTS IMPEDE SEPARATION

Managers would run some firms badly if ownership separated from control. Effective corporate and securities laws constrain controllers' stealing, but do much less to directly induce them to operate their firms well. A related-party transaction can be attacked or prevented where corporate law is good, but an unprofitable transaction law leaves untouched, with managers able to invoke the business judgment rule to ward off direct legal scrutiny.

Consider a society (or a firm) where managerial agency costs from dissipating shareholder value would be high if there is separation, but low if there is no separation, because a controlling shareholder can contain those costs. When high but containable by concentration, concentrated shareholding ought to persist *even if corporate law fully protects minority stockholders from the ravages of dominant stockholders.* Blockholders would weigh their costs in maintaining control (in lost liquidity, lost diversification, etc.) versus their potential loss in value from managerial agency costs. Control would persist even if corporate law were good. The quality of conventional corporate law becomes irrelevant in determining the degree of separation: whether quality is low or high, separation will be minimal.

This is a simple point, and it is needed to explain the data that we look at in Chapter 25.

24.2. IMPROVING CORPORATE LAW *WITHOUT* INCREASING SEPARATION

The argument that variance in managerial agency costs can drive ownership structure *even if conventional corporate law is quite good* can be stated formally. High managerial agency costs preclude separation *irrespective of the quality of conventional corporate law.*

1. *The model.* Let:

A_M = The managerial agency costs to shareholders from managers dissipating shareholder value, to the extent avoidable via concentrated ownership.

C_{CS} = The costs to the concentrated shareholder in holding a block and monitoring (that is, the costs in lost liquidity, lost diversification, expended energy, and, perhaps, error).

When A_M is high, ownership persists in concentrated form whether or not law successfully controls the private benefits that a controlling shareholder can siphon off from the firm.

V = Value of the firm when ownership is concentrated.

B_{CS} = The private benefits of control, containable by corporate law.

Consider the firm worth V when ownership is concentrated. Posit first that managerial agency costs are trivial even if the firm is fully public. As such, the private benefits of control, a characteristic legally malleable and reducible with protective corporate law, *can* determine whether ownership separates from control. Consider the controller who owns 50 per cent of the firm's stock. As such he obtains one-half of V, plus his net benefits of control. (In this simple first model, the value of the firm remains the same whether it has a controlling stockholder or is fully public.) He retains control when the following inequality is true:

$$V/2 + B_{CS} - C_{CS} > V/2. \tag{1}$$

The left side is the value to the controlling stockholder of the control block: half the firm's cash flow plus the private benefits diverted from minority stockholders, minus the costs of maintaining the block (in lost diversification and liquidity). The right side is the value he obtains from selling the block at its full pro rata value to the public. Equation (1) states that as long as the private benefits of control exceed the costs of control, then concentrated ownership persists. Because corporate law can dramatically shrink the private benefits, B_{CS}, corporate law matters quite a bit in equation (1). This is the conventional theory that we shall next amend.[1]

We amend by introducing A_M, managerial agency costs from dissipating shareholder value. If those managerial agency costs are non-trivial, then the controller's proceeds from selling into the stock market would be $(V - A_M)/2$. Concentration persists if and only if

$$V/2 + B_{CS} - C_{CS} > (V - A_M)/2. \tag{2}$$

Re-arranging: concentration persists if the net benefits of control ($B_{CS} - C_{CS}$) are more than the controller's costs of diffusion ($A_M/2$):

$$B_{CS} - C_{CS} > -A_M/2. \tag{3}$$

Or, further rearranging, concentration persists if:

$$B_{CS} + A_M/2 > C_{CS}. \tag{4}$$

Quality-of-corporate-law theory predicts that diffusion does not occur when $B_{CS} > C_{CS}$, with corporate law the means of containing B_{CS}. But we now can see the limits to the theory: true, without agency costs, A_M, the level of private benefits, B_{CS}, can determine whether ownership diffuses or concentrates.

But with A_M high, diffusion will not occur *even if B_{CS} is zero, because A_M could take over and drive the separation decision.* B_{CS}, the controlling shareholder's private benefits, are relatively unimportant if A_M is very high. Only when $A_M \to 0$ do legally malleable private benefits kick in as the critical determinant.

2. *An example.* Agency costs as impeding separation can be exemplified. Firm has value V of 150 under concentrated ownership, 100 if diffusely owned. Managers will not steal (law is good enough here), but they will be loose with shareholders' investment in the firm. Unlike a controlling shareholder, they will over-expand, react slowly to changing markets, and avoid the tough decisions. Hence $A_M = 50$. Consider two levels of private benefits to the controlling shareholder: in one it is high, equal to one-third of the firm; in the other B_{CS} is low, equal to zero.

---

[1] On the right-side of the equation: to get full pro-rata value, the controller would have to stabilize diffuse ownership, via voting caps, poison pills, or other means. When he or she cannot stabilize it, the right-side of the equation would have to be reduced to reflect the lower price wary buyers would pay. But as the private benefits term approaches zero (and the value to diffuse shareholders of stabilizing diffusion declines concomitantly), this adjustment would also approach zero.

On the left-side of the equation: some private benefits are matters of taste, preferences for power, family recognition in a family firm, etc. These are not readily containable by law; they might be better analyzed here as part of the costs of control, C_{CS}, as mitigating the usual costs (lost diversification, liquidity, etc.). They also might vary from firm to firm and nation to nation. And the capacity to offload illiquidity and non-diversification might vary similarly. Where risks can be hedged, owners should indulge themselves and keep control more readily than where they cannot. When a controller mismanages more than a professional manager would, C_{CS} rises.

Table 24.1. *When Agency Costs High, Private Benefits to Controlling Shareholder Irrelevant: Concentration Persists Even if Law Drives Down Private Benefits of Control*

	V, firm's value to shareholders	Value to 50% owner	Value to minority shareholders	Notes
Private benefits low: $B_{CS} = 0$				
Concentrated ownership	150	75	75	
Diffuse ownership ($A_M = 50$);				Management
controller sells block for 50	100	50	50	loses A_M
Private benefits high: $B_{CS} = 1/6$ of V				
Concentrated ownership	150	100	50	
Diffuse ownership ($A_M = 50$);				Raider grabs 33
controller sells block for 33	100	33	33	(and perhaps A_M)

Separation *loses* shareholders 50 in profits. Because those lost profits (A_M) are high, at 50, they would seek, and pay for, a structure that would preserve those profits for shareholders. If blockholding avoids A_M (which it does as the model defines A_M: the agency costs that blockholding would avoid), and if the costs of blockholding, C_{CS}, are low, blockholding persists *irrespective of whether private benefits, B_{CS}, are 50, 25, or zero.*

True, if the costs of blockholding exceed A_M, or if the managers can (unusually) pay the original controllers for A_M, or if the efficiency benefits of diffuse ownership overwhelm A_M, then private benefits once again become relevant. The most plausible scenario under which they become relevant is, again, when $A_M \to 0$. But when A_M, the containable managerial dissipation, is very high, this managerial agency cost is the principal determinant of separation, of the quality of the securities market, and, to the extent corporate law is demand-driven, even of the quality of corporate law.

24.3. CORPORATE LAW'S LIMITED CAPACITY TO AFFECT AGENCY COSTS

One might reply that core corporate law when improved reduces *both* the controlling stockholder's private benefits (B_{CS}, by reducing the controller's capacity to siphon off value) *and* managerial agency costs (A_M, by reducing the managers' capacity to siphon off benefits for themselves).

1. *The business judgment rule.* This criticism is both right and wrong, but mostly wrong. The reason it is mostly wrong is simple. Managerial agency costs are the sum of managers' thievery (unjustifiably high salaries, self-dealing transactions, etc.) *and* their mismanagement. Economic analyses typically lump these together and call them 'agency costs'. But agency costs come from stealing *and* from shirking. It is correct to lump them together in economic analyses *as a cost to shareholders,*

because both costs are visited upon shareholders.[2] But it is incorrect to think that law affects each cost to shareholders equally well.

The standard that corporate law applies to managerial decisions is, realistically, no liability at all for mistakes, absent fraud or conflict of interest.[3] *But this is where the big costs to shareholders of having managerial agents lie, exactly where the core of corporate law falls into an abyss of silence.*

Conventional corporate law does very little, maybe nothing, directly to reduce shirking, mistakes, and bad business decisions that squander shareholder value. Elaborate doctrines shield directors and managers from legal action. Unless the directors have conflicts of interest or acted fraudulently, the business judgment rule is nearly insurmountable in America. When that rule is in play, judges shield directors and managers from legal inquiry.

Consider this statement from a respected Delaware chancellor:

There is a *theoretical* exception to [the business judgment rule, protecting directors and managers from liability,] that holds that some decisions may be so 'egregious' that liability... may follow even in the absence of proof of conflict of interest or improper motivation. *The exception, however, has resulted in no awards of money judgments against corporate officers or directors in [Delaware].* . . . Thus, to allege that a corporation has suffered a loss... does not state a claim for relief against that fiduciary *no matter how foolish the investment* . . . [4]

As I said, one does not exaggerate much by saying that American corporate law has produced only one major instance in which non-conflicted managers were held liable for mismanagement: *Smith* v. *Van Gorkom*,[5] a decision excoriated by managers and their lawyers, and promptly overturned by the state legislature.[6]

Nor should we think, 'Oh, this is just a gap in American law, one that could be filled if other institutions fell short in allaying these managerial agency costs. If the other institutions failed, corporate law would, and could, jump in.' One *would not* want the judge in there, regularly second-guessing managers any more than one

---

[2] Eugene Fama, 'Agency Problems and the Theory of the Firm', 88 J. *Pol. Econ.* 288 (1980) (agency costs come from 'shirking, perquisites or incompetence').

[3] Michael P. Dooley and E. Norman Veasey, 'The Role of the Board in Derivative Litigation: Delaware Law and the Current ALI Proposals Compared', 44 *Bus. Law.* 503, 521 (1989) (Veasey is now the Delaware Supreme Court Chief Judge); Joseph W. Bishop, Jr 'Sitting Ducks and Decoy Ducks: New Trends in the Indemnification of Corporate Directors and Officers', 77 *Yale L.J.* 1078, 1099 (1968) (managers without a conflict of interest always win); Edward B. Rock and Michael L. Wachter, 'Islands of Conscious Power: Law, Norms and the Self-Governing Corporation', 149 *U. Pa. L. Rev.* 1619, 1664–68 (2001).

[4] Gagliardi v. TriFoods Int'l, Inc., 683 A.2d 1049, 1052 (Del. Ch. 1996) (Allen, J.) (emphasis supplied).

[5] 488 A.2d 858 (Del. Sup. Ct. 1985). And not just Delaware and not just recently: '[I]t is only in a most unusual and extraordinary case that directors are held liable for negligence in the absence of fraud, or improper motive, or personal interest.' Bayer v. Beran, 49 N.Y.S.2d 2, 6 (N.Y. Sup Ct. 1944).

[6] Del. Corp. Code § 102(b)(7). And 38 legislatures, aghast at the possibility of directorial liability if their courts followed Delaware in *Smith* v. *Van Gorkom*, passed similar exemptive legislation. See D. Gordon Smith, 'The Shareholder Primacy Norm' 23 J. *Corp. L.* 277, 289 n.52. Corporate casebooks have to go back quite far to find other judicial attacks on managerial error, much less find managerial defeats. Shlensky v. Wrigley, 237 N.E.2d 776 (Ill. App. 1968); Dodge v. Ford Motor Co., 170 N.W. 668 (Mich. 1919).

would want the commissar or the bureaucrats in there directing the managers. Most American analysts assume that it would be costly if judges regularly second-guessed managers' non-conflicted business decisions.[7]

2. *Errors by controlling shareholders.* One might refine this analysis by adding a term to account for controlling shareholder error. One could, but the costs of these errors would be smaller than legally uncontrollable managerial error, and, even if not, less likely to affect the diffusion decision. (The controlling stockholder might put up with his own errors if he enjoys control, i.e., the sign of C_{CS} could flip.) True, similar legal doctrines (the business judgment rule) shield the controlling shareholder from lawsuits for a non-conflicted mistake. But because the controlling stockholder owns a big block of the company's stock, it internalizes much of the cost of any mistake (unlike the manager). Because the controlling stockholders, in contrast to the managers, bear the costs of their errors, they immediately internalize their errors, unlike managers who must be made indirectly to internalize them (via incentive compensation, labor market constraints, and the like). Controlling shareholders who make undue errors can sell their firm.[8] Only if the compensating gains (such as power, prestige, and pride of ownership) exceed the costs of their errors (and the other costs of carrying the block), do they keep that block of stock. Managers who make errors do not face such immediate constraints and incentives.

Simply put: controlling stockholders impose the full cost of their stealing on diffuse stockholders but absorb half the cost of their own mismanagement. Controlling managers impose the cost of their dissipation, as well as of their thievery, on diffuse stockholders. Law reduces stealing, not unconflicted dissipation and mismanagement. The point is not that founders and blockholders never waste or make mistakes, but that they bear much of the cost of their waste, while managers do not.

24.4. LAW'S INDIRECT EFFECT ON AGENCY COSTS

We have thus far focused on the effects on separation of conventional corporate law, the law of fiduciary duties, of derivative suits, and of corporate waste. Conventional corporate law can reduce stealing and, where it or a substitute fails to, separation should not be wide. But even if law succeeds, managerial agency costs to shareholders could be high and, when high, ownership cannot readily separate. Institutions other than conventional corporate law raise, lower, and control these managerial agency costs, reducing them via competitive markets,

---

[7] See Joy v. North, 692 F.2d 880 (1982) (Winter, J.).

[8] That is, controlling stockholders might fall asleep, not manage, give away the store, or retire from active management without giving up their position to those who would manage. Cf. Harold Demsetz, 'The Structure of Ownership and the Theory of the Firm', 26 *J. L. & Econ.* 375 (1983). The usual economically-oriented analysis is that they internalize these costs and, prior to falling asleep, sell out their stock unless the shirking managers would cost them more than their sleepiness.

shareholder wealth maximization norms, incentive compensation, hostile take-overs, and corporate transparency.

For these institutions, law is also relevant. But its relevance is indirect. True, law can potentially encompass everything in a society. Law could ban the institutions that indirectly reduce agency costs. Anything can be taxed, destroyed, and prohibited.

1. *Through takeover law*. The relevant law here closest to the core of corporate law is takeover law. Takeovers are heavily law-influenced. True, private actors must commence the takeover, but then the judge and takeover law make it harder or easier for them to succeed. But takeover law—a type of corporate law—only goes so far. First, there's that persistent and substantial premium. For quite some time an offeror has had to offer a 50 per cent premium over the pre-offer trading price in the United States. Even if takeovers flatly barred managers from mismanaging the firm anything beyond that premium, then although takeovers keep managers within a 50 per cent boundary, other institutions (like product market competition, incentive compensation, professionalism, etc.) would be the institutions that kept most managers from straying so far. Takeovers would set an outer boundary, but other institutions must be doing the rest of the work. And since 50 per cent of firm value is quite a lot, those other, non-corporate law institutions are not trivial.

One might reply here by saying that American takeover law is lax, and gives managers too much discretion. Better takeover law—such as that embodied in the British takeover code—would do the job better, keep managerial agency costs low, and facilitate separation.

This kind of rebuttal has two deep problems though: American takeover law might well fail to measure up for shareholders, but America has now and has long had one of the strongest ranges of ownership separation. Even if takeover law in the United States was, and is, imperfect for shareholders, of the world's richest nations, it is the United States where separation is strongest. This combination would, again, suggest that corporate law (here, in the guise of takeover law) is not always the essential ingredient.

Moreover, comparing the United States here with Britain is instructive. Critics of American corporate law often point to the British City takeover code as about as good as we can get. But how much does that improved takeover law get Britain? I know of no deep measurement, so I undertook one of my own, measuring the premium in hostile offers. The Thomson Financial data yielded the typical premium for the United States—50 per cent. And for Britain over the same time period, the premium turned out to be less—40 per cent.

That 10 per cent differential should not be belittled. Ten per cent better management—if that's what better British law would yield—is huge. But 40 per cent, the residual, is much more. And for that big residual, *other* institutions must do the job, and these are institutions, such as product market competition and the like, that get even further afield from core corporate law.

2. *Through antitrust law, tax law, and other institutions*. So, although ordinary but mistaken managerial business decisions and corporate transactions are immune from any direct judicial attack, other institutions in society affect these

decisions and transactions; and law can facilitate or ban these other institutions. But in each case, the other institution is the primary control, with law just assisting or impeding. For insider thievery, basic corporate law is a primary deterrent. The judge bars the transfers, recovers the diverted value for the injured, and punishes the wrong-doer. The judge intervenes directly. But for the indirect constraints, the judge does not attack directly.

Consider product market competition, shareholder primacy norms, professionalism, incentive compensation, and transparency. Strongly competitive markets, for example, can be prodded along by good antitrust law, or lost by bad antitrust law.[9] But the primary constraint is the product market, not law, and law only acts as a secondary, and perhaps sometimes inconsequential, means of enhancing or demeaning product competition.

And shareholder primacy norms, for example, can be facilitated or demeaned by legal pronouncements. But the norm, not the pronouncement, is the direct means to affect managerial performance. Or incentive compensation can be spurred, or taxed. But once again, it is not the tax rule that spurs managers directly, but the incentive compensation.

Although law affects these institutions, law's effects here differ from the effects of conventional corporate law. First off, they do not directly invoke the current core explanation for good corporate law, namely that it grows out of common law and the judge's capacity to stop transactions that divert corporate value into the controller's bank account. Most importantly, law here does not attack the cost to shareholders directly (as law does when the judge punishes a controlling shareholder who diverts value to herself). Law's role is not to attack directly but to enhance or impede the private institutions that would reduce the dissipation. More generally, several of these institutions have the potential to be politically charged, and in other nations one or the other or all of them have been politically charged in a way that the core corporate law of fiduciary duties rarely is.

24.5. EVEN IF LAWS CRITICALLY AFFECT BOTH TYPES OF AGENCY COSTS

One might reject the proposition that law is secondary in inducing good management for shareholders. Law affects these other institutions that control managerial agency costs (competition, compensation, and so on), and one might believe these laws, even if indirect, to be nevertheless important for managerial agency costs.

But even so the structure of my argument persists: *different* institutions and *different* laws affect managerial agency costs than the institutions and laws that affect insider machinations. The two sets are *not* identical. They barely overlap. If one society does better with one set than with the other, the degree of diffusion

---

[9] Strongly competitive capital markets can also constrain managers, but I do not add capital markets to the list where corporate law influence is weak.

will be deeply affected. Corporate law might minimize insider transactions, but the *other* laws might fail to reduce managerial agency costs.

Or, assume arguendo that corporate law, broadly defined, can if 'unleashed' affect both private benefits and managerial agency costs. However if *other* institutions *also* affect managerial agency costs, then corporate law could be perfect but these *other* institutions would affect the strength of ownership separation, via their effect on raising or lowering managerial agency costs.

Distant stockholders have two main worries: the level of managerial agency costs from misdirection is one; the level of insider machinations is another. The severity of each would differ in differing institutional settings, unless serendipitously they both worked identically well or badly. And there is reason to think that the difference in severity widens and contracts around the world, depending on which cost to shareholders a society best minimizes.

24.6. PRECISION IN DEFINING AGENCY COSTS AND PRIVATE BENEFITS

B_{CS} we have defined as the private benefits that a controller can grab from the firm by diverting value away from the firm's stockholders. A typical such diversion would be for the controller to fully own a private entity that sells product to the firm at inflated prices. Dissipating shareholder wealth is not the actor's goal; shifting that wealth to himself or herself is.

But to be precise here, dissipation *would* be a secondary result. To make the transfer from the firm into her own pocket, the controller might have to distort the firm's operations. But her primary goal is to divert, not to dissipate.

A_M we have defined as the value that managers can dissipate in the firm, due to mistaken management. They might over-invest, under-invest, or mis-invest. They might over-pay suppliers or fail to adopt profitable technologies. They might react too slowly to changing market conditions.

But to be precise here as well, diversion could still be a secondary result here, too. The dissipation occurs because the managers could work a little harder, or a little longer, or take on the tough decisions. But they do not. Their action is a kind of self-dealing, in that they benefit from the easier life. But the primary effect of A_M is to dissipate value; the diversion that managers get by working a little less hard is secondary to the dissipation of shareholder value.

24.7. AMBIGUITY IN RECENT LEGAL THEORY: WHEN DOES BETTER CORPORATE LAW REDUCE SEPARATION?

So, when we observe concentrated ownership in rich nations, a currently-popular theory has it, it is probably because they failed to build the needed corporate law.

The relationship will be roughly linear: if other basic conditions are equal (state of the economy, level of technology, etc.), a nation whose corporate law better protects minority stockholders induces stronger securities markets and more diffuse ownership. Conversely, all else equal, a nation that poorly protects stockholders yields more concentrated ownership and weaker securities markets.

Thus far we have seen that a corporate-law-focused theory risks omitting half of what is important to the separation decision, namely the potential variation in managerial *dissipation* of shareholder value, costs to shareholders that American corporate law does not directly control and indeed costs about which it *avoids* inquiry, avoiding it via doctrines such as the business judgment rule. Adding potential managerial dissipation back in makes the demand for separation vary widely even if corporate law protects minority stockholders from thievery and thereby eliminates any private benefits of control.

1. *Offsetting effects.* There is more. Thus far I have accepted the recent wisdom that strengthening corporate law facilitates separation across-the-board in rich, developed nations as well as in transition and developing ones. But even if managerial agency costs are constant (at any initial level of ownership concentration), a theory of separation based on corporate law is softer here than the recent literature has it. Improving corporate law in the world's richest nations *is in theory as likely to increase blockholding as to decrease it.*

Recall the core corporate law argument from Part II. If minority stockholders are unprotected by corporate law, they do not buy or only buy at a discount. With private benefits of control high, the controller *must* hold onto control, because those benefits cannot be sold (other than by selling the block intact), lest someone else be able to grab those benefits of control.

In such settings, distant investors invest reluctantly, fewer firms go public, and those that do retain a concentrated owner. For some firms, in some nations, when those firms do go public, they set up roadblocks to a raider entering, via poison pills, capped voting, and mandatory bid rules. (Managers oftentimes seek such rules to entrench themselves, but such rules keep nasty raiders out as well.)

Consider the firm that is public, with pills, caps, and other charter terms that keep raiders out. Consider two nations, A and B, with A protecting minority stockholders imperfectly but better than B. (Or consider a nation, A, that is moving through law-reform from imperfect but not atrocious minority protection to better minority protection.) *The minority protection argument tells us that minorities would feel more comfortable in 'protective' nations, such as B, or the reformed A, than in non-protective nations, such as the old A.* Hence, if law were the driving force, the 'better' corporate and securities law nations could, all else equal, end up with *more* blockholders in those firms that go public. More controllers would be willing to go public, because investors, feeling well protected, would pay full pro rata value for the minority stock that they would buy. More public firm stockholders would be willing to accept a blockholder, because better law would lower the blockholder's capacity to rip them off.

Blockholders provide critical good services to the firm and one powerful bad service: the good ones are monitoring managers,[10] facilitating information flow from inside the firm to capital owners,[11] and making implicit deals with stakeholders when soft deals are efficient;[12] their one big bad activity is their stealing from the minority stockholders. But if a nation's laws limit their potential to do bad without diminishing their ability to do good, then one could expect that nation's firms to get *more* blockholders, not fewer.

2. *Illustrating the countervailing movement.* Consider the impact of corporate law improvement on three categories of large-firm ownership:

1. diffuse;
2. public, but with a dominant stockholder; and
3. privately-held.

The quality-of-corporate-law thesis assumes that law reform would, monotonically, increase diffusion. Without satisfactory corporate law protections, diffuse ownership would be unstable, with a raider able to capture control and siphon off private benefits. Large owners (in categories 2 or 3) therefore cede control only reluctantly. If a nation improves its corporate law, that reluctance diminishes. Firms move from categories 2 and 3 to category 1.

Consider a nation that has workable but flawed corporate law. Some firms are fully public firms in category 1, but most large firms stay in categories 2 or 3. Corporate law has gaps but it is good enough for some public firms, and a few firms are public with diffuse ownership. The diffuse firms use contract to keep out future blockholders, for example by using capped voting that stops blockholders from taking control. Some firms are sufficiently valuable when fully public that they can absorb the costs of these barriers to controller entry. But most firms stayed in categories 2 or 3, because the dominant owner cannot cheaply enough construct structures that minimize any future grab for the private benefits of control. (Think France, Belgium, or, as usually viewed, Germany.)

Corporate law (or a substitute, or its enforcement) improves.[13] Current discourse focuses on the motivations of the owners in the middle category—those in

---

[10] Andrei Shleifer and Robert W. Vishny, 'Large Shareholders and Corporate Control', 94 *J. Pol. Econ.* 461, 465 (1986) ('our analysis indicates that [by monitoring managers] large shareholders raise expected profits and the more so the greater their percentage of ownership'); Marianne Bertrand and Sendhil Mullainathan, 'Agents With and Without Principals', 90 *Am. Econ. Rev. Papers & Proc.* 203 (2000). (managers in firms with blockholding stockholders have less performance-based pay than managers in firms with blockholders).

[11] Mark J. Roe, *Strong Managers, Weak Owners: The Political Roots of American Corporate Finance* 260–1 (1994) (large owners can mitigate); Jeremy C. Stein, 'Efficient Capital Markets, Inefficient Firms: A Model of Myopic Corporate Behavior', 104 *Q. J. Econ.* 655 (1989) (diffuse ownership creates informational inefficiencies).

[12] Cf. Andrei Shleifer and Lawrence Summers, 'Breach of Trust in Hostile Takeovers', in *Corporate Takeovers: Causes and Consequences* 33–56 (ed. by Alan J. Auerbach) (1988).

[13] Path-dependent drags will impede legal change and if change starts anyway path dependence will slow it. Mark J. Roe, 'Chaos and Evolution in Law and Economics', 109 *Harv. L. Rev.* 641 (1996); Lucian A. Bebchuk and Mark J. Roe, 'A Theory of Path Dependence in Corporate Ownership and Governance', 52 *Stan. L. Rev.* 127 (1999). Here I simply show that even without path-dependent impediments, improving law propels the firms in several directions, not just the one conventionally assumed.

category 2 that fear a loss of private benefits. No longer so fearing, they relinquish control. Ownership diffuses.

This is surely one logical effect of improving corporate law. But it is not the only effect. Consider first those firms that are already public. They have devices that minimize the intrusion of blockholders, to impede a raider from entering to siphon off private benefits. But with private benefits less available, the firm could drop its barriers to entry, as the siphoning—possible when corporate law was weak—is less important when improved corporate law reduces the private benefits. A block-holder can enter if it can add value.[14]

This might be especially so if the reason the firm moved from category 2 to category 3 was *because* the existence of private benefits reduced total firm value. That is, if shareholders and dominant stockholders were always wary, always wrestling for position, and sometimes engineering value-decreasing transactions (by the blockholder to siphon off value, or by the blockholder to 'warranty' to outsiders that it would not siphon off value and that hence the outsiders should pay full pro rata value) then the firm had reason to move to diffuse ownership as the less costly alternative. With this drag on the value of category 2 firms—blockholder versus diffuse stockholder infighting and bonding—removed, the firm could stabilize with a blockholder. (We could use the inequalities in the earlier model: improving corporate law reduces C_{CS} by eliminating the costs of conflict, the resulting sub-optimal operating strategies, etc. Law by lowering those costs of concentration would make concentration more viable for more firms.)

Firms would move to the public-but-with-dominant-stockholder category via other channels. Firms might be privately held—in category 3—because their owners refused to sell out any of their stock at a discount. They might refuse to sell for more than one reason: (1) the outsiders and private owner might not agree on the expected level of future private benefits, stymieing a deal that facilitates the initial sale of stock, and (2) if the firm went public anyway, the total value of the firm might decline as the controllers would know they would have to take on value-reducing transactions to keep their private benefits (or to warranty to minority stockholders that they would not take them).

But with corporate law improved, the blockholder could sell, and investors could buy, confident that future rip-offs would be minimal. With future rip-offs minimal, value-decreasing transactions could not occur (or would occur less frequently and less severely). Hence, more initial public offers would happen. And with future rip-offs minimal, the sellers and investors could focus on fundamental value, instead of the future division of the pie, in pricing the stock in the firm's initial public offer and thereafter.

To illustrate this with numbers, consider a nation with thirty large firms. Ten are diffusely-held, ten are public but with blockholders, ten are fully private. In the commonly used indices of diffusion, this nation would have a 0.5 index of

---

[14] Not all will, of course. Path dependence and positional advantage will deter many. The point is that the pressures here from improving corporate law do not all point toward greater diffusion.

diffusion among public firms (i.e. of the twenty largest public firms, ten have blockholders).

Corporate law then improves. As suggested by current theory and intuition then, five of the blocks diffuse in the public firms with blocks. Ownership for these five fully separates. Owners can at last sell out at full value, because they do not have to worry about a future raider grabbing control and the concomitant private benefits.

If that were the only move, then the standard index of diffusion would jump to 0.75.

But consider the ten firms that were fully public. Five now can afford blockholders because the dissipation of value from infighting would decline, and the blockholder would add value. They can remove their caps and pills, allowing blockholders to enter. If this were the second move, then the index would, when the smoke cleared and all the separation adjustments were made, *end up right back where it began, at 0.5.*

But that is not all. Of the ten firms that were fully private (in category 3), five owners decide that they can take the firm public and, under the newly-improved corporate law regime, investors readily buy up the minority stock. When this third set of transactions is completed, that nation would have ten fully public firms and fifteen public but block-held firms. Five firms would remain completely private. The index of diffusion would have *dropped* from 0.5 to 0.4.[15] Improving corporate law would thereby *reduce* the density of separation in that nation's public firms.[16]

To summarize: *one* effect of improving corporate law is that public firms with blockholders could more easily transit to fully diffuse firms. This is just as current theory, intuition, and policymaking would predict. But that is only one of the effects; overall, improving corporate law has ambiguous effects on diffusion.

This may not just be theory: 'The mean percentage of common stock held by a [U.S.] firm's officers and directors as a group rose from 13 per cent in 1935 to 21 per cent in 1995. Median holdings doubled from 7 per cent to 14 per cent.'[17] As corporate law improved in the United States in the twentieth century through

---

[15] Because the standard index only looks at the twenty largest firms, we assume here that the size distribution is random. Hence, the top twenty would include four of the previously public firms and four of the old public but concentrated firms that went diffuse. The public but diffuse category would include four diffuse firms that took on a now more-trusted blockholder, four that stayed with their old structure, and four previously private firms that decided they could now handle an initial public offering but would stay with block ownership.

[16] In addition, some diffusely-held firms might go private. They did not do so before because of reasons that improved corporate law reduces: (1) the firm's charter barred going private because when corporate law was weak going private was too dangerous in its potential to rip-off public stockholders. And (2) the engineers of a going private transaction would have been reluctant to take their firm private, because they would have had more difficulty doing a later initial public offering of stock when it became warranted. Exit barriers (i.e. via going public later) are entry barriers (i.e. to taking the firm private now). But with corporate law improved, these two considerations fade in importance. Bottom line: improving corporate law could decrease the incidence of diffusion in public firms from 0.5 to 0.25.

[17] Clifford G. Holderness, 'A Survey of Blockholders and Corporate Control', 9 FRBNY *Econ. Pol. Rev.* 51 (April 2003).

Table 24.2. *Indeterminate Effect of Better Corporate Law in an Already-Rich Nation*

	Type of firm ownership			Index of concentration of public firms
	Diffuse public	Blockholder but public	Fully private	
Time 1. Country begins with serviceable but not excellent corporate law				
1. Initial ownership distribution	10	10	10	0.5 (10/20)
Time 2. Corporate law improves				
2a. 5 blockholders sell out	15 ⟵ 5		10	0.75 (15/20)
2b. Caps, pills removed; 5 public firms get blocks	10 ⟶ 10		10	0.5 (10/20)
2c. 5 fully private go public but blockholder remains	10	15 ⟵	5	0.4 (10/25)
2d. 5 fully public go fully private in LBOs	5	15	10	0.25 (5/20)

better securities laws and enforcement, for example, from passable to very good, blockholding increased.

* * *

More starkly: concentrated blockholders have two major roles inside the firm: they steal from stockholders; and they monitor managers. Minority stockholders would see a trade-off and reduce the price they would pay accordingly: pay more to the extent monitoring raises firm value, but less to the extent the blockholder steals from the minority. But if law limits the negative possibility—less, or no, shareholder stealing, because law protects the minority stockholders—then that good law should make stockholders *more* comfortable, *not less* comfortable, with blockholders. Private owners would feel *more* comfortable in selling some stock because they would be able to get full, pro rata value for it, rather than the discount that buyers would insist upon in bad-law regimes. Improving corporate law should, in such settings, all else equal, *increase*, not decrease, the incidence of blockholding.

This offsetting effect from improving corporate law does not tell us that improving it is potentially bad. (Getting more public firms for a nation and separating ownership from control is not inherently good.) Ownership choice and shareholder welfare expand by improving corporate law. But one could not measure the increased quality of corporate law by measuring the change in the number of public firms and the density of separation over time. Corporate law might improve, *and its very improvement might diminish the density of separation*.

24.8. LIMITS TO THE PURELY LEGAL THEORY

Thus, using purportedly poor minority protection from a controller's diversion of value to explain why blocks persist in Russia is convincing, but for Western Europe is fuzzy, or for a few nations may be wrong. If blocks persist in the wealthy West, one cannot a priori know whether they persist because minority stockholders fear the controller, or because they fear the *managers*, who might so dissipate shareholder value that they run the firm into the ground if a controlling stockholder disappears. Even if better corporate law usually increases diffusion in rich nations with adequate but not outstanding corporate law (a proposition open to theoretical challenge),[18] concentration might be due to high managerial agency costs and have little to do with how well core corporate law constrains insider machinations.

If distant shareholders fear unrestrained managers, the controller cannot sell stock at a high enough price and thus she keeps control to monitor managers or to run the firm.

* * *

Beyond that line demarcating corporate law's limits is a region in which this book's political theory is operating, and probably operating quite strongly. Where politics makes managers less sure allies of owners, the potential managerial agency costs (if ownership separates) would rise. The high managerial agency costs would not be from laziness or mistake: managers there could work hard, be capable, and so on. But the *direction* in which they would move the firm would not always be purely in shareholders' interests. Hence, managerial agency costs, not of a general kind but of a specific, politically-induced kind, would rise.

The idea here is not that, say, business schools and managers' leadership skills are weak in these countries (although perhaps schools there do not inculcate shareholder primacy as strongly), but that managers in such countries are pressed to run the firm other than purely in shareholder interests. A_M, broadly interpreted, is higher in nations where such political pressures are higher.

---

[18] See section 24.7, just preceding.

25

Its Limits: Data

If we could measure the quality of corporate law, then we could see whether ownership is concentrated where corporate law protects shareholders and diffuse where it does not. True, if diffusion correlated with high-quality law, the primacy of the law-as-cause thesis would not be proven: when ownership is made diffuse for some other reason (say, technology or politics) then the diffuse owners may demand legal protections. Corporate law might, as we've said before, sometimes follow market development, not precede it. But if, among the satisfactory corporate law nations, ownership were still concentrated in several, we would need more than just the legal theory to explain the result. And the data show that several nations in the wealthy West have strong corporate law protections but weak ownership separation. Corporate law cannot explain these results well, or at all. More is needed to explain them satisfactorily.

25.1. Measuring Quality
25.2. Data: Good Corporate Institutions, Weak Separation

25.1. MEASURING QUALITY

1. *Corporate law: what counts?* Judging how well corporate law protects minority stockholders across nations by examining their corporate law is hard. Not only must one judge which laws are critical (how did Britain succeed without a derivative suit, the very institution that plaintiff-oriented counsel in the U.S. would cite as a sine qua non?; and one that France, seen as a weak corporate law nation by American analysts, allows?[1]), but interaction effects can make a rule that is a loophole in one nation into a roadblock in another. Or a protection might be

---

[1] 1. Art. 200 of Decree No. 67–236 March 23, 1967 in *'Journal Officiel de la République Française'*, 24 March 1967, 2858; Art. L225–252 of the French Code de Commerce (codifying Art. 245 of Law No. 66–537 of 24 July 1966); Arndt Stengel, 'Directors' Powers and Shareholders: A Comparison of Systems,' *I.C.C. L. Rev.*, No. 2, at 52 (1998) (Germany). Germany has the derivative suit in theory (in that the company must bring suit when 10% of the stockholders seek that it do so), but in practice it is left unused. Id.

missing, but an even stronger substitute present. Moreover, the rules-on-the-books could be identical in two nations but the quality of enforcement (because of a corrupt, incompetent, or inefficient judiciary or regulatory system) might make the bottom line protections differ greatly. Or *practices* not required by a nation's corporate law could protect shareholders: a legal index might look bad, but the reality could be the opposite if contractual understandings or business practices counteract a deficient corporate law.

Undaunted by lawyers' skepticism that one can qualitatively assess corporate law directly, several finance-oriented students of corporate governance built legal indices for many nations. They have accomplished a major undertaking, one that should embarrass many (of us) corporate law professors who have not even attempted what the financial economists have completed. They have argued convincingly that corporate law institutions are weak in many third world and transition nations, that these weaknesses correlate with weak securities markets, and that the legal institutions are so decrepit that the public firm cannot arise or, if created by government fiat, cannot persist.[2] These studies could be interpreted (and have been interpreted), less convincingly, to suggest that weak corporate law is the primary culprit for the weak securities markets on the European continent. Not only do corporate players in France, Germany, and Sweden think their corporate law is fine, but they sometimes proclaim its superiority in some dimensions over the American variety.[3]

The indexers consciously do not seek to measure the bottom-line quality of, say, American corporate law but use a handful of proxies. Possibly the index focuses on rules that are not right at the core of shareholder protections, but rather on proxies for a total set of institutions that protect shareholders, a set for which there might be more direct measures. Improving the measurement is possible.[4]

---

[2] Rafael La Porta, Florencio Lopez-de-Silanes, and Andrei Shleifer, 'Corporate Ownership Around the World', 54 *J. Fin.* 471, 492 (1999); Rafael La Porta *et al.*, 'Law and Finance', 106 *J. Pol. Econ.* 1113, 1136–37 (1998); Rafael La Porta *et al.*, 'Legal Determinants of External Finance', 52 *J. Fin.* 1131, 1138 (1997), and the followers. Economically less-developed countries have added reasons why they have undeveloped securities markets. Good securities and corporate rules might come with wealth, and not the other way around. Corporate law rules might be implemented late in a nation's economic development.

[3] André Tunc, 'A French Lawyer Looks at American Corporation Law and Securities Regulation', 130 *U. Pa. L. Rev.* 757 (1982) (French law bans dangerous transactions that American judges weigh, balance, and sometimes approve); Stengel, supra, note 1, at 49, 52 (1998) ('In Germany the liability rules are . . . strict. For instance, the burden of proof is reversed. As soon as the plaintiff shows that the director did not comply with his duties and the company was damaged, the burden is reversed and he then has to prove that he was not at fault.'); cf. Jonas Agnblad, Erik Berglöf, Peter Högfeldt, and Helena Svancar 'Ownership and Control in Sweden—Strong Owners, Weak Minorities, and Social Control' in *The Control of Corporate Europe* 228, 229 (ed. by Fabrizio Barca and Marco Becht) (2001) (hard to find even anecdotes of flagrant insider machinations in Sweden).

[4] Wall Street lawyers, for example, might have reservations about heavily using pre-emptive rights, cumulative voting, and the minimum percentage needed to call a special shareholder meeting—items not likely to be near the top of most American lawyers' lists of Delaware corporate law's most important legal protections—and of abandoning Delaware law for the index where it seems silent. (The index uses Delaware corporate law except on the minimum percentage needed to demand a meeting. La Porta, *et al.*, 'Law and Finance', supra, note 2, at 1128 n.6.) Delaware allows

Organized qualitative analysis challenges legal academics' preference for nuance, anecdote, and discussion.[5] But anecdotes abound, and one can find anecdotes of fleeced minority stockholders on both sides of the Atlantic.[6] One can list differing rules, but it is difficult to know (1) which rules are substitutes and, hence, which countries truly have gaps in protection; (2) which rules really count; (3) the extent to which players follow announced rules; and (4) whether the rules in focus are the kind that securities market players demand up front as necessary to build securities markets, or whether the rules are just the polish on financial markets that comes once deep securities markets exist for other reasons. Some rules are window-dressing, some rules really bind. Which is which?

2. *Corporate law: the bottom-line.* Can we *measure* the bottom-line, overall quality of corporate law? If we knew the nation-by-nation average premium for control and could compare it to the value of the traded stock, we would have a bottom-line number for the value of control in a firm. In nations where the premium is high, we would surmise corporate law or its enforcement is inferior; in nations where that premium over the price available to diffuse stockholders is low, we would surmise corporate law is superior.

Consider a firm worth $100 million, with a 51 per cent blockholder who values that block at $60 million and minority stock that trades for an aggregate value of $40 million. If we can observe those numbers, we have roughly measured the value of control: the controller plausibly pays the 10 per cent premium (measured as a percentage of total firm value) because he or she can divert 10 per cent of the firm's value from minority stockholders into his or her own pocket. If one could measure this difference across nations, then one would have a 'bottom-line' number indicating the value of control. If the quality of corporate law were the, or a, principal determinant of separation, then nations with high gaps between the value of control and the value of the minority stock would have more concentrated ownership than nations where that gap is small.[7]

---

firms to decide the issue by specifying a low percentage in their charter, a right that, I understand, firms rarely use. Sticking with Delaware here would have made Delaware corporate law protection look mediocre, when it is probably pretty good. The point is not that Delaware is bad—the index probably hits the right bottom line—but that developing an accurate index is hard, not a task law professors would relish and one that law professors have thus far avoided.

For a critique more skeptical than mine of the index, see Detlev Vagts, 'Comparative Corporate Law—The New Wave', in *Festschrift for Jean-Nicolas Druey* 595 (ed. by Rainer Schweitzer and Urs Gasser) (2002). Vagts argues that the coding judgments for the German index are incorrect. For instance, although German stockholders are viewed as unable to vote by mail, most send their instructions in to their bank (by mail) and the bank then votes on behalf of the stockholders. Hence, German corporate law is 'better' than the index suggests.

[5] E.g. Tunc, supra, note 3.

[6] Cf. Floyd Norris, 'Perelman's Plan: Take Profits While Public Owners Suffer', *N.Y. Times*, 24 Nov. 2000, at C1; James B. Stewart, *Den of Thieves* 119–27 (1992) (machinations of Victor Posner in NVF, DWG, Pennsylvania Engineering, APL, Royal Crown, and Sharon Steel).

[7] The measurement of the private benefits of control and, hence, of law's ability to keep those benefits low will be imperfect. Some of the premium could come from the cost of assembling a block. Some of the premium may come from the controller's power to decide, say, when to sell, although the sale would be made at a fair price for all. If the transaction costs are high, then a

25.2. DATA: GOOD CORPORATE INSTITUTIONS, WEAK SEPARATION

1. *Trading control blocks*. We have data on the value of a control block. Researchers have looked at the premium paid for a voting block over the pre-trading price. In the United States, it was found to be about 4 per cent of the firm's value.[8] For Italy parallel research suggests a premium of 25 per cent or more,[9] a premium consistent with the quality-of-corporate-law theory (since ownership is concentrated there and corporate law said to be poor).

But in Germany, the control block premium was recently, and surprisingly, found to be less than 4 per cent of the firm's value,[10] inconsistent with the corporate law theory, because German ownership is quite concentrated.[11] To be sure here, the data could understate the private benefits: benefits might have already been taken before the sale and, hence, the sales price would not reflect them. And firms for which blocks are sold could be those with low private benefits, while those where diversion is high do not trade. But even the reduced fact remains that, for those blocks sold, the future private benefits the market expects to be extracted are about equal to those expected in American block trades.

So, the block premium in Germany is about 4 per cent of firm value; that in the United States is 4 per cent. We should pause at this finding for Germany. That German number casts doubt on the pure-form of the law-driven theory, because Germany, the world's third largest national economy, has very concentrated ownership. If control blocks trade at such a low premium there, perhaps something else is driving the concentration.

---

pre-assembled block should command a premium because it side-steps the transaction costs. Hence, high premia may overstate law's weakness because some fraction of the premium comes from unrelated transaction costs, not from uncontrolled private benefits.

[8] Michael J. Barclay and Clifford Holderness, 'Private Benefits from Control of Public Corporations', 25 *J. Fin. Econ.* 371 (1989); Michael J. Barclay, Clifford Holderness, and Dennis Sheehan, 'The Block Pricing Puzzle' (University of Rochester Simon School of Business Working Paper FR 01–05, March 2001) (3% for 1978–97 sample).

[9] Giovanna Nicodano and Alessandro Sembenelli, 'Private Benefits, Block Transaction Premiums and Ownership Structure' (University of Turin Working Paper, Jan. 2000). See also Luigi Zingales, 'The Value of the Voting Right: A Study of the Milan Stock Exchange Experience', 7 *Rev. Fin. Stud.* 125 (1994) (premium for dual-class voting stock).

[10] Julian Franks and Colin Mayer, 'Ownership and Control of German Corporations', 14 *Rev. Fin. Stud.* 943, 968–9 (2001).

[11] Franks and Mayer show that big blocks trade at an average premium of 13.85% over the price of the minority stock. Non-selling stockholders gain over time about 2.34%. That means that, net, the selling blockholder gets 11.61% more than the minority stockholders (from 13.85% minus 2.34%). Since the average size of the block is 36.32% of the firm's issued stock, the new blockholder pays 4.05% of the firm's value to the old blockholder, to the exclusion of the minority stockholders (from 36.32% of 11.61%). If this represented the total private benefits of control (no more and no less), then the private benefits would be about 3.8% of the firm's value. (If the firm's total value is 100 + the private benefits of 4.05, the diversion would be 4.05/104.5, or 0.38.) Conceptually, a premium of 10% for half of the company's stock indicates the controller could grab 5% of the firm's value for itself.

An explanation for Germany is that German codetermination—by which labor gets half of the seats in boardrooms of large firms—fits snugly with concentrated shareholding as a counter-balance in large, especially large smoke-stack, industries.[12] That 4 per cent premium is *less* than the decline in shareholder value measured when Germany enhanced its codetermination statute in 1976 and increased employee representation in the boardroom from one-third to one-half.[13]

The low German 4 per cent control premium also shows why constructing an index for corporate law quality is so hard. To divert big value, the controlling shareholder typically needs a big transaction—a buyout, a merger, a related party sale of good or services. And to get a big transaction through a firm, one needs board approval and, hence, a compliant board. Because the majority stockholder in the United States typically appoints the entire board, it is plausible to expect that an American majority stockholder can readily control a compliant American board. But in Germany the controller can *never* control the full board, because their law mandates that labor gets half of it, and the practice is that banks holding their brokerage customers' proxies get some of it. Other German corporate law features might be weak, thereby generating a low 'index' of corporate law protections. But even so, the German blockholder may be stymied in pushing a related-party transaction through because he or she *cannot* control the full German board. Interaction effects impede putting our finger on the one or two key features that indicate whether technical corporate law is overall good or bad.

True, this German data does not end inquiry: the research, using tests that indirectly measure the efficacy of corporate law institutions, could be reversed or deepened as researchers refine their techniques. But the basic fact persists that the best data we now have does not show corporate law to be uniformly wretched in continental Europe, and thus something other than poor corporate law could be impeding separation. And even if we learned that corporate law were indeed uniformally wretched, the theoretical issue would still persist: corporate law is not enough to induce separation, and if the other institutions—namely those that would mitigate managerial agency costs—are not in place, then the true cause, or at least another cause, for weak separation may lie outside corporate law. Joint forces are at work, and a fix of corporate law alone (if it indeed needed fixing) would not induce separation.

Thus the new German data on control block premium, if it holds up, presents a counter-example, and a very big one, to the law-driven theory. Counter-examples

---

[12] Mark J. Roe, 'German Codetermination and German Securities Markets', in *Employees and Corporate Governance* 194 (ed. by Margaret M. Blair and Mark J. Roe, 1999).

[13] Felix R. FitzRoy and Kornelius Kraft, 'Economic Effects of Codetermination', 95 *Scand. J. Econ.* 365 (1993); Gary Gorton and Frank A. Schmid, 'Class Struggle Inside the Firm: A Study of German Codetermination' (National Bureau of Economic Research Working Paper, Oct. 2000); Frank A. Schmid and Frank Seger, 'Arbeitnehmermitbestimmung, Allokation von Entscheidungsrechten und Shareholder Value', 5 *Zeitschrift für Betriebswirtschaft* 453 (1998); but see Theodor Baums and Bernd Frick, 'The Market Value of the Codetermined Firm', in *Employees and Corporate Governance* 206 (ed. by Margaret M. Blair and Mark J. Roe, 1999); Bernd Frick, Gerhard Speckbacher, and Paul Wentges, 'Arbeitnehmermitbestimmung und moderne Theorie der Unternehmung', *Zeitschrift für Betriebswirtschaft* 745–63 (1999).

are important, but perhaps there is some German-specific factor, not replicated elsewhere, that could make the theory generally true, but just inapplicable in Germany. To check, we turn to other data.

2. *Dual class common stock.* Corporate law's effectiveness can be roughly measured otherwise. Some firms issue dual class common stock. In its most basic form, class A stock votes, class B stock does not, but both have the same dividend rights. (Variations abound.) A controller cannot reap benefits by controlling the class B stock, but can by controlling the class A stock. Both are formally entitled to the same cash coming out from the company. If the value of class A stock is higher than that of class B's, we have a measure of the value of control and of the value that the controller can surreptitiously divert from outside shareholders to herself. If we could systematically measure the differences from one nation to another nation, then we could measure the value of control and, hence, the quality of corporate law in controlling the ravages of a dominant stockholder, as one Nobel Prize winner sought to do a few years ago.[14]

More specifically: posit that a $100 million company issues 500,000 shares of class A stock, which vote, and 500,000 shares of class B stock, which do not. If the diversionary benefit of control is near zero, then class A and class B stock should trade at the same price. If weak law allows the controlling shareholder to divert $10 million in value from the minority stockholders into his own pocket, then the class A stock should trade for about $60 million in the aggregate, the class B for $40 million. The quality-of-corporate-law theory would then predict that, in gross, as the value of control went up, ownership concentration would increase. And vice versa: as the value of control decreased, controllers would loosen their grip and ownership would diffuse.

Unpublished voting premium data has recently become available. Table 25.1 shows the voting premium in the world's richer nations. Italy's and France's voting premium is high, America's low—a difference consistent with the legal theory, as Italy is reputed to have poor protections and has concentrated ownership, and the United States the converse. But this new data increases the tension for the legal theory; Germany is a weak corporate law nation in the finance economists' indices, but the dual class numbers here *again* show it protects non-voting stockholders rather well, vindicating defenders of the quality of German corporate law. And four Scandinavian nations all have *very* concentrated ownership but protect minority stockholders well.

This dual class premium data casts some doubt on whether a uni-variable model is enough to explain the richer nations' degree of ownership separation. True, the data is sparse. And further confirmation, with data collected by other

---

[14] Franco Modigliani and Enrico Perotti, 'Protection of Minority Interest and the Development of Security Markets', 18 *Managerial & Dec. Econ.* 519, 525 (1997). Modigliani and his co-author sought to prove that the dual class premium varied with the quality of a nation's security market. They had a smaller, and less up-to-date sample of seven nations' voting premia. The current dual class data better measures the premia and the implied quality of legal protections, but as we shall see shortly the new premia data still does not predict the degree to which ownership separates from control.

Table 25.1. *Voting Premium and Ownership Concentration*

Country	Voting premium	Portion of large firms that are widely-held
Australia	0.23	0.65
Canada	0.03	0.60
Denmark	0.01	0.40
Finland	0.00	0.35
France	0.28	0.60
Germany	0.10	0.50
Italy	0.29	0.20
Norway	0.06	0.25
Sweden	0.01	0.25
Switzerland	0.05	0.60
United Kingdom	0.10	1.00
United States	0.02	0.80

Source: Voting premium data comes from Tatiana Nenova, 'The Value of Corporate Votes and Control Benefits: A Cross-Country Analysis' (Harvard University Working Paper, 21 Sept. 2000); the ownership concentration data comes from La Porta *et al.*, Corporate Ownership, supra, note 2. The percentage of widely-held firms for a nation is the percentage of the nation's twenty largest firms that lack a 20% or larger blockholder. Technical cautions are discussed below in the text.

researchers, would be needed before drawing even tentative conclusions. The number of observations—a dozen or so of the richer nations—is low.

And, the dual class data as measuring the value of control is soft. If the controller has a majority of the class A voting stock, then the researchers are observing the trading value of the minority stockholders on the class A level, and comparing that data to the trading value of the non-voting class B stock. But the minority class A stockholder is not a controller; it just has a chance of sometime joining a control block.[15]

Improvements in time in *some* aspects of corporate law could actually widen the disparity between voting and non-voting stock: posit that there are uncontrolled private benefits. The minority class A does not get them, so the difference between the traded A shares and the non-voting B shows up as small: *both* have been victimized by shifts in value to the controller (who owns a majority of A), but the trading values show no voting stock premium, because the minority in A are not needed by a controller to assume control. Assume next that that nation *thereafter* presents a mandatory bid rule, one that requires an outsider to bid for all of the voting stock A at the same price when seeking control, but that does not require a bid for B. This means that the controller must share any sale premium with the

---

[15] Statistical analyses could try to control this problem, by observing the value of the vote when control is incomplete, i.e. what's the premium for the minority of stock A when there's a 40% shareholder? The incomplete control means that the other stock's vote *could* be decisive for a controlling coalition. See Tatiana Nenova, 'The Value of Corporate Votes and Control Benefits: A Cross-Country Analysis' (Harvard University Working Paper, 21 Sept. 2000); Zingales, supra, note 9. Such calculations are inherently imprecise.

minority voting stock (driving up its price) but not with the non-voting stock. The disparity in value between A and B might widen even as one aspect of corporate law was improved.

Thus while this is the best dual class data set available, it is imperfect for our purposes. We can take comfort in that ancillary information comports with the numbers. The American premium is low, and U.S. corporate and securities law is usually seen as highly protective. The Swedish premium is low as well, and Swedish researchers assert that there are not even anecdotal instances of controllers shifting value to themselves. Two Scandinavian researchers tell us that 'the value of control does not derive from the possibility to expropriate the fringe of minority shareholders... [but] has to be motivated by some other economic motives.'[16] Other Swedish researchers report that

Outside shareholders do not refrain [from] investing on the Stockholm Stock Exchange since 55% of the Swedish population own shares...and 33% of outstanding shares are owned by foreign investors.... [T]he ratio of the stock market capitalization held by minority share-holders in relation to GDP...is 0.51 for Sweden compared to 0.58 for the U.S.... [I]t is not likely that weak investor protection has hampered financial market development in Sweden....[17]

The other Scandinavian nations have similar reputations, and they also have low premiums. Moreover, the leading blockholding Swedish investor typically uses dual class stock, but not in a way that locks up control: the Wallenberg family holding company does not take majority control but more typically ends up with 5 per cent of the cash flow and 25 per cent (not a majority) of the votes,[18] leaving potential control in the other 75 per cent of the votes. And although the German voting premium is low compared to the usual prejudice, it also comports with the more direct measure of control block premiums recently measured by two leading financial researchers, at roughly 5 per cent of the firm's value.[19] Thus the rankings seem roughly in order, and they may be hazily sketching for us something important about how corporate law quality is not enough to determine the depth of a securities market in the world's richest nations.[20]

[16] Clas Bergström and Kristian Rydqvist, 'The Determinants of Corporate Ownership—An Empirical Study on Swedish Data', 14 J. Banking & Fin. 237 (1990) (emphasis supplied).

[17] Martin Holmén and Peter Högfeldt, 'Corporate Control and Security Design in Initial Public Offerings' 38, 39 (Stockholm School of Economics Working Paper, 15 Dec. 1999) (emphasis supplied).

[18] Eric Leser and Anne-Marie Rocco, 'Les Wallenberg veulent faire cohabiter capitalisme familial et mondialisation', Le Monde, 24 Nov. 2000, at 23.

[19] Franks and Mayer, supra, note 10, at 968–69. They attribute ownership concentration though to the high private benefits of control, although the number they found is on the low side world-wide. Other researchers have recently found German bankers able to extract little or nothing in the way of private benefits of control. Gary Gorton and Frank A. Schmid, 'Universal Banking and the Performance of German Firms', 58 J. Fin. Econ. 29, 70 (2000).

[20] And, as long as the 'real' premium varies in tandem from nation to nation then, even if under-stated, the comparisons can be made. We can take some further comfort from the data in that a well-known winner of the Nobel Prize thought it the best available way to measure legal quality. He was, however, working with what has become stale data. Modigliani and Perotti, supra, note 2, at 524–25.

Other data is available. When blockholders sell their blocks, they presumably get a premium for the private benefits of control where corporate law is weak. A low premium ought to indicate good corporate law. I have used the premium on sale-of-control in Table 22.2 (on the right side) and Table 22.3 (in the third row) as an indicator of minority stockholder protection. Although it does better than the voting premium data in predicting separation, it only weakly predicts ownership separation in the wealthy West. Indeed, the political measures—GINI, employment protection, and political scientists' rankings—are usually better at predicting separation and often dominate these legal measures.

* * *

To repeat a proviso: I hardly mean that this data tells us that high-quality corporate and securities law is irrelevant. Rather, some rich nations do protect minority stockholders, *but ownership still remains close* and securities ownership does *not* diffuse. The point in this Part is *not* that good corporate law is irrelevant in the world's richer nations—it keeps the costs of running a big enterprise low— *but when it is already pretty good, subtle gradations in its quality do not determine whether ownership diffuses.* Something else is much more important, with the leading alternative hypothesis being that high managerial potential to dissipate value precludes separation even if corporate law quality is high.

3. *And the not-so-rich nations?* One might observe that many poorer nations have decrepit corporate law institutions. This is true, and possibly weak corporate law is keeping them back, but even there the coincidence of bad law and a bad economy does not tell us enough. To learn that, say, Afghanistan has poor corporate law does not tell us as a matter of logic whether the absence of public firms is primarily due to its weak corporate law or, as one would suspect as a matter of judgment, to its *other* weak institutions. If the other institutions, particularly the other property rights institutions, are decrepit, these may be, and one suspects are, the critical debilities preventing Afghanistan from developing both the wealth and sufficiently complex private institutions that ready it for public firms and ownership diffusion. Only *then* when it gets that far, will we be able to tell whether weak corporate law holds it back further. The omitted variable in some of the legal theory conjectures might be weak property rights institutions generally, with weak corporate law institutions just being a visible, and perhaps minor, surface manifestation of the deeper weakness.

4. *Enforcing contracts.* Bad law sufficiently explains weak securities markets where law is *so* weak that even *basic contracts* cannot be enforced—as they cannot be in contemporary Russia, many transition economies, and significant parts of the less developed world—thereby rendering complex corporate institutions impossible.[21] This is important because (1) the quality of contract law one would surmise correlates with the quality of corporate law, and (2) much that is useful in

---

[21] Bernard S. Black and Reinier Kraakman, 'A Self-Enforcing Model of Corporate Law', 109 *Harv. L. Rev.* 1911 (1996) (Russia); Jeffrey D. Sachs and Katharina Pistor, 'Introduction: Progress, Pitfalls, Scenarios, and Lost Opportunities', in *The Rule of Law and Economic Reform in Russia* 1, 3 (ed. by Jeffrey D. Sachs and Katharina Pistor, 1997).

corporate law can be built out of good contract law, either directly by public authorities or indirectly by private parties.

Many of the same nations that by measurement have good corporate law *also* have good contract law. All the Scandinavian nations, Germany, and several other continental European countries enforce contract *as well as* the United States does.[22] This casts more doubt on whether the quality-of-corporate-law thesis explains enough of why ownership separates or does not in the world's richer nations. Contract law seems good, and corporate law, which also seems good, is in many dimensions a special form of contract law. Nations that can build one business law institution should be able to build the other, if they wanted to. And the rudiments of a corporate law can, in primitive form, be built out of contract.

Studies of business climate are consistent: continental Europe and the Anglo-Saxon basic *business* institutions are generally seen as *equally* business-friendly, but the continental European *labor* markets are seen as much *less* business-friendly.[23]

Nor is it logically correct to assume that where corporate rules are weakly enforced, that weakness is the *primary* cause for weak stock markets in nations that have already built satisfactory contract and property institutions. Were the demand for diffuse ownership sufficiently strong in such nations, investors and firms could try to build the institutions needed for good securities markets. If societies that successfully built *other* complex business and legal institutions, especially those that effectively enforce commercial contracts, did not try to build these corporate law institutions, then a deeper reason might explain why they did not try.

Thus, one could synthesize the legal and the politically-driven managerial agency cost theories into a two-step argument: when corporate law, contract law, and court systems are decrepit, public firms will not emerge because the system fails to protect minority stockholders. This probably describes Russia, some transition nations, and some developing nations. Such nations might fail to build good corporate law because of generalized institutional failure, manifested in an inability to build good property and contract institutions, or because of a specific, local institutional inability to build good corporate law institutions. But when either contract or basic corporate law becomes satisfactory, as it is in several Western European nations and the United States, then whether a nation builds on what it has (by writing complex contracts, by further improving corporate law, or by developing the ancillary institutions such as stock exchanges or effective

---

[22] Gerald P. O'Driscoll, Kim R. Holmes, and Melanie Kirkpatrick, *2001 Index of Economic Freedom* 18 (2001) (Denmark, Finland, Germany, Norway, Sweden, and the United States protect private property and contract strongly and have largely efficient legal systems). The index, a crude one, purports to measure both property rights and 'the ability of individuals and businesses to enforce contracts'. Id. at 57. Cf. Ross Levine, 'Law, Finance, and Economic Growth', 8 *J. Fin. Intermediation* 8, 14–15, 20 (1999) (risk that government will not respect a contract it has signed: low for the United States, but *lower* for France, Germany, and Scandinavia).

[23] Jeffrey D. Sachs and Andrew M. Warner, 'Executive Summary', in *World Economic Forum, The Global Competitiveness Report* 1998, at 24.

intermediaries) becomes a question of whether the underlying politics—and the underlying potential for low managerial agency costs to shareholders—make it profitable for the players to do so.

APPENDIX

Table 25.2. *Law, Via Voting Premium, as Inconclusive in Predicting Separation*

Explanatory power of voting premium in 12 rich nations	Coefficient	Adj R-sq	t-stat
top20	0.01	−0.10	0.01
top10	0.09	−0.10	0.10
med20	−1.24	0.15	−1.72
med10	−0.67	0.08	−1.39
Dom Mkt Cap/GDP	−0.55	−0.02	−0.87

26

The Quality of Corporate Law and Its Limits

Good corporate law helps to build large firms, securities markets, and structures with ownership separation. The world is a complex place, and there is room for more than one important explanation for what allows ownership separation. But good corporate law is insufficient to induce separation, because corporate law does not seek to control managerial agency costs from poor decisions, only the costs to minority stockholders from insider thievery. The latter is important, but there is much more to running a firm than avoiding diversions of value. In nations and firms in which managerial agency costs would remain high in the public firm, ownership separation will proceed only haltingly, or not at all.

I have not here denied the value of strong corporate law that protects distant stockholders, nor denigrated its usefulness in building efficacious business enterprises, nor refuted its academic utility in explaining some key aspects of corporate differences around the world, especially in transition and third world nations. It is valuable in protecting distant shareholders, as it is often the lowest cost means to protect them. It is useful in thereby building big firms. And it is helpful in explaining corporate structures in the world's developing and transition economies, many of which cannot yet establish good enforceable corporate rules. It may interact to some extent with economic conditions even in the world's richer nations by lowering the costs of going public and separating ownership from control.

I have instead examined the limits to the quality-of-corporate-law argument. High-quality corporate law is insufficient to induce ownership separation in the world's richest, most economically-advanced nations. Technologically-advanced nations in the wealthy West can have the potential for fine corporate law in theory, and several have it in practice, but ownership will *not* separate from control if managerial agency costs are high. And managerial agency costs, unlike insider self-dealing, are not closely controlled by corporate law. Indeed corporate law's business judgment rule has corporate law avoid dealing with managerial agency costs. If law is still relevant, the laws involved would be elsewhere in the system, including antitrust laws, tax laws on incentive compensation, and the like.

An academic theory explaining corporate structures as deriving primarily from corporate law's shareholder protections leaves too many unanswered questions. Why does strong, pro-minority shareholder corporate law not lead to *more* blockholders, instead of fewer, because distant minority stockholders would have *less* to fear of controllers' trampling as law improved? Why do some rich nations lacking even *a single anecdote* of over-reaching behavior by controllers nevertheless lack strong separation? Why are there so many rich nations with low control benefits by measurement, high-quality corporate institutions by anecdote, and much minority stock by statistical comparison, yet without ownership separating from control?

By examining a restricted sample of the world's richest nations we can move toward two conclusions, one strong and the other weak. The strong one focuses on rich nations in the wealthy West: studies that examine corporate law the world-over over-predict the importance of corporate law in the world's richest nations. These nations—where contract can usually be nicely enforced—should not have much trouble developing satisfactory corporate law or good substitutes. Some, by measurement, already have. If ownership still has not separated widely there, then other institutional explanations are probably in play. The weak conclusion focuses on the world's transition and developing nations. We cannot conclude that improving corporate law is irrelevant for them, because we have only examined here the restricted set of the world's richest nations. But it is possible that the development agencies may laudably do everything right in getting the corporate law institutions of these nations ready for ownership separation, and no one might come to the party.

The quality of conventional corporate law does not fully explain why and when ownership concentration persists in the wealthy West, because *corporate law does not even try directly to control managerial agency costs from dissipating a firm's value.* The American business judgment rule keeps courts and law out of basic business decisions and *that* is where managers can lose, or make, the really big money for shareholders. Non-legal institutions principally control these costs. In nations where those *other* institutions, such as product competition or incentive compensation, fail or do less well, managerial dissipation would be higher and ownership cannot as easily separate from control as it can where dissipation is lower. Corporate law quality can be high, private benefits of control low, but if managerial agency costs from dissipation are high, separation will not proceed.

Even if we believed law to be critical to building these *other* institutions, my analysis would persist because *different* laws support the agency cost controlling institutions (antitrust and product market competition; tax law and incentive compensation, etc.). Even when we expand corporate law into its broadest possible terms, we see that two problems must both be resolved inside the firm before ownership can separate: the private benefits of control must be reduced *and* managerial agency costs must be acceptably low after separation. Even if legal institutions lowered both equally—a dubious equality, I have argued—the problem of differing levels in the two costs to shareholders would persist. If variation in *other* institutions raises one greatly—say, pushing up the level of managerial agency costs—then separation could be stymied. If the other institutions vary widely enough, corporate law—even corporate law writ wide—would no longer primarily determine the degree of separation.

A nation need not both deter grabbing insiders and motivate managers equally; and to the extent that it does one better than the other, it affects concentration and diffusion: the diffusion decision is based on the *sum* of private benefits of control and managerial agency costs. Even if traditional corporate law drives private benefits to zero, concentration should persist if managerial agency costs are high.

Data is consistent. Several nations have, by measurement, good corporate law (or at least well-protected minority shareholders), but not much diffusion and separation. These nations also have a high potential for managerial agency costs: relatively weaker product market competition and relatively stronger political pressures on managers to disfavor shareholders.

The quality of a nation's corporate law cannot be the only explanation for why diffuse Berle-Means firms grow and dominate. Perhaps, for some countries at some times, it is not even the principal one.

VII

UNIFYING TWO POLITICAL THEORIES

Democracies everywhere rein in shareholders. Political stability may historically have been impossible where they were not reined in. Or, at least, pure shareholders usually lacked the votes to get their agenda through without compromise. So they did not get a pure shareholder agenda through, and they compromised. But the way shareholders were reined in has differed around the world: financial institutions in the United States were hamstrung from playing a big role inside the large industrial firm, but the range of actions that shareholders' representatives could take vis-à-vis labor was not hemmed in. In much of the rest of the world, labor markets have been more protected, with the range of action for shareholders restricted, but without restrictions on financial institutions that were as tight as they had been in the United States. In some nations, governments played a large role in the economy, often protecting some classes of workers from corporate change. The politics of cabining in shareholders has differed around the world, not just in degree but also in kind, and these differences deeply affected corporate governance structures.

27

....

Populism and Socialism in Corporate Governance

American-style populism and European-style social democracy are differing sides of the same political coin. The polity pays up to affect corporate governance institutions. The deep structure of the political goal has been similar—reining in capital—but the means and degree have differed. And these differences have deeply affected corporate governance, militating toward differing ownership and govern-ance structures.

Democratic polities have a hard time reconciling themselves with pure, strong shareholder values. Democracy usually wedges open gaps between shareholders and the firm, although the means of wedging the two apart, and the size of any gap, differ from nation to nation. Pure shareholder voice can be muffled in some nations, by, say, suppressing one breed of shareholder, such as the powerful financial institution with a strong say inside the industrial firm. American-style populism did this. Or the range and force of capital can be constricted by rules, norms, or labor structures that preclude shareholders from rapidly laying off employees or quickly changing the nature of the work place. Continental-European-style social democracy did this. Or a society can set up informal constraints so that a wide class of employees cannot be fired. Post-war Japan did this.

Each political impulse calls forth distinctive corporate ownership structures: once financial institutions are suppressed, then as long as capital is otherwise free to tie managers to shareholders, the diffusely-held public firm prospers. Once labor is strongly protected and capital is restricted from acting too negatively on labor, that tends to call forth fewer diffuse-held public firms, especially if the means that would make managers loyal to shareholders are denigrated.

In each case what is at work is a democratic polity's reluctance to facilitate strong, unmodulated shareholder voice.

* * *

The goal here has not been to show some gross inefficiency in one corporate governance system or another. Concentrated ownership looked good in the 1980s, when German and Japanese industry seemed to out-compete several American industrial sectors. Diffuse ownership looks good now, as it is associated with advanced technologies and rapid adaptation. Lost in the debate is the possibility that each has some advantages, for some industries, for some firms, for some periods of the firms' life cycle. Politics, by skewing firms to one type of ownership and governance system, probably denies each some variety in organizational form.

* * *

Capital movement is fluid and can be channeled. Capital, corporate structure, and financial flows attract political attention, and the political result deeply affects the organization of the large firm. In the United States, populist politics historically suppressed powerful financial institutions and their voice inside the large firm.[1] This suppression especially affected the structure of the very largest firms, because the largest American firms were (and for the most part still are) too large for even the richest American families to take and retain long-term big blocks; for many of the biggest firms, only financial institutions could.[2] Complementary pro-shareholder institutions developed to support distant shareholding in public firms, both in those public firms that were very large and in those that were merely large, and hence the public firm dominates in the United States.[3] In contrast, modern European social democratic politics pressed on invested capital, and weakened or barred those complementary institutions that support the diffusely-owned public firm. Hence, close ownership, both family and institutional, has thus far persisted in Europe.

---

[1] Mark J. Roe, *Strong Managers, Weak Owners: The Political Roots of American Corporate Finance* 1–101 (1994).

[2] A look at the Forbes list of richest Americans quickly tells us why: the richest for the most part already have big blocks in a single firm (Gates in Microsoft; Dell in Dell). For them to take a big block of stock in another firm, they would have to give up the block they have. In effect the 'supply' of very rich people is small in relation to the supply of very large firms.

[3] Roe, supra, note 1, at 7–8.

Conclusion

Political conditions affect whether the large public firm can arise and prosper, and whether ownership can easily separate from control. In the United States these conditions have been in place for quite some time; in contrast, modern continental social democracies historically mixed badly with the American-style public firm.

The American-style public corporation is a fragile contraption, filled with contradictions, easy to destabilize and destroy. Although it dominates American business, due to its counter-balancing ability to agglomerate capital and efficiently spread private risk, it needs multiple preconditions to arise, survive, and prosper. One powerful precondition is that shareholders if they disperse can remain assured of managerial loyalty, an assurance that a social democracy reduces, or destroys.

True, the benefits with which the public firm is associated—innovation, competition, and high technology, for example—might be obtained without ownership separation and public firms. Innovation, competition, and efficient production can be reached in different organizations. Nations that deny themselves one organizational form do not condemn themselves to economic backwardness, but leave themselves without one tool in the organizational toolkit. Public firms and the capacity to go public can motivate entry, can enhance product market competition, and can democratize the appearance of business. But all these can be accomplished otherwise, although perhaps occasionally at higher technical cost. (And, similarly, nations that overly fragment institutional shareholding and financial voice inside the corporate boardroom deny themselves a different tool.)

Moreover, this is hardly a reason to criticize social democracies. What gets lost in shareholder tools may be gained on the shop floor; net efficiency effects may be zero. And the solidarity and equality in these nations may make more citizens happier, and those societies may in the long run be more stable and productive than they would be otherwise. Many European players, even managerial players, believe this to be so.[1] Citizens in nations with a yearning for stability, perhaps one created by gloomy destructive histories, may get special value from the stability of a social democracy.

[1] Michel Albert, *Capitalisme contre capitalisme* 169–92 (1991).

But productivity effects and the *overall* value of a social democracy are not the principal lines of thought here. The story here is not the normative one of which is better, but the positive one of why we see corporate differences that cannot be fully explained without looking at a society's political foundations. The key point is that for a nation to create public firms and deep securities markets it needs more than just the right legal institutions; rather, it faces a problem that goes to the core of that society's social and political organization. As such, reformers have thus far often found technical solutions frustrating or impossible to implement; and, even if implemented, the technical reforms have sometimes had little effect unless and until the underlying political reality changed. One may see little demand for the institutions that support securities markets until a social democracy has softened enough to lay the political foundation for making public firms viable. That softening may have happened in Europe during the past decade; in the United States that social democracy never existed.

Capital markets and institutions, managerial markets and institutions, and labor markets and institutions interrelate. Some types fit well together, complementing one other, and some do not. Politics can determine one type of the three and thereby indirectly determine the other two, because sometimes only a restricted set of the others fits the one that politics determined. America's historical antipathy to private institutional power over-emphasized one kind of capital market, and thereby affected the managerial institutions of the public firm.[2] European politics affected labor institutions and these in turn affected managerial institutions and capital structure. Had American labor institutions differed—had the United States been more of a social democracy—the public firm would have had a harder time in the United States and may have evolved as a minor rather than a major American business institution.

So, to restate, the fewer public firms and historically shallower security markets in France, Germany, and the rest of continental Europe have often been seen as technical results, as deriving from the inability to build the needed *institutional* prerequisites. Accounting needs to be transparent. Culture that leads the upper middle class in Europe to avoid owning stocks and that calls forth too few entrepreneurs is blamed. Securities laws need revamping; insider traders must be jailed when discovered. And, most recently, analysts have discovered minority stockholder protection as a fundamental prerequisite to public firms and deep securities markets.

Some technical problems are important, others are surmountable. France and Germany have built good bureaucracies, staffed by capable and motivated professionals. If securities laws determine the differences in securities markets, then one wonders why and how 'technical' law could be the difference here, because France and Germany are often better than the United States at drafting and implementing comprehensive statutory schemes and then building government agencies to enforce them.

---

[2] Mark J. Roe, *Strong Managers, Weak Owners: The Political Roots of American Corporate Finance* xiii–xvi, 283–87 (1994).

Technical institutions that support the large public firm are useful, but for the world's wealthier democracies, their construction is hardly rocket science. Several already have them. When the political will is there, they usually can get built. The lack of political will in modern times in the rich democracies is manifested in social democracy. And in some nations the technical institutions are there, but if the political configuration is not conducive, ownership does not separate from control. Visions of what makes for a good society differ, and those differing visions lead to differing corporate organization.

If the wealthier democratic nations often do not build the corporate stockholder protections, or if securities markets do not flourish even when they do, then other explanations must account for their inaction. *The demand for those institutions might be low, because other institutions—namely, social democracy itself—render public firms less valuable to diffuse shareholders.* When blocks persist, one cannot tell a priori whether distant stockholders fear dominant stockholders or fear high managerial agency costs in public firms. If they fear high managerial agency costs, blockholding would tend to persist as that nation's shareholders' best way to control managerial agency costs.

This result is not merely technical, arising just from the accidents of which technical institutions a society has built. And, hence, no change will be purely technical either. The result maps back to a society's political condition: social democracies raised the managerial agency costs to shareholders in the public firm. They exacerbated managerial tendencies to expand unprofitably, to avoid risk at all costs, and to avoid biting the bullet and forcing organizational change when markets and technologies shifted. In each case incumbent employees often preferred that these changes not go forward; incumbent employees have had a strong political voice in social democracies; and owners and managers have had a rougher time bringing about organizational change in the social democracies.

Political differences among the world's rich democracies explain much about their corporate differences. Social democracies wedged open the gap between shareholders and managers in public firms, by raising agency costs higher and reducing the efficacy of the techniques that would control them. This wedge has been small in the United States, and we have thereby uncovered the critical precondition to the separation of ownership from control and, hence, of the rise and persistence of the dominant form of business organization in the United States: namely the historical absence of a strong social democracy.

* * *

Corporate governance can be analyzed solely in terms of the inner workings of the corporation: the mechanical requirements for the board of directors, the degree to which minority stockholders are protected from insider machinations, the degree to which incentive-compatible compensation is implemented, the quality of specialized committees, the quality of securities law disclosure and insider-trading enforcement, etc.

The fragile ties between managers and diffuse shareholders are all too easy to sever. Not all societies favor shareholders. Some fray the ties between managers and shareholders, because they dislike many ways that managers act for share-holders. Such societies can induce unconstrained managers to expand firms even when not profitable to do so, to go slow in downsizing when the firm is misaligned with its product market, and to shy away from profitable risks that could disrupt the work place. If they push managers to expand, go slow, and avoid risk, then diffuse shareholders will find their stock less valuable than if the firm could find a way to avoid these pressures. Diffuse stockholders will be fewer than in societies without such pressures. And if the modern tools that align managers with share-holders in the United States are also denigrated—incentive compensation, hostile takeovers, shareholder primacy norms, and transparency—then diffuse stock-holders have a doubled-up reason to be wary.

The corporation is part of a larger society. One recalls Pierre Trudeau's comment about what it was like for Canada to be right next to the United States, which I mentioned in this book's Introduction. It is like sleeping next to an elephant, Trudeau said. Even if the elephant is benign, even if it is paying little attention to you, slight movements during the elephant's sleep could have a very large effect.

For corporate governance, the elephants are labor markets, politics, and capital and product markets. Small changes in any, and especially small changes in polit-ical results, can make for big changes in how corporate governance looks.

Or to use another metaphor: if one wants to understand the flow of the world's waters in rivers, bays, and oceans, then attending to viscosity, rainfall, erosion, and so on is important. Some of these one can control; some one cannot. But one cannot fully understand the water's movements without understanding the huge gravitational pull of the moon, and the concomitant tidal effects. The moon's pull is unseen, unchangeable by humans, but powerful. For corporate governance the moon's pull comes from politics.

ACKNOWLEDGEMENTS

For a conference I organized as part of Columbia Law School's Sloan Project on corporate governance in March 1997, I invited two dozen corporate law scholars to pick a country, speculate on what was missing from corporate governance analysis in that country, and consider how that reflected on corporate governance elsewhere. I chose Germany and speculated how codetermination could fit with weak boardrooms and concentrated ownership. That sketch eventually became the core of Chapter 4 of this book. This book expands on that assertion, with a view that the formal institution is not needed to yield similar effects. Politics affects corporate governance.

Two deans, David Leebron and Robert Clark, and two foundations, Sloan at Columbia and Olin at Harvard, supported this research. Several colleagues read the underlying articles. I thanked them then, and I thank them here again. Several, including Lucian Bebchuk, Ronald Gilson (my co-author of the article on Japanese lifetime employment), Victor Goldberg, and Jeffrey Gordon, commented on more than one of the underlying articles. Victor Brudney, Gérard Hertig, Michelle Jewett, Mark Ramseyer, and Detlev Vagts read and critiqued the entire manuscript, Margaret Blair, Einer Elhauge, Howell Jackson and Lorenzo Stanghellini parts of it.

David Musson from Oxford University Press and Colin Mayer from Oxford's Business School gave me the opportunity to collect these thoughts in the Clarendon Lectures on Management in May 1999. The book focuses on, and expands upon, the second of the three lectures.

Portions of this book draw on these prior articles:

1. 'Political Preconditions to Separating Ownership from Control', 53 *Stanford Law Review* 539 (2000).
2. 'Rents and their Corporate Consequences', 53 *Stanford Law Review* 1463 (2001).
3. 'Corporate Law's Limits, 31 *Journal of Legal Studies* 233 (2002).
4. 'The Shareholder Wealth Maximization Norm and Industrial Organization', 149 *University of Pennsylvania Law Review* 2063 (2001).
5. 'The Political Economy of Japanese Lifetime Employment', in *Employees and Corporate Governance* (with Ronald Gilson) (Margaret M. Blair & Mark J. Roe, eds, 1999).
6. 'Lifetime Employment: Labor Peace and the Evolution of Japanese Corporate Governance', 99 *Columbia Law Review* 508 (1999) (with Ronald Gilson).

7. 'German Securities Markets and German Codetermination', 98 *Columbia Business Law Review* 167 (1998).
8. 'Backlash', 98 *Columbia Law Review* 217 (1998).
9. 'From Antitrust to Corporate Governance: The Corporation and the Law, 1959–1995', in *The American Corporation Today*, 102–27 (Carl Kaysen, ed., 1996).

BIBLIOGRAPHY

Books, Manuscripts, and Journal Articles

Agnblad, Jonas, Erik Berglöf, Peter Högfeldt, and Helena Svancar. 'Ownership and Control in Sweden: Strong Owners, Weak Minorities, and Social Control'. In *The Control of Corporate Europe*, edited by Fabrizio Barca and Marco Becht, at 228. New York: Oxford University Press, 2001.

Albert, Michel. *Capitalisme contre Capitalisme*. Paris: Editions du Seuil, 1991.

Alesina, Alberto, Rafael Di Tella, and Robert MacCulloch. 'Inequality and Happiness: Are Europeans and Americans Different?' Cambridge, Mass.: National Bureau of Economic Research, 2001 (Working Paper No. 8198).

André, Thomas J. 'Some Reflections on German Corporate Governance: A Glimpse at German Supervisory Boards'. 70 *Tulane Law Review* 1819 (1996).

Aoki, Masahiko. 'The Japanese Firm as a System of Attributes: A Survey and Research Agenda'. In *The Japanese Firm: The Sources of Competitive Strength*, edited by Masahiko Aoki and Ronald Dore, at 11. New York: Oxford University Press, 1994.

—— 'Toward an Economic Model of the Japanese Firm'. 28 *Journal of Economic Literature* 1 (1990).

—— Paul Sheard, and Hugh T. Patrick. 'The Japanese Main Bank System: An Introductory Overview'. In *The Japanese Main Bank System: Its Relevance for Developing and Transforming Economies*, edited by Masahiko Aoki and Hugh T. Patrick, at 3. New York: Oxford University Press, 1994.

Araki, Takashi. 'Flexibility in Japanese Employment Relations and the Role of the Judiciary'. In *Japanese Commercial Law in an Era of Internationalisation*, edited by Hiroshi Oda, at 249. Boston: Graham & Trotman/M. Nijhoff; Norwell, 1994.

Association Française des Entreprises Privées. *Recommendations of the Committee on Corporate Governance Chaired by M. Marc Viénot*. Paris: Mouvement des Entreprises de France, July 1999.

Barclay, Michael J. and Clifford G. Holderness. 'Private Benefits from Control of Public Corporations'. 25 *Journal of Financial Economics* 371 (1989).

—— and Dennis P. Sheehan. 'The Block Pricing Puzzle'. Rochester, NY: Simon School of Business, University of Rochester, March 2001 (Working Paper No. FR 01–05).

Barucci, Piero and Antonio Magliulo. *L'Insegnamento Economico e Sociale della Chiesa (1891–1991)*. Milan: Mondadori, 1996.

Bauer, Michel and Benedicte Bertin-Mourot. *Administrateurs et Dirigeants du CAC 40*. Paris: CNRS Observatoire des Dirigeants, October 1997.

Baums, Theodor and Bernd Frick. 'The Market Value of the Codetermined Firm'. In *Employees and Corporate Governance*, edited by Margaret M. Blair and Mark J. Roe, at 206. Washington, DC: Brookings Institution, 1999.

Bebchuk, Lucian Arye. 'A Theory of the Choice Between Concentrated and Dispersed Ownership of Corporate Shares and Votes'. Cambridge, Mass.: Harvard Law and Economics Working Paper, October 1998.

—— 'A Rent-Protection Theory of Corporate Ownership and Control'. Cambridge, Mass.: Harvard Law and Economics Working Paper, 1999.

—— Jesse Fried, and David I. Walker. 'Executive Compensation in America: Optimal Contracting or Extraction of Rents?' Cambridge, Mass.: Harvard Law School Working Paper, 2001.

—— and Mark J. Roe. 'A Theory of Path Dependence in Corporate Ownership and Governance'. 52 *Stanford Law Review* 127 (1999).

—— Reinier Kraakman, and George Triantis. 'Stock Pyramids, Cross-Ownership, and Dual Class Equity: The Creation and Agency Costs of Separating Control from Cash Flow Rights'. In *Concentrated Corporate Ownership*, edited by Randall K. Morck, 295. Chicago: University of Chicago Press, 2000.

Becht, Marco and Ailsa Röell. 'Blockholdings in Europe: An International Comparison'. 43 *European Economic Review* 1049 (1999).

Becker, Gary Stanley. *The Economics of Discrimination*. Chicago: University of Chicago Press, 1957.

Bergström, Clas and Kristian Rydqvist. 'Ownership of Equity in Dual-Class Firms'. 14 *Journal of Banking and Finance* 255 (1990).

—— —— 'The Determinants of Corporate Ownership: An Empirical Study on Swedish Data'. 14 *Journal of Banking and Finance* 237 (1990).

Bertrand, Marianne and Sendhil Mullainathan. 'Agents With and Without Principals'. 90 *American Economic Review Papers and Proceedings* 203 (2000).

—— —— 'Is There Discretion in Wage Setting? A Test Using Takeover Legislation'. 30 *Rand Journal of Economics* 535 (1999).

Bianco, Magda and Paola Casavola. 'Italian Corporate Governance: Effects on Financial Structure and Firm Performance'. 43 *European Economic Review* 1057 (1999).

Bishop, Joseph W., Jr. 'Sitting Ducks and Decoy Ducks: New Trends in the Indemnification of Corporate Directors and Officers'. 77 *Yale Law Journal* 1078 (1968).

Bisogni, Giovanni Battista. 'Autonomia ed eteronomia nella disciplina dei rapporti associativi della publicly held corporation'. *Rivista delle società*, No. 116, 649 (1997).

Black, Bernard S. 'The Core Institutions That Support Strong Securities Markets'. 55 *Business Lawyer* 1565 (2000).

—— and Reinier Kraakman. 'A Self-Enforcing Model of Corporate Law'. 109 *Harvard Law Review* 1911 (1996).

Blake, Harlan M. and William K. Jones. 'In Defense of Antitrust'. 65 *Columbia Law Review* 377 (1965).

Bogenschütz, Eugen and Kelly Wright. 'A Look at Germany's New Reduction Tax Act 2001'. 21 *Tax Notes International* 499 (2000).

Boorstin, Daniel J. *The Genius of American Politics*. Chicago: University of Chicago Press, 1953.

Calomiris, Charles W. 'The Costs of Rejecting University Banking: American Finance in the German Mirror, 1870–1914'. In *Coordination and Information: Historical Perspectives on the Organization of Enterprise*, edited by Naomi R. Lamoreaux and Daniel M. Raff, at 257. Chicago: University of Chicago Press, 1995.

Carli, Guido and Paolo Peluffo. *Cinquant'anni di vita italiana*. Rome; Bari: Laterza, 1993.

Carlin, Wendy and Colin Mayer. 'Finance, Investment and Growth'. Oxford: University College and Said Business School Working Paper, 18 October 1998.

Carpenter, Robert E. and Laura Rondi. 'Italian Corporate Governance, Investment, and Finance'. 27 *Empirica* 365 (2000).

Castles, Francis G. and Peter Mair. 'Left–Right Political Scales: Some "Expert" Judgments'. 12 *European Journal of Political Research* 73 (1984).

Cella, Gianprimo. 'Criteria of Regulation in Italian Industrial Relations: A Case of Weak Institutions'. In *State, Market, and Social Regulation: New Perspectives on Italy*, edited by Peter Lange and Marino Regini, at 167. New York: Cambridge University Press, 1989.

Chandler, Alfred D., Jr. *Scale and Scope: The Dynamics of Industrial Capitalism*. Cambridge, Mass.: Belknap Press, 1990.

—— and Herman Daems. 'Introduction'. In *Managerial Hierarchies: Comparative Perspectives on the Rise of Modern Industrial Enterprise*. Cambridge, Mass.: Harvard University Press, 1980.

Channon, Derek F. *The Strategy and Structure of British Enterprise*. Boston: Graduate School of Business Administration, Harvard University, 1973.

Chiesi, Antonio and Alberto Martinelli. 'The Representation of Business Interests as a Mechanism of Social Regulation'. In *State, Market, and Social Regulation: New Perspectives on Italy*, edited by Peter Lange and Marino Regini, at 187. New York: Cambridge University Press, 1989.

Cioffi, John W. 'State of the Art: A Review Essay on Comparative Corporate Governance: The State of the Art and Emerging Research'. 48 *American Journal of Comparative Law* 501 (2000).

Clift, Ben, Andrew Gamble and Michael Harris. 'The Labour Party and the Company'. In *The Political Economy of the Company*, edited by John Parkinson, Andrew Gamble and Gavin Kelly, at 51. Oxford; Portland, Ore.: Hart, 2000.

Coffee, John C., Jr. 'Liquidity Versus Control: The Institutional Investor as Corporate Monitor'. 91 *Columbia Law Review* 1277 (1991).

—— 'The Future as History: The Prospects for Global Convergence in Corporate Governance and Its Implications'. 93 *Northwestern University Law Review* 641 (1999).

—— 'The Rise of Dispersed Ownership: The Roles of Law and the State in the Separation of Ownership and Control'. 111 *Yale Law Journal* 1 (2001).

Commons, John R. 'History of Labor in the United States: 1896–1932'. In *III Classics in Institutional Economics: The Founders, 1890–1945*, edited by Malcolm Rutherford and Warren J. Samuels, at 438. London; Brookfield, Vt.: Pickering & Chatto, 1997.

—— 'Is Class Conflict in America Growing and Is It Inevitable?' In *III Classics in Institutional Economics: The Founders, 1890–1945*, edited by Malcolm Rutherford and Warren J. Samuels, at 112. London; Brookfield, Vt.: Pickering & Chatto, 1997.

Contini, Giovanni. 'The Rise and Fall of Shop-Floor Bargaining at Fiat, 1945–1980'. In *The Automobile Industry and Its Workers: Between Fordism and Flexibility*, edited by Steven Tolliday and Jonathan Zeitlin, at 144. Cambridge: Polity Press, 1986.

Conyon, Martin J. and Joachim Schwalbach. 'Corporate Governance, Executive Pay and Performance in Europe'. In *Executive Compensation and Shareholder Value: Theory and Evidence*, edited by Jennifer Carpenter and David Yermack, at 13. Dordrecht; Boston: Kluwer Academic Publishers, 1999.

Cusack, Thomas R. 'Partisan Politics and Public Finance: Changes in Public Spending in the Industrialized Democracies, 1955–1989'. 91 *Public Choice* 375 (1997).

Dahrendorf, Ralf. 'The Third Way and Liberty: An Authoritarian Streak in Europe's New Center'. *Foreign Affairs*, Sept./Oct. 1999, at 13.

Daines, Robert. 'Does Delaware Law Improve Firm Value?' 62 *Journal of Financial Economics* 525 (2001).

Demsetz, Harold. 'The Structure of Ownership and the Theory of the Firm'. 26 *Journal of Law and Economics* 375 (1983).

Dooley, Michael P. and E. Norman Veasey. 'The Role of the Board in Derivative Litigation: Delaware Law and the Current ALI Proposals Compared'. 44 *Business Lawyer* 503 (1989).

Dyck, Alexander and Luigi Zingales. 'Why Are Private Benefits of Control so Large in Certain Countries and What Effect Does This Have on their Financial Development?' Cambridge, Mass.: Harvard Business School, 2001 (working paper).

Edwards, Franklin R. 'Managerial Objectives in Regulated Industries: Expense-Preference Behavior in Banking'. 85 *Journal of Political Economy* 147 (1977).

Edwards, Jeremy and Klaus Fischer. *Banks, Finance and Investment in Germany*. Cambridge, UK.; New York: Cambridge University Press, 1994.

Eisenstadt, S. N. and Eyal Ben-Ari (eds.) *Japanese Models of Conflict Resolution*. London; New York: K. Paul International; New York, 1990.

Elbaum, Bernard and William Lazonick. *The Decline of the British Economy*. New York: Oxford University Press, 1986.

Emmons, William R. and Frank A. Schmid. 'Universal Banking, Control Rights, and Corporate Finance in Germany'. 80 *Federal Reserve Bank of St. Louis Review*, July/Aug. 1998, at 19.

Enriques, Luca. 'Off the Books, but on the Record: Evidence from Italy on the Relevance of Judges to the Quality of Corporate Law'. Bologna, Italy: University of Bologna. Working Paper, 2001.

Fama, Eugene F. 'Agency Problems and the Theory of the Firm'. 88 *Journal of Political Economy* 288 (1980).

Fanto, James A. 'The Role of Corporate Law in French Corporate Governance'. 31 *Cornell International Law Journal* 31 (1998).

FitzRoy, Felix R. and Kornelius Kraft. 'Economic Effects of Codetermination'. 95 *Scandinavian Journal of Economics* 365 (1993).

Fligstein, Neil and Frederic Merand. 'Globalization or Europeanization: Evidence on the European Economy Since 1980'. Berkeley: University of California at Berkeley. Working Paper, April 2001.

Foreman-Peck, James and Leslie Hannah. 'Britain: From Economic Liberalism to Socialism— And Back?' In *European Industrial Policy: The Twentieth-Century Experience*, edited by James Foreman-Peck and Giovanni Federico, at 18. New York: Oxford University Press, 1999.

Francis, Arthur. 'Families, Firms and Finance Capital: The Development of UK Industrial Firms with Particular Reference to Their Ownership and Control'. 14 *Sociology: Journal of the British Sociological Association* 1 (1980).

Franks, Julian and Colin Mayer. 'Ownership and Control of German Corporations'. 14 *Review of Financial Studies* 943 (2001).

Freeman, Richard B. and James L. Medoff. *What Do Unions Do?* New York: Basic Books, 1984.

Frick, Bernd, Gerhard Speckbacker and Paul Wentges. 'Arbeitnehmermitbestimmung und moderne Theorie der Unternehmung'. 69 *Zeitschrift für Betriebswirtschaft* 745 (1999).

Gamble, Andrew, Gavin Kelly, and John Parkinson. 'Introduction: The Political Economy of the Company'. In *The Political Economy of the Company*, edited by John Parkinson, Andrew Gamble and Gavin Kelly. New York: Oxford University Press, 2000.

Garon, Sheldon M. *The State and Labor in Modern Japan*. Berkeley: University of California Press, 1987.

Garonna, Paolo and Elena Pisani. 'Italian Unions in Transition: The Crisis of Political Unionism'. In *Unions in Crisis and Beyond: Perspectives from Six Countries*, edited by Richard Edwards, Paolo Garonna, and Franz Tödtling, at 114. Dover, Mass.: Auburn House Publishing Company, 1986.

Garvey, Gerald T. and Peter Swan. 'The Interaction Between Financial and Employment Contracts: A Formal Model of Japanese Corporate Governance'. 6 *Journal of the Japanese and International Economies* 247 (1992).

Gilson, Ronald J. and Mark J. Roe. 'Lifetime Employment: Labor Peace and the Evolution of Japanese Corporate Governance'. 99 *Columbia Law Review* 508 (1999).

Ginsborg, Paul. *A History of Contemporary Italy: Society and Politics, 1943–1988*. London: Penguin, 1990.

Goergen, Marc and Luc Renneboog. 'Strong Managers and Passive Institutional Investors in the United Kingdom'. In *The Control of Corporate Europe*, edited by Fabrizio Barca and Marco Becht, at 259. New York: Oxford University Press, 2001.

Gordon, Andrew. 'Contests for the Workplace'. In *Postwar Japan as History*, edited by Andrew Gordon, 373. Berkeley: University of California Press, 1993.

—— *The Evolution of Labor Relations in Japan: Heavy Industry, 1853–1955*. Cambridge, Mass.: Council on East Asian Studies, Harvard University, 1985.

Gorton, Gary and Frank A. Schmid. 'Class Struggle Inside the Firm: A Study of German Codetermination'. Cambridge, Mass.: National Bureau of Economic Research, October 2000. (Working Paper No. 7945).

—— —— 'Universal Banking and the Performance of German Firms'. 58 *Journal of Financial Economics* 29 (2000).

Graham, Andrew. 'The UK 1979–95: Myths and Realities of Conservative Capitalism'. In *Political Economy of Modern Capitalism: Mapping Convergence and Diversity*, edited by Colin Crouch and Wolfgang Streeck, 117. London; Thousand Oaks, Calif.: Sage, 1997.

Gros-Pietro, Gian Maria, Eduardo Reviglio, and Alfio Torrisi. *Assetti Proprietari e Mercati Finanziari Europei*. Bologna: Il Mulino. 2001.

Hall, Brian J. and Jeffrey B. Liebman. 'Are CEOs Really Paid Like Bureaucrats?' 113 *Quarterly Journal of Economics* 653 (1998).

Hamilton, Alexander, James Madison, and John Jay. *The Federalist Papers*. Cutchogue, NY: Buccaneer Books, 1992.

Hannah, Leslie. 'Mergers, Cartels and Concentration: Legal Factors in the U.S. and European Experience'. In *Law and the Formation of the Big Enterprises in the 19th and Early 20th Centuries: Studies in the History of Industrialization in Germany, France, Great Britain, and the United States*, edited by Norbert Horn and Jürgen Kocka, at 306. Göttingen: Vandenhoeck and Ruprecht, 1979.

—— 'Visible and Invisible Hands in Great Britain'. In *Managerial Hierarchies—Comparative Perspectives on the Rise of the Modern Industrial Enterprise*, edited by Alfred D. Chandler, Jr. and Herman Daems, at 41. Cambridge, Mass.: Harvard University Press, 1980.

Hannan, Timothy H. and Ferdinand Mavinga. 'Expense Preference and Managerial Control: The Case of the Banking Firm'. 11 *Bell Journal of Economics* 671 (1980).

Hart, Oliver D. 'The Market Mechanism as an Incentive Scheme'. 14 *Bell Journal of Economics* 366 (1983).

Hartz, Louis. *The Liberal Tradition in America: An Interpretation of American Political Thought Since the Revolution*. New York: Harcourt, Brace, 1955.

Hiwatari, Nobuhiro. 'Employment Practices and Enterprise Unionism in Japan'. In *Employees and Corporate Governance*, edited by Margaret M. Blair and Mark J. Roe, at 275. Washington, DC: Brookings Institution, 1999.

Hofstadter, Richard. *The American Political Tradition*. New York: A. A. Knopf, 1948.

Holderness, Clifford G., 'A Survey of Blockholders and Corporate Control'. 9 *FRBNY Econ. Pol. Rev.* 51 (April 2003).

Holmén, Martin and Peter Högfeldt. 'Corporate Control and Security Design in Initial Public Offerings'. Stockholm: Stockholm School of Economics, 15 December 1999.

Hopt, Klaus J. 'The German Two-Tier Board: Experience, Theories, Reforms'. In *Comparative Corporate Governance: The State of the Art and Emerging Research*, edited by Klaus J. Hopt, Hideki Kanda, Mark J. Roe, Eddy Wymeersch, and Stefan Prigge, at 227. New York: Oxford University Press, 1998.

Horn, Norbert and Jürgen Kocka. *Law and the Formation of the Big Enterprises in the 19th and Early 20th Centuries: Studies in the History of Industrialization in Germany, France, Great Britain, and the United States*, edited by Norbert Horn and Jürgen Kocka, at 306. Göttingen: Vandenhoeck and Ruprecht, 1979.

Hoshi, Takeo. 'Evolution of the Main Bank System in Japan'. In *The Structure of the Japanese Economy: Changes on the Domestic and International Fronts*, edited by Misuaki Okabe, at 287. Basingstoke: Macmillan, 1995.

Hüffer, Uwe (ed.) *Aktiengesetz*. Munich: C. H. Beck, 1995.

Huntington, Samuel P. *American Politics: The Promise of Disharmony*. Cambridge, Mass.: Harvard University Press, 1981.

'Italy'. In *Encyclopaedia Britannica Online* (accessed 3 August 2001).

Jacoby, Sanford M. 'Employee Representation and Corporate Governance: A Missing Link'. 3 *University of Pennsylvania Journal of Labor and Employment Law* 449 (2001).

Jagannathan, Ravi and Shaker B. Srinivasan. 'Does Product Market Competition Reduce Agency Costs?' 10 *North American Journal of Economics and Finance* 387 (1999).

Jensen, Michael C. 'Agency Costs of Free Cash Flow, Corporate Finance, and Takeovers'. 76 *American Economic Review* 323 (1986).

Kandel, Eugene and Neil D. Pearson. 'The Value of Labor Force Flexibility'. Rochester, NY: Simon School of Business Working Paper, University of Rochester, 20 June 1995.

Karier, Thomas. 'Unions and Monopoly Profits'. 67 *Review of Economics and Statistics* 34 (1985).

Kaysen, Carl (ed.) *The American Corporation Today*. New York: Oxford University Press, 1996.

Kindleberger, Charles P. *Economic Growth in France and Britain, 1851–1950*. Cambridge, Mass.: Harvard University Press, 1964.

Kirk, Neville. *Change, Continuity and Class: Labour in British Society, 1850–1920*. Manchester, England; New York: Manchester University Press, 1998.

Kwoka, John E., Jr. 'Monopoly, Plant, and Union Effects on Worker Wages'. 36 *Industrial and Labor Relations Review* 251 (1983).

La Porta, Rafael, Florencio Lopez-de-Silanes, and Andrei Shleifer. 'Corporate Ownership Around the World'. 54 *Journal of Finance* 471 (1999).

—— —— and Robert Vishny. 'Investor Protection and Corporate Governance'. 58 *Journal of Financial Economics* 3 (2000).

—— —— 'Law and Finance'. 106 *Journal of Political Economy* 1113 (1998).

—— —— 'Legal Determinants of External Finance'. 52 *Journal of Finance* 1131 (1997).

Lester, Richard A. 'A Range Theory of Wage Differentials'. 5 *Industrial and Labor Relations Review* 483 (1952).

Levine, Ross. 'Law, Finance, and Economic Growth'. 8 *Journal of Financial Intermediation* 8 (1999).

Levy, Jonah D. *Tocqueville's Revenge: State, Society, and Economy in Contemporary France*. Cambridge, Mass.: Harvard University Press, 1999.

Libecap, Gary D. *Contracting for Property Rights*. New York: Cambridge University Press, 1989.

Locke, Richard M. 'The Political Embeddedness of Industrial Change: Corporate Restructuring and Local Politics in Contemporary Italy'. In *Transforming Organizations*, edited by Thomas A. Kochan and Michael Useem, at 28. New York: Oxford University Press, 1992.

Magnani, Marco. 'Alla ricerca di regole nelle relazioni industriali: breve storia di due fallimenti'. In *Storia del Capitalismo Italiano dal Dopoguerra a Oggi*, edited by Fabrizio Barca, at 501. Rome: Donzelli, 1997.

Maier, Charles S. *In Search of Stability: Explorations in Historical Political Economy*. New York: Cambridge University Press, 1987.

—— 'Preconditions for Corporatism'. In *Order and Conflict in Contemporary Capitalism*, edited by John H. Goldthorpe, at 39. Oxford: Clarendon Press, 1984.

—— *Recasting Bourgeois Europe: Stabilization in France, Germany, and Italy in the Decade After World War I*. Princeton, NJ: Princeton University Press, 1975.

Marchetti, Piergaetano. 'Diritto societario e disciplina della concorrenza'. In *Storia del Capitalismo Italiano dal Dopoguerra a Oggi*, edited by Fabrizio Barca, 467. Rome: Donzelli, 1997.

Martins, Joaquim Oliveira, Stefano Scarpetta, and Dirk Pilat. 'Mark-up Pricing Ratios in Manufacturing Industries: Estimates for 14 OECD Countries'. Paris: Organization for Economic Cooperation and Development, Econ. Dept, 1996 (Working Paper No. 162).

Mesnooh, Christopher J., 'Stock Options in the United States and France: A Comparative Regard'. MTF-L'AGEFI, No. 102. Nov./Dec. 1998, 59.

Milgrom, Paul and John Roberts. 'Complementarities and Systems: Understanding Japanese Economic Organization'. 9 *Estudios Económicos* 3 (1994).

Modigliani, Franco and Enrico Perotti. 'Protection of Minority Interest and the Development of Security Markets'. 18 *Managerial and Decision Economics* 519 (1997).

—— —— 'Security Versus Bank Finance: The Importance of a Proper Enforcement of Legal Rules'. Cambridge, Mass.: MIT Sloan School of Management, 1998.

Morck, Randall K. 'Introduction'. In *Concentrated Corporate Ownership*, edited by Randall K. Morck, at 1. Chicago: University of Chicago Press, 2000.

Mosk, Carl. *Competition and Cooperation in Japanese Labour Markets*. New York: St. Martin's Press, 1995.

Mülbert, Peter O. *Empfehlen sich gesetzliche Regelungen zur Einschränkung des Einflusses der Kreditinstitute auf Aktiengesellschaften?: Gutachten E für den 61*. Deutschen Juristentag. Munich: Beck, 1996.

Nenova, Tatiana. 'The Value of Corporate Votes and Control Benefits: A Cross-Country Analysis'. Cambridge, Mass.: Harvard University Economics Working Paper, 21 Sept. 2000.

Nickell, Stephen J. 'Competition and Corporate Performance'. 104 *Journal of Political Economy* 724 (1996).

Nicodano, Giovanna and Alessandro Sembenelli. 'Private Benefits, Block Transaction Premiums and Ownership Structure'. Turin, Italy: University of Turin Working Paper, Jan. 2000.

Nishiguchi, Toshihiro. *Strategic Industrial Sourcing: The Japanese Advantage*. New York: Oxford University Press, 1994.

Nyman, Steve and Aubrey Silberston. 'The Ownership and Control of Industry'. 30 *Oxford Economic Papers*, n.s. 74 (1978).

O'Driscoll, Gerald P., Kim R. Holmes, and Melanie Kirkpatrick. *2001 Index of Economic Freedom*. Washington, DC: The Heritage Foundation, 2001.

Organization for Economic Co-operation and Development, *The OECD Jobs Study: Evidence and Explanations, Pt. II: The Adjustment Potential of the Labour Market*. Paris: Organization for Economic Co-operation and Development, 1994.

——*Financial Market Trends, No. 69*, February 1998.

Pagano, Marco and Paolo Volpin, *The Political Economy of Corporate Governance*. Salerno, Italy: Universita Degli Studi di Salerno Working Paper. October 1999.

Palmer, John. 'The Profit-Performance Effects of the Separation of Ownership from Control in Large U.S. Industrial Corporations'. 4 *Bell Journal of Economics and Management Science* 293 (1973).

Pinto, Arthur R. and Gustavo Visentini (eds.) *The Legal Basis of Corporate Governance in Publicly Held Corporations: A Comparative Approach*. The Hague; Boston: Kluwer Law International, 1998.

Pistor, Katharina. 'Codetermination: A Sociopolitical Model with Governance Externalities'. In *Employees and Corporate Governance*, edited by Margaret M. Blair and Mark J. Roe, 163. Washington, DC: Brookings Institution Press, 1999.

Polanyi, Karl. *The Great Transformation*. New York: Rinehart and Co., 1944.

Popkin, Samuel L. 'Public Choice and Peasant Organization'. In *Toward a Political Economy of Development: A Rational Choice Perspective*, edited by Robert H. Bates, 245. Berkeley: University of California Press, 1988.

Porter, Michael E. 'The Microeconomic Foundations of Economic Development'. In *The Global Competitiveness Report*, at 38. Geneva: World Economic Forum (1998).

Portolano, Alessandro. 'The Decision to Adopt Defensive Tactics in Italy'. 20 *International Review of Law and Economics* 425 (2000).

Posner, Richard A. 'The Social Costs of Monopoly and Regulation'. 83 *Journal of Political Economy* 807 (1975).

——*Antitrust Law: An Economic Perspective*. Chicago: University of Chicago Press, 1976.

Price, John. *Japan Works: Power and Paradox in Postwar Industrial Relations*. Ithaca, NY: ILR Press, 1997.

Przeworski, Adam. 'Socialism and Social Democracy'. In *The Oxford Companion to Politics of the World*, edited by Joel Krieger, *et al.*, at 832. New York: Oxford University Press, 1993.

Raff, Daniel. 'Wage Determination Theory and the Five-Dollar Day at Ford'. 48 *Journal of Economic History* 387 (1988).

Rajan, Raghuram G. and Luigi Zingales. 'The Great Reversals: The Politics of Financial Development in the 20th Century'. Chicago: University of Chicago Working Paper, February 2001.

Rathenau, Walther. *Die Neue Wirtschaft*. Berlin: S. Fischer, 1918.

Reyneri, Emilio. 'The Italian Labor Market: Between State Control and Social Regulation'. In *State, Market, and Social Regulation: New Perspectives on Italy*, edited by Peter Lange and Marino Regini, at 129. New York: Cambridge University Press, 1989.

Reynolds, Lloyd George. *The Structure of Labor Markets: Wages and Labor Mobility in Theory and Practice*. New York: Harper, 1951.

Rock, Edward B. and Michael L. Wachter. 'Island of Conscious Power: Law, Norms, and the Self-Governing Corporation'. 149 *University of Pennsylvania Law Review* 1619 (2002).

Roe, Mark J. *Strong Managers, Weak Owners: The Political Roots of American Corporate Finance*. Princeton, NJ: Princeton University Press, 1994.

——'Takeover Politics'. In *The Deal Decade: What Takeovers and Leveraged Buyouts Mean for Corporate Governance*, edited by Margaret M. Blair, at 321. Washington, DC: Brookings Institution, 1993.

—— 'Backlash'. 98 *Columbia Law Review* 217 (1998).

—— 'From Antitrust to Corporate Governance?—The Corporation and the Law: 1959–1994'. In *The American Corporation Today*, edited by Carl Kaysen. New York: Oxford University Press, 1996.

—— 'German Codetermination and German Securities Markets'. In *Employees and Corporate Governance*, edited by Margaret M. Blair and Mark J. Roe, 194. Washington, DC: Brookings Institution Press, 1999.

—— 'Political Preconditions to Separating Ownership from Corporate Control'. 53 *Stanford Law Review* 539 (2000).

—— 'Chaos and Evolution in Law and Economics'. 109 *Harvard Law Review* 641 (1996).

—— 'Rents and Their Corporate Consequences'. 53 *Stanford Law Review* 1463 (2001).

—— 'The Shareholder Wealth Maximization Norm and Industrial Organization'. 149 *University of Pennsylvania Law Review* 2063 (2001).

Rose, Nancy L. 'Labor Rent Sharing and Regulation: Evidence from the Trucking Industry'. 95 *Journal of Political Economy* 1146 (1987).

Ruback, Richard S. and Martin B. Zimmerman. 'Unionization and Profitability: Evidence from the Capital Market'. 92 *Journal of Political Economy* 1134 (1984).

Ruggiero, Eugenio. 'Italy'. In *The Legal Basis of Corporate Governance in Publicly Held Corporations: A Comparative Approach*, edited by Arthur R. Pinto and Gustavo Visentini, 79. The Hague; Boston: Kluwer Law International, 1998.

Sachs, Jeffrey D. and Andrew M. Warner. 'Executive Summary'. In *The Global Competitiveness Report 1998*, 24. Geneva: World Economic Forum, 1998.

—— and Katharina Pistor. 'Introduction: Progress, Pitfalls, Scenarios, and Lost Opportunities'. In *The Rule of Law and Economic Reform in Russia*, edited by Jeffrey D. Sachs and Katharina Pistor, at 1. Boulder, Colo.: Westview Press, 1997.

Salinger, Michael A. 'Tobin's *q*, Unionization, and the Concentration–Profits Relationship'. 15 *Rand Journal of Economics* 159 (1984).

Schattschneider, E. E. *The Semisovereign People: A Realist's View of Democracy in America*. New York: Holt, Rinehart and Winston, 1960.

Schimmelmann, Wulf von. 'Unternehmenskontrolle in Deutschland'. In *Finanzmärkte*, edited by Bernhard Gahlen, Helmut Hesse, and Hans Jürgen Ramser, 7. Tübingen: Mohr Siebeck, 1997.

Schmid, Frank A. and Frank Seger. 'Arbeitnehmermitbestimmung, Allokation von Entscheidungsrechten und Shareholder Value'. 5 *Zeitschrift für Betriebswirtschat* 453 (1998).

Scott, John. 'Corporate Control and Corporate Rule: Britain in an International Perspective'. 41 *British Journal of Sociology* 351 (1990).

Shirer, William L. *The Collapse of the Third Republic—An Inquiry into the Fall of France in 1940*. New York: Simon & Schuster, 1969.

Shleifer, Andrei and Lawrence H. Summers. 'Breach of Trust in Hostile Takeovers'. In *Corporate Takeovers: Causes and Consequences*, edited by Alan J. Auerbach, 33. Chicago: University of Chicago Press, 1988.

Shleifer, Andrei and Robert W. Vishny. 'Large Shareholders and Corporate Control'. 94 *Journal of Political Economy* 461 (1986).

Smith, D. Gordon. 'The Shareholder Primacy Norm'. 23 *Journal of Corporate Law* 277 (1998).

Stanghellini, Lorenzo. 'Corporate Governance in Italy: Strong Owners, Faithful Managers. An Assessment and a Proposal for Reform'. 6 *Indiana International & Comparative Law Review* 92 (1995).

Stein, Jeremy C. 'Efficient Capital Markets, Inefficient Firms: A Model of Myopic Corporate Behavior'. 104 *Quarterly Journal of Economics* 655 (1989).

Stengel, Arndt. 'Directors' Powers and Shareholders: A Comparison of Systems'. *International Company and Commercial Law Review*, February 1998, at 49.

Stewart, James B. *Den of Thieves*. New York: Simon & Schuster, 1991.

Stimson, S. C. 'Social Democracy'. In *The New Palgrave: A Dictionary of Economics*, edited by John Eatwell, Murray Milgate, and Peter Newman, 395. Vol. 4. London: Macmillan, 1987.

Sutton, Francis X., Seymour E. Harris, Carl Kaysen, and James Tobin. *The American Business Creed*. Cambridge, Mass.: Harvard University Press, 1956.

Szewczyk, Samuel H. and George P. Tsetsekos. 'State Intervention in the Market for Corporate Control: The Case of Pennsylvania Senate Bill 1310'. 31 *Journal of Financial Economics* 3 (1992).

Tilly, Richard. 'Banks and Industry: Lessons from History'. In *European Economic Integration as a Challenge to Industry and Government: Contemporary and Historical Perspectives on International Economic Dynamics*, edited by Richard Tilly and Paul J. Welfans. New York: Springer, 1996.

Tolliday, Steven and Jonathan Zeitlin, (eds.) *The Automobile Industry and Its Workers: Between Fordism and Flexibility*. Cambridge: Polity, 1986.

Treu, Tiziano. 'Employment Protection and Labor Relations in Italy'. In *Employment Security and Labor Market Behavior: Interdisciplinary Approaches and International Evidence*, edited by Christoph F. Buechtemann, at 385. Ithaca, NY: ILR Press, 1993.

Tullock, Gordon. 'The Welfare Costs of Tariffs, Monopolies, and Theft'. 5 *Western Economic Journal* 224 (1967).

Tunc, André. 'A French Lawyer Looks at American Corporation Law and Securities Regulation'. 130 *University of Pennsylvania Law Review* 757 (1982).

Turner, Frederick Jackson. *The Frontier in American History*. New York: H. Holt and Co., 1920.

Vagts, Detlev. 'Comparative Company Law—The New Wave'. In *Festschrift for Jean-Nicolas Druey*, edited by Rainer Schweitzer and Urs Gasser. Zurich: Schulthess Juristische Medien, 2002.

Viscusi, W. Kip, John M. Vernon, and Joseph E. Harrington, Jr. *Economics of Regulation and Antitrust*. 2nd ed. Cambridge, Mass.: MIT Press, 1995.

Weiss, Leonard W. 'Concentration and Labor Earnings'. 56 *American Economic Review* 96 (1966).

Weiss, Linda. *Creating Capitalism: The State and Small Business Since 1945*. New York: B. Blackwell, 1988.

——and John M. Hobson. *States and Economic Development: A Comparative Historical Analysis*. Cambridge, Mass.: Polity Press. 1995.

Windolf, Paul. 'The Governance Structure of Large French Corporations: A Comparative Perspective'. New York: Columbia Law School Sloan Project on Corporate Governance, 1998.

Yamamoto, Kiyoshi. *Toshiba Sogi (1949-Nen)*. Tokyo: Ochanomizu Shob, 1983.

Zingales, Luigi. 'The Value of the Voting Right: A Study of the Milan Stock Exchange Experience'. 7 *Review of Financial Studies* 125 (1994).

Official Documents

France. Art. 200. Decree No. 67–236 of March 23, 1967. *Journal Officiel de la République Française*, 24 March 1967, 2858.

France. Art. L225–252 Code de Commerce. (Art. 245. Law No. 66–537 of July 24, 1966 *Journal Officiel de la République Française*, 26 July 1966, 6420).

Delaware Code Annotated (Michie).

Germany. *The German Stock Corporation Act* [Aktiengesellschaft. 1965], edited by Hannes Schneider and Martin Heidenhain. 2nd ed. Boston: Kluwer Law International, 2000.

Cases

Bayer v. Beran, 49 N.Y.S.2d 2 (N.Y. Sup. Ct. 1944).

Dodge v. Ford Motor Co., 170 N.W. 668 (Mich. 1919).

Gagliardi v. TriFoods Int'l, 683 A.2d 1049 (Del. Ch. 1996).

Joy v. North, 692 F.2d 880 (2d Cir. 1982).

Shlensky v. Wrigley, 237 N.E.2d 776 (Ill. App. 1968).

Smith v. Van Gorkom, 488 A.2d 858 (Del. Sup. Ct. 1985).

United States v. Socony-Vacuum Oil Co., 310 U.S. 150 (1940).

Other Official Publications

France. Ministère de l'Economie, des Finances et de l'Industrie. *Rapport au Premier Ministre sur l'épargne salariale*. Paris: Documentation Française, 2000.

Marini, Philippe, sénateur. *La modernisation du droit des sociétés: rapport au Premier Ministre*. Paris: Documentation Française, 1996.

Germany. Monopolkommission. *Wettbewerbspolitik in Netzstrukturen: Hauptgutachten 1998–1999*. Baden-Baden: Nomos, 2000. (Hauptgutachten der Monopolkommission No.13).

Germany. Monopolkommission. *Marktöffnung umfassend verwirklichen: Hauptgutachten 1996–1997*. Baden-Baden: Nomos, 1998. (Hauptgutachten der Monopolkommission No. 12).

Newspaper and Magazine Articles

Andrews, Edmund L. 'A French Concoction—Totalfina's Acquisition of Elf May Be Only a Prelude'. *New York Times*, 21 September 1999, C1.

'Banque: Le Coup de Poker de la BNP'. *Le Monde* (Paris), 11 March 1999, 1.

Bostnavaron, François. 'Le dépôt de bilan de la compagnie AOM-Air Liberté paraît imminent—Les deux actionnaires, Swissair et Ernest-Antoine Seillière, refusent toujours de recapitaliser l'entreprise'. *Le Monde* (Paris), 16 June 2001, 19.

—— 'Le PDG d'AOM-Air Liberté décide de déposer le bilan de la compagnie aérienne'. *Le Monde* (Paris), 17–18 June 2001, 16.

Boston, William. 'Hostile Deal Could Breach German Resistance'. *Wall Street Journal*, 17 November 1999, A17.

Bowley, Graham. 'Hoechst launches stock option scheme'. *Financial Times* (London), 13–14 September 1997.

Colombani, Jean Marie, Eric Le Boucher, and Arnaud Leparmentier. '[Interview with] Gerhard Schröder, [Chancelier de la République Fédérale d'Allemagne:] Je ne pense plus souhaitable une société sans inégalités'. *Le Monde* (Paris), 20 November 1999, 3.

'Des réactions politiques et syndicales sévères'. *Le Monde* (Paris), 11 September 1999, 16.

Docquiert, Jacques. 'En raison de l'opposition des Allemands—Le Parlement européen rejette l'harmonisation des OPA'. *Les Echos* (Paris), 5 July 2001, 1.

Edmondson, Gail, 'France: A CEO's Pay Shouldn't Be a Secret', *Business Week*, 9 August 1999, 47.

'Europe's Capital Markets: Takeover Troubles'. *The Economist*, 12 May 2001, 14.

'Europe—A French Lesson', *The Economist*, 1 July 2000, 47.

Faujas, Alain. 'Français, Allemands et Italiens n'attendent rien de bon des entreprises'. *Le Monde—Economie* (Paris), 1 June 1999, IV.

Fressoz, Françoise and Jean-Francis Pécresse. 'Licenciements: Jospin évite la crise mais mécontente les partenaires sociaux'. *Les Echos* (Paris), 14 June 2001, 4.

Friedman, Milton. 'The Social Responsibility of Business Is to Increase Its Profits'. *New York Times Magazine*, 13 September 1970, 32.

Goldstein, Peter. 'Compensation Packages for Executives Aren't All Alike—Base Pay Converges in Europe, but Bonuses and Stock Options Vary'. *Wall Street Journal* (Europe), 22 December 1998, 4.

Halstead, Richard. 'Steel Is Put to the Sword'. *Independent* (London), 23 March 23 1997, 3.

Kamm, Thomas. 'French Bill Takes Aim at Takeovers in Wake of Recent Merger Battles'. *Wall Street Journal* (Europe), 16 March 2000, 2.

Katz, Alan. 'Shareholders Gain Voice in France, but Socialist Tradition Talks Back'. *Wall Street Journal*, 13 February 1998, B7E.

Kuttner, Robert, 'Soaring Stocks: Are Only the Rich Getting Richer?—Illusion: Despite Appearances, Equity Ownership Is Still Highly Concentrated—While Most Americans' Earnings Are Stagnant', *Business Week*, 22 April 1996, at 28.

Latour, Almar and Greg Steinmetz. 'Swedish Giant: Barnevik Sets About Task of Preserving Wallenberg Empire'. *Wall Street Journal*, 18 May 1998, A1.

Lemaître, Frédéric. 'Le succès de l'actionnariat salarié bouleverse le capitalisme français'. *Le Monde—Entreprises* (Paris), 2 March 1999.

Leparmentier, Arnaud. 'L'Allemagne industrielle de nouveau conquérante'. *Le Monde* (Paris), 28 November 1998, 1.

'Les stock-options seraient moins imposées et plus "transparentes"'. *Le Monde* (Paris), 10 December 1998, 9.

Leser, Eric and Anne-Marie Rocco. 'Les Wallenberg veulent faire cohabiter capitalisme familial et mondialisation'. *Le Monde* (Paris), 24 November 2000, 23.

Liener, Gerhard, 'The Future of German Governance'. *Corporate Board*, May/June 1995, at 1.

Lomazzi, Marc. 'Polémiques sur la débâcle d'AOM-Air Liberté'. *La Tribune* (Paris), June 18, 2001, 3.

Mabille, Philippe. 'Stock-options: Vers des prélèvements allégés et une transparence accrue'. *Les Echo* (Paris), 9 December 1998, 2.

Malingre, Virginie. 'Les députés PS acceptent le dispositif stock-options préconisé par M. Fabius'. *Le Monde* (Paris), 28 April 2000, 9.

—— and Michel Noblecourt. 'Les députés PS veulent taxer davantage les stock-options'. *Le Monde* (Paris), 15 October 1999, 8.

'Management and Labor Join Forces to Stiff-Arm Raiders in Pennsylvania', *Corporate Control Alert*, January 1990, at 1.

Mandraud, Isabelle and Caroline Monnot. [Interview with Guillaume Sarkozy]. 'Toutes ces dispositions vont nuire aux négociations sociales d'entreprise . . .'. *Le Monde–Economie* (Paris), 19 June 2001, III.

Mauduit, Laurent. 'Le gouvernement diffère la réforme fiscale des stock-options'. *Le Monde* (Paris) 9 January 1999, 7.

—— 'M. Jospin ouvre avec précaution le dossier de l'épargne salariale'. *Le Monde* (Paris), 29 January 2000, 6.

Meller, Paul. 'European Parliament Rejects Measure to Ease Takeovers'. *New York Times*, 5 July 2001, C1.

Morio, Joël. 'Comment démarrer en bourse'. *Le Monde—Argent* (Paris), 7 May 2001, 1.

Münchau, Wolfgang. 'German Executives Discover a Nice Little Extra: Moves Towards Share Options for Top Managers are Likely to Provoke Controversy'. *Financial Times* (London), 24 April 1996, 23.

—— 'Europe Reinvented: Pondering the Power of the Market, in Europe's New Capitalism'. *Financial Times* (London), 8 February 2001, Pt 4, 2.

Noblecourt, Michel. 'François Hollande: Pour une extension des stock-options à l'ensemble du personnel'. *Le Monde* (Paris), 7 October 1999, 6.

Norris, Floyd. 'Perelman's Plan: Take Profits While Public Owners Suffer'. *New York Times*, 24 November 2000, C1.

Orange, Martine. 'La fin de l'exception française?' *Le Monde* (Paris), 30 March 1999, 19.

Owen, David. 'Michelin Slips After Provisions'. *Financial Times*, 15 March 2000, 32.

Oyama, David I. 'French Socialists Back Steeper Taxes on Options Gains'. *Wall Street Journal*, 27 April 2000, A17.

Pons, Frédéric. 'Un brin d'éthique dans les fusions.'. *Liberation* (Paris), 16 March 2000, 25.

Prudhomme, Cécile. '[Interview with] Bill Crist, président de CalPERS: "Danone n'a pas réduit ses effectifs en réponse à une demande d'un fonds de pension." ' *Le Monde* (Paris), 7 May 2001, 16.

Rhoads, Christopher and Vanessa Fuhrmans. 'Stakeholders Yield to Shareholders in the New Germany'. *Wall Street Journal* (Europe), 21 June 2001, 1.

Ryback, Timothy W., 'The Man Who Swallowed Chrysler'. *The New Yorker*, November 16, 1998, at 80.

Schilling, Florian. 'Der Aufsichtsrat ist für die Katz'. *Frankfurter Allgemeine Zeitung*, 27 August 1994, 11.

Steinmetz, Greg and Matt Marshall. 'Krupp Suspends Hostile Bid for Thyssen'. *Wall Street Journal*, 20 March 1997, A13.

Stüdemann, Frederick. 'Steeled for a Battle'. *Financial Times* (London), 22–3 March 1997, 9.

Sullivan, Andrew. 'The End of Britain'. *New York Times Magazine*, 21 February 1999, 39.

Wayne, Leslie. 'Takeovers Face New Obstacles—Pennsylvania Effort Raises Broad Issues'. *New York Times*, 19 April 1990, D1.

Williams, Eileen J. 'Focus: Mergers and Consolidations'. *BNA's Corporate Counsel Weekly*, 24 March 1999, 8.

Woodhead, Michael. 'A Pyrrhic Victory for Germany'. *Sunday Times* (London), 30 March 1997, §3, 7.

'Workers' rights in the EU–Inform, consult, impose'. *The Economist*, 16 June 2001, 79.

Xan, Smiley. 'They're (nearly) all centrists now—Italian survey special section'. *The Economist* (London), 7 July 2001, 6.

Index